INDIA REMEMBERED

INDIA REMEMBERED

Second Edition

with an Introduction by
NARAYANI GUPTA

PERCIVAL SPEAR
and
MARGARET SPEAR

Orient BlackSwan

ORIENT BLACKSWAN PRIVATE LIMITED

Registered Office
3-6-752 Himayatnagar, Hyderabad 500 029 (A.P.), India
e-mail: centraloffice@orientblackswan.com

Other Offices
Bangalore, Bhopal, Bhubaneshwar, Chennai,
Ernakulam, Guwahati, Hyderabad, Jaipur, Kolkata,
Lucknow, Mumbai, New Delhi, Patna

First Published by Sangam Books India Pvt Ltd 1981
An Imprint of Orient Blackswan Pvt Ltd
Second Edition 2010

ISBN 978 81 250 3960 0

Typeset by
Le Studio Graphique, Gurgaon 122 001
in Adobe Garamond Pro 11/14
Printed at
Yash Printographic
Noida

Published by
Orient Blackswan Private Limited
1/24 Asaf Ali Road
New Delhi 110 002
e-mail: delhi@orientblackswan.com

To

All Servers of India

Contents

Introduction to Second Edition[*]

The year before Percival Spear passed away, he presented an autographed copy of *India Remembered* to the India International Centre (IIC) library. This eminently readable book is the last of his four books on Delhi. It is a tribute to the city he met at the age of twenty-three and which stayed with him all his life. His account is beautifully complemented by that of his wife, Margaret. Written with characteristic modesty, it is in no sense an autobiography of the historian. Of Margaret Spear's life, we know even less.

Spear was born on 2 November 1901 in Bath, England. He read history and theology at Cambridge. He travelled to India in 1924, the year in which E.M. Forster, another Cambridge scholar, twenty-two years his senior, published *A Passage to India*—a classic novel on India. He joined St Stephen's College as a lecturer, teaching British and European history but soon developed an interest in the history of modern India. For his doctoral thesis he researched the social life of the British in India in the eighteenth century. His thesis, completed in 1931, was published the next year as *The Nabobs: A Study of the Social Life of the English in Eighteenth Century India*, a delightful book which has not dated.

In 1933, 'Dr Spear ... undertook a sentimental journey to England with happy results. We congratulate him on his engagement to Miss Dorothy Margaret Perkins of Stoke Ash, Suffolk. We wish we could tell our readers more about Dr Spear's fiancée, but our

* I thank Dr David Baker for sharing material from the St Stephen's College Magazine and the archives of the Cambridge Mission to Delhi.

attempts to question him on the subject have ... resulted only in mutual embarrassment' (wrote the *St Stephen's College Magazine*). In their memoir, both Percival and Margaret describe in happy detail how they set up home in Delhi, and how much they enjoyed living in the city. 'In this atmosphere and with these neighbours ... we came to feel at one with the Indian people.'

Margaret Spear was clearly as happy in Delhi as her husband was. Her delight in its lively streets—'Such an utter contrast to the dull regimentation of the West'—may be explained by the fact that her childhood had been spent in the West Indies. Her training in theatre probably accounts for her easy ability to relate to different kinds of people—there is a delightful description of life in a nearby village, and of their bundling the village children into their car and taking them to see the Civil Lines bungalows. She was quick to notice how when they passed the Harijan Basti at Kingsway Camp they called out "Gandhi*ji ki Jai*!"—'one of the most moving of all such demonstrations that I saw in India'.

The descriptions draw in the reader as well to enjoy the city. Of Chandni Chowk Spear writes, 'The houses spread out into court after court with open verandahs and *neem* trees. From the roof of one of them the old city looked like a garden city.' Of Hauz Khas, 'The buildings gave dignity, calm and repose, the raised bank a sense of space and perspective, and the crops life and colour.' Spear was polite about the brand new city designed by Lutyens, but said tongue-in-cheek, 'It will take many years of encroachment to convert the whole into a bureaucratic slum' (what a phrase !). He was more severe in his comment on 'the fatal measure ... to build "types" according to status'. During the War the disadvantages of this kind of layout became clear—the streets which had houses of senior officials had telephone connections, while the others had none at all.

His interest in Delhi was not confined to exploring the monuments. He wanted the College Social Service League (founded by Rev. Ireland and Mr Sharp) to be active in 'the old Moghul city with its suburbs which, until very recently, had been neglected by the administration in favour of the new ... It is easy to understand that Delhi city is now one of the most congested and unhealthy cities in the world'. He pointed out that 'the composition of the population increases its value as a demonstration centre. Hindus and Muslims live there in the proportion of 4 to 3.... The Sikhs have an important temple and a representative residential group ... (while) the Christian community now have about 17,000.... Old Delhi provides a microcosm of ... national life, with its social, communal and religious conflicts and loyalties'.

This book might as well have been called *Delhi Remembered*, though there are accounts of other places too, a particularly vivid one being of Khajjiar and Chamba. The Spears enjoyed holidays at hill stations, though Margaret does not seem to have gone on the trips to historic places that her husband organised for his students.

The Delhi that the Spears had known changed irrevocably in 1947. The tragic fallout of the decision to partition the country must have caused great sorrow to Spear. We do not have access to the letters he wrote to his friends in Delhi, but can get a sense of his anxiety in this letter from David Raja Ram, who had succeeded S.N. Mukarji as Principal. On 6 October 1947 he wrote to Spear, 'We rejoiced to find our Hindu students volunteering to ... serve the Muslims in the Refugee camp.... All our Muslim students who were in the Purana Qila were able to get away to their homes.' Shortly after, Spear received a letter from Karachi (dated 18 October) from I.H. Qureshi, whom he had appointed as a colleague in the history department. 'It is a source of great satisfaction to have friends like you to whom one can turn for advice, help and solace. Please understand that I would have accepted your most generous offer of monetary help if I had needed it, but I have no financial worry.... The question is shall I throw away my specialized knowledge of Indo-Muslim history? It seems doubtful that any Pakistani university can absorb me in the near future....' He added bitterly, 'Among my own losses, the most hard to bear is that of my books, notes, my indices ... my Persian manuscripts, pictures, rare volumes ... and imagine my colleagues planning the loot and the students executing it.'

Years later, in the 1970s, Spear's visit to Delhi left him amazed at the changes. As he writes in the Preface, 'We had lived in what is virtually a different age.'

Spear is remembered as a historian, but in his lifetime he was loved as a teacher. To find out more about Spear the teacher, we have to turn to the entry on him in the *Dictionary of National Biography* written by a fellow-historian, Dr Kenneth Ballhatchet. There are also nuggets of information in old issues of the *St Stephen's College Magazine*, meticulously trawled by Dr David Baker, an Australian scholar, who in the 1960s joined the Department of History of St Stephen's College where Spear had begun his career.

St Stephen's College had three passions—theatre, cricket, and the History Society. In 1934 the college magazine wrote 'with great satisfaction (about) the acquisition to the life of the College ... as a result of Dr Spear's marriage. Mrs Spear ... has provided another home where members of the staff and students are always welcome. She is a charming lady endowed with gifts which have already been of considerable assistance to the Shakespeare Society and in the judging of our Elocution Prizes'. Spear himself was not professionally involved in theatre as Margaret was, but he was game to participate, as in the Shakespeare Society spoof on an Urdu play, a pantomime for the Founder's Day Assembly in 1933.

Cricket must have given as much enjoyment to Spear as to anyone else, but his passion was tennis. He and his two colleagues were described as losing themselves in the game so completely that 'but for their "white" faces, we would have found difficulty even in recognizing them'.

The founding of the History Society was Spear's greatest contribution to the college. In 1926 the Society reported, 'It would be difficult to say how great a support and guidance he has afforded to the Society.... He has not only revived it but ... brought it to its present strong position'. It also led him to identify what was to become his chief area of interest. 'A few days before his departure to England on two years' leave he delivered a magic-lantern lecture on Mughal architecture' (how evocative the term "magic-lantern" in contrast to "powerpoint"!). This interest was later to be translated into two books—*Delhi: An Historical Sketch* (1937) and *Delhi: Its Monuments and History* (1943).

His return to Delhi was marked by renewed activity. 'Ever since 1928, we have been probably the most active Society in the College.... The activities of the Society are simply envied by the sister-societies associated with (the) College', and 'have given us more real education than a score of books'. It is of little wonder, when we read of the range of their interests—in 1928 they had readings of "Joan of Arc", a demonstration of the Battle of Waterloo by Messrs. Sarkar, Spear and Winsor, a moonlight picnic at Humayun's Tomb, and a well-attended discussion on "Dominion Status or Independence for India". In the summer of 1930 the Nationalist Society was set up "to meet the heartfelt desire of the students to express their nationalistic feelings". Its members had to take a pledge to support the *swadeshi* movement. Spear gave them a lecture on "the difference between non-violence and coercion"—how one wishes one had the text! Nationalistic fervour was also given ballast by trips to Mohenjodaro and Taxila, to Ajanta and Ellora, and most memorably by visits to the historic areas around Delhi. The moonlight picnic at Humayun's Tomb seems to have been an annual event, for there is an account of one in June 1934. 'Besides light refreshment and cold drinks we were delightfully entertained by Dr Spear with his flute, and with his short discourse on the history of domes and Mughal gardens.'

A Leverhulme Fellowship for two years (1937–39) enabled Spear to take a second break from teaching, and the leisure to work on *India During Bentinck*, and to research for a book on the later Mughals. At that time he could not have foreseen that he would not return to St Stephen's. As their war service, he and Margaret in 1940 joined the staff of the Director-General of Information in India, later to become part of the Department of Information and Broadcasting. Later Margaret was appointed librarian, and her husband deputy-director of counter-propaganda. In 1943 he became deputy secretary in the Ministry of Information and Broadcasting and, in 1944, the Government Whip in the Legislative Assembly.

If St Stephen's had to give up Spear in 1938, Delhi said farewell to Percival and Margaret at the end of the War. In 1945 he was appointed Bursar and Fellow of Selwyn College, Cambridge. 'I left India 17 years ago, but India has never left me.' His *India, Pakistan and the West* was published in 1949 in the Home University series. He carried Delhi back with him. His classic *Twilight of the Mughuls* was published in 1951. 'Everyone, I suppose, has their kinks, their interest or taste for which there is no rational explanation. In my case it was the Mughals. Indian friends would say that this reflected a previous Mughal incarnation.' *Twilight,* arguably the finest book on the subject, portrayed the life of the people of the city, and of its rulers, and ended by endorsing F.W. Buckle's argument that the East India Company had had no right to try the King of Delhi since he was not a British subject.

Back in Cambridge, Spear's academic work moved to a wider plane—he completed three histories of modern India—the third part of the *Oxford History of India* of Vincent Smith, the India volume in the University of Michigan's History series, and the second volume of the Pelican *History of India.* In 1961 he published *Factors in Indian History*, and in 1975 a book on Clive. As a visiting professor at Berkeley he helped the University of California to set up its course of South Asian Studies. He returned to teaching in 1963, for the next six years, and is remembered as a generous and encouraging teacher. Pulled back to his enduring passion, he planned a large history of Delhi, which he was not able to complete.

In 1979, three years before the end, he was invited as guest of honour at a seminar on Delhi held at the University of Wisconsin, the proceedings of which were later published as a festschrift (*Delhi Through the Ages,* edited by Robert Frykenberg, Delhi, 1987).

My own acquaintance with Spear began in 1963 when I wrote to him enquiring about the possibility of getting admission to a D.Phil programme in Cambridge. He replied in detail, and with characteristic courtesy, concluded encouragingly, 'To be accepted as a research student is not as difficult as for the History Tripos, so that I hope you may have success in your application.' As it turned out, I did not follow this up, but when I registered to work for a Ph.D. in Delhi in 1967, I chose the history of modern Delhi as my subject. This took me back to *Twilight of the Moghuls*, and after a year of leafing through records in the National Archives, I tried one hot summer to make sense of them and write an article. This I sent to Professor Spear, and I still have the note with his meticulous comments and, most important, his encouraging suggestion that I might try to publish it. I first met him in 1970, when I paid him a visit in Selwyn College. We had a friendly chat over a pot of tea which he brewed carefully, reminding one of Mr Chips. In 1981, when my husband, children and I were in Cambridge, we were invited to tea with the Spears. Thinking it would be difficult for the elderly couple to organise a child-friendly tea, we took along a bag of cake and biscuits, only to be put to shame by seeing a large roundtable in a cosy and cluttered sitting-room, groaning under cakes of every shade of icing, and jolly biscuits in animal-shapes. We carried away the image of a happy smiling couple that remained with us when we heard the next year, in December 1982, that the last of the Mughals had left this world.

January 2010 NARAYANI GUPTA

Percival Spear Remembered

Dr Percival Spear was an unforgettable and admirable person and a much loved and respected teacher.... Being his student I too carry with me the indelible impressions of his personality.

I vividly recall the day in October 1929, when I first attended his history class. It was a unique piece of methodical, yet inspired teaching. He created immense interest and insight into the subject. His lectures ended with a recapitulatory note and a revisionary question on the topic. Dr Spear was an excellent adviser regarding books and references.... In the Maitland House library which had an open shelf system individual students worked in the small cubicles. When we submitted our researched work, in his tutorials, Dr Spear carefully went through our papers and made his studied observations and suggestions before returning them to us.

This had a very healthy and creative effect. Further, he had the unique faculty of planning his lectures in such a manner that he could take both the "Pass" and the "Honours" group combined into one, and yet to their best advantage.

Still more important were the excursions that Dr Spear conducted for us, to the various historical monuments in and around Delhi. I can vividly remember those Sunday outings when he showed to us the significance of each stone, in the architectural, political and social development of Delhi. To him every stone had a story to tell: the story of Delhi through various periods—the Khilji, the Tughlaq, the Lodhi, the Grand Mughal and the Later Mughal.... It is perhaps these forays into the past—with his pupils, and sometimes just by himself, dressed in *sherwani* and *churidars*—that gave birth to his book *Delhi and its Surroundings*.

One such excursion, I recollect, was to the Tughlakabad fort in January 1930. There we hoisted the National Congress Flag, the same day when on the banks of the Ravi, Pandit Nehru had hoisted the flag, and pledged complete freedom as the goal of India. Dr Spear actively participated and shared the aspirations of his students assembled there.

This approach to history was unbiased and pragmatic and he succeeded in generating a similar environment around him. Thus it was that when we discussed politics, it was without any rancour or prejudice on either side. A true teacher, he identified himself with the social and cultural life of the college. It is delightful to recall the vision of Dr Spear in white muslin *dhoti* and *kurta*, playing his flute, in the Saturday concerts.

His lively and innovative teaching, I am sure, has converted many into fans of history. I am one of them. At a personal level, he achieved the same with his warmth and concern for his pupils. How can I forget his warm hospitality, when years later I was in the UK on an educational assignment in 1958–59. He also offered me all possible help as the then Chairman of the Cambridge Syndicate. To his many fortunate pupils, he was a true friend, philosopher and guide.

Extract from an obituary by S.P. Sharma (a student of Percival Spear) published in the *Stephanian* XCII, May 1983

Preface to First Edition

This book is one of memories and reflections. Memories, because they are pleasant to recall and reflections because, now that our life in Indian is a completed whole, as is the British period of Indian history, one is increasingly inclined to seek the meaning which underlies it all.

There is another consideration. Our memories of India together cover half the twenties, the thirties and half the forties of this century. It is a long time ago and apart from political changes, others in the social sphere have been drastic. Not only World War II with its dislocation of society, but Independence, the Nehru regime with its economic, social and political developments, have changed the face of the country. A new India has emerged with new outlooks, new stresses, new hopes and fears.

Consequently we realised we had lived in a world, not only thirty to fifty years in time past, but in what is virtually a different age. The pace of change had quickened; from the deliberation of the tortoise to the rush of the hare, from the creaking of the bullock cart to the speed of the air-liner. Reminiscence could not only record events but could also describe something of a vanished world. Who would believe today, for example, that the New Delhi of the thirties was one of the quietest, most spacious and traffic-free cities in India, that the Delhi of the twenties was still in essence an old-world provincial city, with a sprawling but empty suburb to the south, and a cold weather incursion of "high-ups" to the north, longing to escape from their tents and temporary quarters to the coolness of

Simla each March-April. We can detect few connection links save the eternal Chandni Chowk with its clanging and creeping trams, its incessant chaotic bustle and noise, the majesty of the Jama Masjid, the unending clamour of the railway station.

We saw in those years not only the transformation of Delhi from a provincial city to a metropolis but also the last years of the countryside as it had existed for centuries. On a visit twenty years later we found radical changes here too. The motor-bus had replaced the bullock cart for locomotion, the tube-well was no longer a talking point in New Delhi office and Viceregal speeches, but a fact of experience. Wayside factories, electrification, five-year plans were all to play their part in the change. No longer did our car creep beside a line of a hundred bullock wagons filled with chanting village women in their way to a *mela*, or seek to evade sleeping wagon drivers on the Grand Trunk road by ploughing blind through the dust-track alongside.

The Simla Hills, too, were about to lose the peace, the solemnity, the kindliness of the thirties, leaving only the grandeur of the snow vistas for drivers whose eyes were too intent on the new motor roads to notice them.

When the first of us came to Delhi in 1924, Mahatma Gandhi had just emerged from his first imprisonment and was about to embark on his first great fast. When we joined in setting up house, the Civil Disobedience movement of 1930, had collapsed; India was in a doldrums of repression and realignment. When we left, the British were about to appear victorious in World War II, apparently, for the moment, stronger than they had been for decades. Within these time limits there lies a vanished world; it has been our endeavour to catch something of its nature and its spirit and to pass it on to the present generation.

Cambridge,
December 1980

Percival & Margaret Spear

Part One

First Impressions

I landed in Bombay on 10 February 1924 and left for Delhi the same afternoon. The beauty of Bombay struck me as it does all travellers who approach it by sea. The city itself impressed me as a cosmopolitan rather than oriental city. There were the crowded main streets, the big clocks of offices, the hurrying crowds. There was a general look of white clothes and brown faces, but only the Parsis stood out, with their peculiar mitre-like hats stamping them as an oriental version of the cityman. Some of the buildings were self-consciously eastern, but they had a heaviness which betrayed their Britannic origin and most were merely modern commercial erections. The day was cool by Bombay standards, but when I left by the Frontier Mail at four o'clock the heat in the still air and cloudless sky seemed torrid and stifling. I kept saying to myself, this is the Orient and what you find here is what you have to get used to.

My first railway journey in India has left little on my memory. I have a vague impression of noise, and of extraordinary clamour of every big station we stopped at. This seemed specially the case at night; perhaps the heat restrained the ardour of the platform dwellers by day, for as many seemed to be on the stations as ever got in or out of the train. As the journey wound into central India another and stronger impression of dust was added, one of the most characteristic features of north Indian life as I was soon to find out. Two clearer pictures remain. One was that of the young Muslim who shared the carriage. He looked at me for some time and suddenly said, 'Do you believe in destiny?' I have no memory of my answer except that it was quite unphilosophical. I do remember being taken aback by the nature of the question, coming as it were from the void. But is was not, after all, a bad introduction to the Indian mind. The other was that of walking down the train four times to take meals in the restaurant car. There I found the car filled with young officers returning to the Frontier (the train went on to Peshawar) from leave. One was suddenly in a solid phalanx of the ruling raj, all taking Indian soldier's gup in accented Oxfordese, or exchanging reminiscences of home with its hunting and fishing. An upstanding and vigorous looking crowd, a self-assured and self-absorbed group, with a touch of arrogance and more than a touch of aloofness. Or were they quite so assured as they looked and sounded, and were they, as I was, wondering what lay in front of them and covering it with an air of Spartan olympianism, as I was not?

I think my first impression of Delhi was of light and colour. I arrived at the height of the cold weather when with water anything can be grown. The gardens were ablaze with flowers of all kinds, Indian and English, the flaming cannas and the brilliant creepers adding an extra brilliance to any comparable English scene. Brilliance had replaced both the pastel shades and subdued light of England. The light came from a blazing sun set in a blue sky and clear air. It seemed hard and dazzling, but it had also a curiously exhilarating effect. Except in the most cavernous of the old bungalows, it penetrated everywhere and dominated the verandahs where much work was carried on. It had its complement in the shadows it cast, hard and clear in their turn and forming wonderful mosaics in the interstices of the buildings. This stimulus of the light was certainly a very clear experience. One felt for a long time as though one was on one's toes for some big event, as if something important was just about to happen. Years later I had the same feeling when arriving in San Francisco during a heat wave: the feeling left me as soon as the temperature fell, so it would seem that it was the light and heat rather than the sensation of novelty which was responsible. I remember vividly the starlit nights broken by the singing of crickets and the droning of mosquitoes, and the fresh air of the dazzling mornings. In the afternoons the heat was already rising and I had a feeling of breathless stillness. Again that air of expectancy returned, a feeling shall we say, of waiting for Godot?

I found myself living in a corner of the city close to Kashmere Gate. You had only to cross a long footbridge over the railway to find yourself in a public garden which leads to the main street of the city. In Kashmere Gate itself there was much coming and going for it was at that time the shopping centre for the Delhi Europeans. Delhi was not only quite different to anything in my English experience, but to Bombay as well. A first impression was of thronging life of almost infinite variety and a second, as you looked into the throng a little more closely, of poverty and dirt. I was not so much struck with the colours and dress of the different groups, as with their varied appearance and headgear. The red "flower pot" Muslim hat (made in Italy), its black brother, the little round flat Hindu hat, the white Gandhi cap (not always so white), turbans of all sizes and *topis*, white and otherwise, those without hats at all and the umbrellad Bengali. The clothing did not strike one so much although it was just as varied, because it was mostly of shades of off white (some very off). As a whole it helped to build up the picture of dirt and poverty, while the headgear suggested variety. This absence of colour where it might have been expected led one on to another discovery, the absence of women. A world of white and a world of skirts (*dhotis*) but few women apart from those encased in the *burqa* with its prison like grille for the eyes, and adding, with its deliberate dishevelment and squalor to the general impression of dirt. The few flashing saris in Kashmere Gate were not enough to relieve the strong sense of a man's world.

Then there was the variety of vehicles. Apart from the ubiquitous bicycle, sometimes carrying three or even four persons, and the occasional cars, hooting their way noisily through disregarding crowds, the strongest impression came from the creaking, slow moving bullock carts and the faster two-wheeled tongas. These were passenger vehicles with a dog-cart arrangement of seating beneath a canopy. They were drawn by lean and apparently ill-used ponies driven by dishevelled drivers with rancorous cries and the incessant application of the whip. The scene was completed by the rarer high built camel cart and its disdainful puller.

Apart from the human scene there were certain sights and sounds which have indelibly printed themselves on my mind. At dusk in the cold weather a certain hush seemed to fall on the city. The snorting of the engines in the railway yard would suddenly come across the still air like giant reports, and you could sometimes hear hoarse cries and tonga bells in the Chandni Chowk beyond the yard. The smoke from innumerable fires would hang in the still air to form a pall over the city, as it had done for centuries with wood fires and thousands of open hearths. For a moment or two Delhi put on its Mughal dress and went back to the age of Shah Jahan. The effect was heightened by the muezzin's call to prayer from mosque minarets and rooftops. On those calm evenings the chanted call came clearly across the still air. God is great: God is great; there is no god but God. The call as it came from hundreds of mosques was impressive enough in itself, but to me, a newcomer, it imparted to the whole scene an indefinable sense of otherness. I felt close to a world unseen and magical. A further touch was the appearance of the crescent moon, marking the start of a new Muslim lunar month. The clear air made this appearance a regular and so an abiding impression. At festival times, especially at the end of the month of fasting, the flat roofs would be lined with people looking for the moon, because its appearance would mark the end of the fast and the beginning of the feast. The *mullahs* were calling and the people were looking, for what? Were they searching for the real as one had been told everyone did in India, or were they just waiting for Godot? I did not know, but I was immensely stirred and excited.

A further physical impression was the gardens which surrounded the city. I arrived at the moment when they were at their best, it is true. I was fascinated with their blaze of floral colour, their blending with stately monuments and picturesque ruins, all instinct with history, their spaciousness, their variety and their numbers. Some were in the formal Mughal style, some in British landscape, and some a mixture of the two. Delhi was always a city of gardens and greenery for me, even more than of monuments. I have never seen another which to my mind could compare with it in this respect. The nearest garden to Kashmere Gate was the Qudsia Bagh which ran down to the river Jumna. The river ran through several sandy channels in a bed about half a mile wide. In the cold weather, as I first saw it, it was a placid stream only a few yards wide: in the hot weather it shrank to a trickle; in the rains it would fill the whole bed and often surge out in floods beyond. It was then a turbid rushing mass with a vicious look but in the cold weather, when one walked of an evening to an embankment where one had a vista of water, sand and sky, it was tranquil and remote. Again one had that sense of otherness, of the yonder just beyond the grasp of consciousness. In the great vistas of blue and gold and red one's consciousness was raised and one forgot the milkmen with cans jangling on their cycles, the washerman beating his overloaded donkey, the squalor of the little huts here and there.

While I was stirred and excited by my first contacts with the city and its scene, I was decidedly daunted by my first contact with my English colleagues. The unmarried ones lived in a bungalow opposite the college and it so happened that clerical Brethren were living there too during an interim, while a new house was being built for them. The bungalow was a typical north Indian one, with a large central room lit only by skylights (*roshandans*) and a number of others opening out from them. There also, except one, had only skylights, the outside walls enclosing bathrooms on two sides and a heavy verandah in front. The centre of this verandah was covered by a still heavier porch, well calculated to exclude air as well as light; the two sides had been filled in, the one used as a chapel the other as a living room. This had a low ceiling and a verandah about six feet square and it was my fate to live in it for eight years. It was a repository of dust and smells and a mecca for mosquitoes. The house had a fine platform beyond which you could have views of gardens and the river. But this had become a passage way between two hostels. Beneath were kitchens and servants' quarters for these hostels so that you had a take your views along with a stream of passengers, and rising kitchen and other smells. The house also had a garden once but this had been absorbed for another hostel. So we had dust from one hostel and shade from another smells from behind and noise from the main street in front. In act what had once been a typical north Indian bungalow, not without a certain dignity, had become something of a squalid cave. This was what I thought, but my thoughts were not shared. When I asked for some furniture for my room, which had nothing but a table and a bed, I was firmly told by the John Lawrence admiring English principal that 'one table, one bed, one chair was enough for anyone'. I recollected that Lawrence loved to work by the light of candles stuffed in beer bottles. The candles, yes, but why the beer bottles? Wasn't water enough for him? But the English principal was not amused, I hastened to add that I lived in that room for eight years without mishap, a tribute, I still think, to the intrinsic interest of the work rather than the beauty of the room.

Apart from the intellectual and rather remote Head, the Brethren seemed solemn and uninspiring. They were absorbed in their various jobs, and seemed to cherish a fierce determination to go their own way in spite of being a Brotherhood. They had a capacity for disapproval and handy subjects for it exercise in the young college lecturers only recently out from England. These young men were fresh and lively, a tonic not always relished by the older men, a social diversion for the Indians of the mission. But a group had got together to form a set which behaved more like bloods in a public school than collegians, still less teachers or lecturers. They teased their elders for their Victorianism and their youngers because they were younger. All very harmless and well meant, but not endearing to a newcomer. The group soon broke up but it made its impression. A mark of the house at the time was tension. The Brothers appeared to dislike each other and disapprove of the college men; the college men fretted against Brotherhood rules and brotherly fustiness; we all hated the food but couldn't say much because the cook was a Christian. There was an indefinable air of crisis as though the Mission might come to an end any morning. One learnt later that this was a common feeling in British Indian institutions but it was disturbing at the time.

The college as a whole presented no clear picture at first. There was a throng of white-clad students in a dark and crowded assembly hall, a coming and going into classrooms too small for the classes. There was an air of excitement due to the onset of the examinations. Soon half the students disappeared on "examination leave" to dot the lawns of public gardens with figures hunched over books or wandering in shady spots intoning passages of text books. Then came the examinations in mounting heat with little boys (deputies from elders on more profitable business) falling asleep at the end of ropes to the big cloth fans suspended from the roof, who had to be prodded periodically in order to keep the torrid air moving. With a vacation following it was some months before the college was in full swing again. These first few weeks, however, were enough to show me that Indian students were not to be judged by their English counterparts. They were neither schoolboys nor university students in the English sense, but something distinctive between the two. There was a six year spread of student life. The younger had schoolboy traits such as a fondness for treating chalk as space missiles and the elders were not unlike our graduates. But neither conformed to the English pattern, being in some respects more and in others less mature. But they shared fundamental human features and had no traces of mysticism. I was more conscious at first of the college staff, some twenty or so in number with staff room contacts and what seemed to be constant meetings in very small rooms. Here again was the tension I noted in the mission house. This time it seemed to concern the future of the college. Would the college move out to a new site in the next few months and were the doings of the government and/or the University so iniquitous that the college would shortly have to close down? The Irish Principal certainly seemed to be on edge, but after he had gone on leave the tension remained. One gradually came to realise that this was something one had to live with, specially in the hot weather, just as a hot weather crisis was something one had to expect, to weather and to forget.

I was given senior classes at first, as being better able to understand my English and easier to manage. It was from some of these that I got my first lesson in Indian character and history. Though self-consciously nationalist they were humanly tolerant. After having heard me lecture on European nationalism in the nineteenth century they informed the acting Principal that, 'I would do'. I soon found that we shared a sense of humour and a desire for fair play, and our relations grew very friendly. To one Muslim student I was specially indebted. He was unusual in many ways, for he was an intellectual from the Punjab, tall but sensitive, and willowy, as if he might break in two, and with no love of sport. He had a gentle voice with strong convictions and a rather ingratiating manner which belied a certain wiry strength within. He was one of nature's rationalists so that we at once had common ground for discussing anything. We did not, as my missionary colleagues expected, discuss Muslim theology or the Islamic way of life. Instead he was my mentor on Indian nationalism and my initiator in the Mughal age whose wrecks were strewn around me. During the long hot-weather afternoons we re-catalogued the history section of the college library; then and in evening walks the talk went on. It was my first lesson in seeing India through Indian spectacles, and it was perhaps an advantage that I had at that time little background of formal knowledge. At the very beginning I was able to grasp the modernity of the young Indian mind and the degree to which it had been influenced by the west. It was an incalculable advantage for future understanding.

A little later the first Honours class was enrolled. I remember feeling daunted on facing the first four applicants one of whom, with an unkempt beard seemed to regard me with a disapproving and rather baleful eye. But he soon turned out to be the most intelligent and interesting of the four, the attraction of whose innate good manners was enhanced by a cheerful and friendly disposition. To the political philosopher was now added the lover of nature and life and a further stage of my initiation into Indian things began. I learnt later the cause of the baleful glance on the enrolment day. He had been swept into the first noncooperation movement, and left his college for political propaganda. Gandhi's "independence in one year" was the intoxicant. The movement collapsed and he and his friends were stranded. They could not go back to their old college; the local Hindu College was too Hindu; there was no government college in Delhi and so the only alternative was the mission college. He regarded all Englishmen at the time with deep suspicion as enemies of freedom. But within a year personal contacts changed his outlook so much that he became a leading exponent of understanding both communal and national, without in the least ceasing to be a nationalist. With these two and a few others, I soon had a group which contained, besides these two Hindus, a Sikh and a Christian. I taught them formal History and Political Science, but it was they who graduated me in Indian knowledge.

The first hot weather is a hurdle in any experience of north Indian life. As the thermometer mounted to the nineties in early March one felt that curious feeling of exhilaration mentioned before. The air was warm but crisp and dry. A fall of some thirty degrees by night gave cool starlit evenings and delightfully fresh, crisp mornings. The flowers and creepers blazed, the flowering trees began to bloom. Dust was still scarce. There was a certain breathlessness in the air, a feeling of living at a faster *tempo*. Then as April drew on and the thermometer topped 100 degrees, the great change of life occurred. From the end of March the exodus to Simla took place. The busy clatter at Kashmere Gate was hushed. Europeans grew few. Old Delhi considered that it had come into its own again. Our daily routine changed to make one day into two. The college session lasted from seven to eleven instead of from ten to two. The first main meal was an eleven o'clock breakfast, after which the house was shut up. One worked indoors, had a siesta and reappeared for some four o'clock tea. This was the worst moment of the day when on seemed to reach the world's end; the moment of rising seemed to be the limit of exhaustion. Then we went out, to meetings, to sport, for walks by the river. It was a second day lasting into the night. In April the mornings were still fresh and the evening air cool. In May came the next stage. The hitherto clear air would be filled with dust so that the sky would become leaden and the sun be sometimes hardly visible. Periodically this pall would work up into dust storms with gusts of high wind, choking flurries of dust and perhaps some thunder and a few drops of rain. The mornings lost their freshness and the nights their glamour. The stifling night was the mark of Delhi in May. This went on till the rains came. After they came the heat became humid and the days became stifling too. When the rain came people would climb their roofs and run out into the street with relief to gambol and soak themselves in it.

Then there was the hot weather crisis. During the hot weather term one could be sure that sooner or later some incident would shake the college. The incident might be large or small but the same people who would take it in their stride in the cold weather would now become tense and grave. Emotions would be aroused, suspicious fester and tempers flickers. Then moral principles would be invoked, a sign that matters were coming to a head. During the last weak of term it would often seem as though the college must explode with temper and high principle. But a week after we had scattered all would be forgotten and we would assemble for the next term as though we had never known anything but harmony and peace.

I did not get so far as the rains in my first year for the term then ended at the height of the heat towards the end of May. This gave me my first experience of the hills. I stayed with two Brothers in the lower hills near Simla for a time and then joined a boy scouts camp at a place nearby. There was the night journey in the heavy Indian train in a crescendo of heat, dust and clamour, a sort of fiery initiation for the experience to come, Kalka at the foothills was cool by comparison, but the hill train into which we packed was so small and so crowded that we were if anything, hotter than before. I remember people running to the engine as it stopped at each station to get hot water for shaving or for making tea. When at last we got out there were the pines, the steep slopes rising above us and glimpses of the snows on distant ranges. It seemed like heaven as long as one did not look down the slopes towards the plains where desiccated and prickly cactus emerged from the rising dust haze. The Himalayas impressed me not so much by their height as by their vastness. The snows were nearly always visible, but always in the remote distance. Between lay ridge after ridge, often thickly tree clad, in every direction. The vistas in the Alps or the Rockies are not the same for in the one the breadth of the range is much smaller and in the other the ranges rise more slowly. Another impression was the steepness of the *khud* or hillside, so different to the rounded contours of even the Scottish moors. This seemed to be the case from plains to snows, and wherever the slope was more gentle there were the terraced fields of cultivation, watered with skill and patience by miniature irrigation channels. The great range of hill and sky was a delight and brooding over all was a sense of mystery coming from the peaks of the snowy range. This may be called sentimental but there was nevertheless to me some sense of an overriding presence.

My memory of the scout camp is a confused blur, concerned largely with handing out supplies with measures whose names and English equivalents I could not remember (I was Quartermaster). But thereafter I walked to Simla with an Indian student, a three day trip. This first trek was not very exciting in itself, for the path was rather bare and rocky and ended with a hot climb up an exposed hillside to Jutogh. But it completed my surrender to the hill spirit. The freedom of the air and the hills, the winding hill paths, the nestling hill villages, the squat posting bungalows full of relics of the past worked their charm and made the hills the Shangri-la of my imagination during the rest of my Indian life. I might long for the solace of a Simla restaurant while climbing in the sun to Jutogh, but it was to the hills and the sun that I went back.

The hills gave me something else, my first touch with something of the Indian spirit. The Christian *sadhu*, Sunder Singh was staying near the scout camp site and presided over a *Prem Sabha* to which some of us went. This was a nocturnal devotional meeting popular with Indian Christians, at which there was a mixture of prayer, hymns and talks. I understood little because the proceedings were in Urdu and the meeting did not really get going till midnight when I became drowsy. But I had the honour of sitting next to the bearded *sadhu*. He was clad in saffron and his face shone with light. Though I could not understand his talks I could feel the power and radiance of his spirit, and the experience has remained with me. Not long after he set out on the Hindu pilgrim path on one of his journeys into Tibet from which he never returned. My first visit to Simla made little impression. I approached it from Jutogh, winding up the long tree-lined slope to the flat by the church. One saw little paths leading away down to bungalows with labels Rosemount, Sunny Cottage, and the like. One passed the Viceregal Lodge entrance, some hotels and ugly office buildings and eventually ascended to the shops. The crowd was varied but not strikingly so. What was striking was the double view from plains to snowy range and back again, from wooded Tara Devi to bare Naldera and beyond, as the road followed the knife edge of the ridge. In front stood the tree clad Jakko like a sentinel watching the scene. The town itself below the Ridge held no romance at first glance; it seemed just a shamble of corrugated iron roofs, with rickshaws, pedestrians and timber-laden coolies competing for moving space in the narrow streets. These last left a lasting impression. You would meet them in the roads staggering under great pine logs twenty to thirty feet long fastened to their backs, so that they could only rest by leaning against a bank. All the government furniture, all their files were moved twice a year in this way. the men came from long distances for this and for the rickshaws. Their lives were short and no one cared until an intrepid temperance worked, took up their cause, and became known as the Rickshaw Rani. Their conditions of living were indescribable, but they kept the hillman's cheerfulness; and their devotion to their Rani was touching. Where conditions put the greatest strain on human labour it seemed that this was the method of transport which the then authorities preferred.

Back in the plains Delhi gave me my first glimpse of Indian public life. New Delhi was still a-building and the temporary capital was located in the old Civil Lines which stretched north from Kashmere Gate. Officials camped or lived in jerry-built bungalows each cold weather while the Viceroy lived in an enlarged Circuit House beyond the Ridge of Mutiny fame. There was an Assembly Chamber in a temporary secretariat where I attended debates in the cold weather. The two leading figures on the Indian side were Pundit Motilal Nehru, leader of the newly formed Swaraj or Home Rule party, and Muhammad Ali Jinnah, then leader of the Independents. I remember Motilal as a sturdily-built, rather portly figure clad in immaculate white. From this white surround emerged a square head with a rubicund countenance. He had a powerful voice but a slow and deliberate manner. He was a lawyer making an impressive indictment rather than an orator arousing his followers. Having heard much of silver tongued Indians, I was rather disappointed. At the time he was denouncing the failure of the Montford reforms and charging the government with wanting to go back on them. Jinnah was then important because his group held the balance between the Swarajists and the government. Thin to leanness and icily handsome, he affected at that time an overpowering sartorial elegance in the western manner. His voice was quiet, his gestures few, his manner Olympian and aloof as if he was surveying a world of insects or distastefully prodding with a needle some lifeless scientific exhibit. Perhaps his manner suited the occasion by repaying to the government benches the disdain with which they had until recently regarded the nationalists. But he was no more an orator than Motilal, and disappointed me also. I also remember the slim aristocratic figure and beturbaned of Pundit Madan Mohan Malaviya, the political incarnation of Hindu orthodoxy. His eloquence was real, only it was said that whatever subject he treated, he started with the advent of the Aryans in India. The story was reported that E.S. Montagu, when touring India as Secretary of State, once asked him whether he could become a Hindu. 'No', came the reply, 'not in this life, but if you behave very well where you are, you might stand a chance of reincarnation as an outcaste in your next'. When we rail at the pride of the British in India, we should remember that their's was not the only species of the genus to be found there. On the government side the only man of equal distinction was Sir Malcolm Hailey, who had all the manner and debating skill of his opponents and eloquence as well. All Indians love eloquence even if they don't posses it and they hung on his words with unconcealed delight. Sir Charles MacInnes, the Commerce member, was no debater but he had fluency and lucidity and took the House seriously. Sir A. Muddiman was jolly but not taken seriously. The rest of the government speakers, whatever their abilities, ruled themselves out by their manifest contempt of the House. They were the justification for Jinnah's manner.

Outside the House I saw Gandhi, a little head peeping out from the pillows, just after he had completed his first twenty-one days fast in 1924. C.F. Andrews hovered round like an anxious hen with a sick chicken. People spoke in whispers and sounds were muted; the atmosphere was more of worship even than of affection or respect. I was impressed but perplexed as I think a great many other people were at that time. At about the same time Maulana Muhammad Ali, leader of the Khilafat movement which had just collapsed because of the Turkish abolition of the Califate, visited the college. He was a handsome bearded man with striking eyes and clothed in flowing robes. His speech was easy, his manner ingratiating, that of a willing sufferer for a noble cause. To me he seemed to be too suave to be sincere and too insincere to be noble. In fact I took an instant dislike to him.

After about an year I had an experience which I have always regarded as my introduction to the deeper side of India even though it may be said that the introduction was in fact to something that India has rejected. This was a visit to Taxila, the ruined university town destroyed by the Huns in the fifth century A.D. and excavated by Sir John Marshall. We went in the early spring when the sun was bright but not too hot and the countryside still green. Taxila is set in a natural amphitheatre in the foothills and possesses the remains of several Buddhist monasteries besides the excavated portions of ruined cities. It was these which moved me. Round the stupas and courts of these monasteries were clay images of the Buddha in the Greek Gandhara style some of which the flames of the sack had turned into terra-cotta and preserved through the centuries. To the quiet of the gracious valley and the repose of the monastic courts, was added the assured serenity, the detached compassion and repose of these representations of the Buddha. The calm of the countryside was reinforced as it were, or perhaps found its echo in the stillness of the Buddha and together cast a spell from which I have never escaped. I felt the first glimmerings of what Indians mean by "detachment" and the search for the secret of life. I went back to read all I could about the Buddha and Buddhism; Buddhism as a system remained a story that is told, but the attraction of the Buddha, the incarnation of "Wisdom" as Christ is of "Love" remained. From Buddhism it was a natural step to Hindu thought, to the Upanishads and the Gita. India, which I would have gladly deserted six months before, had captured me in a way only India knows.

The Teacher

The college at which I worked stood at that time near Kashmere Gate, facing St James' Church and close to Colonel Skinner's town mansion, converted into the Hindu College. It was set off by an open space known as the Gracia Park (in honour of the wife of a deputy-commissioner) but now as Azad Park. It was designed in the Victorian Mughal style current in the late nineteenth century as practised by Sir Swinton Jacob, and was not without a certain dignity. This is to say the front was so designed, for the full plan was a victim to lack of resources, iron rods taking the place of carved railings on the side verandahs, bare walls and roof timbers of vaultings and domes elsewhere. It was designed for a hundred students and housed most of my time three hundred or more. There was a small lawn space in front where students could gossip; the Principal's house stood on one side across a tennis lawn while behind and on the other side were low additions for science laboratories. Across the road were two residential hostels, with a house for the unmarried staff between them. The temporary capital was at that time on the north of Kashmere Gate side of Delhi while New Delhi was a-building Kashmere Gate was its shopping centre, so that in the cold season it was an animated spot.

The college opened in the cold weather at 10 a.m. with a college assembly. The hall was crowded and conversation buzzed while a roll call was taken by class lecturers. Then the Principal and staff filed in to a dais, the staff sitting on each side and the Principal at a table in the centre. Notices were given out, praise and blame distributed, references made to "our friends across the way" (Hindu College: example not to be followed), the family spirit (to be cultivated) and nation building. Then came a short pause while the college hoped a holiday might be declared, cricket being the best gamble, and then the college prayers. These were Christian in spirit without the Christian ascription, designed to enable members of all faiths to take part sincerely. The were read sonorously by the Principal ending with the Tagore prayer 'Strike, strike, at the root of penury in our hearts' and 'Into that heaven of freedom let my country awake'. How well we knew 'The dreary desert sand of dead habit' and longed for the 'heaven of freedom' in those moments. But looking back and setting aside the monotony of a too-rigid formula, I think it true to say that this approach to a student body nine-tenths of whom were non-Christian was not without effect. It removed the feeling that they were being "got at" as soon as they set foot in the college, proclaimed the primacy of the spirit in a way all understood, and encouraged a sense of the Beyond in a not notably devotional group. The north Indian, unlike many in other parts of India, has not a very developed religious sense. Many groups round Delhi such as the Jats prided themselves on keeping their Brahmins in order, reminiscent of the way the Celtic Irish looked after their bishops. To many, of course, the occasion was a mere ceremony, to others a bore, to be evaded if possible, but the evidence of old students suggested that it provided for many at least a moment of recollection which was valued and remembered.

After the Assembly came a religious period unless there was an address to the whole college. Sometimes there would be a series of religious addresses, by the staff itself or by some visitor like the evangelist Stanley Jones. It was usual to invite visitors to the college to address it, the cordiality of their welcome being heightened by the knowledge that a religious period would be skipped. The central position of the college in Delhi and its many connections brought it many speakers of distinction. Mahatma Gandhi himself came once in my time. Then we would hear the flute like tones of C.F. Andrews with his flowing beard and shining countenance. In the days before World War I he had been almost the second creator of the college. One eloquent lecturer we had, regularly worked himself up into such passion that at his conclusion he staggered backwards into the supporting arms of adjacent Professors. If the back door of the dais was open on account of the heat there was real hazard; once he fell right through. Once a President of an American University visited the college. He would refer to the students as "babus" pronounced as *baboos* with the accent on the "oo". This is an honourable term in Bengali parlance, but its use in English was often disrespectful and generally resented by Indians. The reiteration of the phrase was bad enough for the student audience, but the speaker's American twang gave to English ears and keen Indian ones the sound of "baboons". The students took it with stoic calm but we English, struggling with mirth and indignation, had a hard time. There was the benevolent Muslim member of council from Madras who spoke for an hour and a half in polysyllable without any apparent punctuation in a dictation speed drawl; and there was the learned archaeologist who gave a lantern lecture on the Indus valley and wanted to read a text in the dark at the same time. Armed with a torch he flashed it to and fro, revealing the dark places of the hall but not of his text. Like the Indus valley script, his meaning remained obscure. The students would behave with exemplary restraint on these occasions, but they had (and probably still have) a habit which was disconcerting to the newcomer. They would walk into a meeting twenty minutes late, sit for five minutes and then march out again. Some would come in time and then walk out within five minutes of the start. I think this habit was partly due to the custom of regarding a public lecture as a *tamasha* or show to be looked at. But another cause was the language difficulty. People would walk out after coming in casually when they found that the proceedings were in English, or in an English which they could not understand. This was not only the Englishman's

English but the south Indian's English as well. The south Indian's tendency to add an "a" to the final consonant of words and to run sentences into one syllabic omnibus was mercilessly mocked and inimitably parodied by the north Indians. One could always raise a smile by referring to the "governmenta".

The religious period lasted about twenty minutes, when the Christian faith was expounded by the Christian staff. These classes were voluntary in the sense that you could contract out, and from the fact that disciplinary action was rarely taken if you absented yourself. In these circumstances it was surprising that so many attended. They were the most difficult classes of the day, but attention could usually be obtained for the exposition of the gospels, and in the hands of an able teacher could be tense and wrapt in the case of St John. Here were touched hidden cords of sympathy with the imbedded presuppositions of Indian thought.

There followed the English classes which all had to attend, and then the subject lectures, until about one o'clock. In the hot weather term (May–June) the college opened at 7 a.m. and finished by 11 a.m. so that the students could return before the greatest heat. The question of holidays was then acute, made the more serious by the fact that most of the great Hindu festivals which were public holidays occurred in the cold weather. The Muslim ones went round the calendar and they were usually absent too. The rule was that a pretext must be found but wide latitude of choice was permissible. Once, on a particularly hot June day, I declared a holiday to celebrate the battle of Waterloo, and for a few moments there was unwonted enthusiasm for a British success.

College life did not end with the classes. In the afternoons there was an active programme of games—tennis cricket, football and hockey—on the spacious tree-lined sports ground outside Kashmere Gate. Tennis had most votaries and a high standard, but cricket had pride of place. Introduced as a nostalgic exercise by the first English lecturers, cricket had long been adopted by the Indian public as its own. Its skill, its subtlety and craft combined with its leisureliness to give it an irresistible attraction. The most enthusiastic supporter of all was the Indian Principal. The annual contest with the Hindu College was more of a gladiatorial show than a game. The rival principals sat amid mounting tension on opposite sides of the field surrounded by their supporters, like generals of old time contending armies. Only elephants were wanting to complete the similitude of Mughal rivals for the throne. The two teams had lesser durbars in other corners of the field. Each ball was like the discharge of a gun and each knock a knell for the other side. The students of both colleges cheerfully lined the sides of the field and there was usually shocked surprise on our side at the behaviour of the other. We could usually count on two or three day's holiday unless disaster overtook our team in the first few hours.

In the evenings there was much activity with college societies of various kinds. A third of the students lived in nearby hostels and more than another third in the city, so that access was easy. The college encouraged the students to study their own religions as well as Christianity and so there were Muslim and Hindu religious associations. Every year a "Gita" class was started but it was rarely heard of after Christmas. The fact was that the north Indian-Hindu was not particularly religious. The only way to arouse much interest in his religion was by giving him the impression you were attacking it. There were literary societies. There was the inevitable Bengali association and there were the dramatic societies. The Urdu society put on shows from time to time which could be uproariously funny, but also seemed to be in need of censorship. Later it was led by a literary young lecturer[1] who wrote his own plays. He sought to introduce contemporary social themes into his plays, the central figure of which was always a "serious young man" caught on the horns of some social dilemma and moving reflectively to disaster. "*Afsos! afsos*!" (alas! alas!) is the word which lingers in the mind from these performances. Like other would-be tragic writers my friend could write farces with effortless ease.

But the dramatic thunder was stolen by the Shakespeare Society[2] started in the year of my arrival by a young English lecturer to whom Shakespeare, Wordsworth and Shelley formed a trio almost as important as the Trinity. His lectures on these poets attained such a pitch of intensity that when once a rustic student who was hard of understanding murmured, 'five minutes more', it was taken as sacrilege. The lecturer gathered up his books and swept out. The class was dumbfounded; it was only after a sorrowful deputation had assured him that no disrespect was intended to Wordsworth and that the young delinquent was too ignorant to realise the enormity of what he had done, that he consented to continue the course. Our students lacked neither humour nor a sense of the ridiculous. This incident is a testimony to the power which intense conviction can wield. Our Shakespearian was an excellent producer; he had the genius of an infinite capacity for taking pains, and the gift of getting people to work together. The large casts occupied a number of people; the frequent and prolonged rehearsals kept interest alive while the ultimate public performances set the seal of achievement on the whole effort. There is no doubt that this was one of the most vital parts of the college life. The Indian love of Shakespeare is as genuine as their love of cricket.

About a third of the students lived in hostels in charge of Christian superintendents. Two of these had about forty members each and one was smaller. One had an entrance which looked like a Mughal afterthought, with nothing more behind than a yard lined with verandahed rooms. The other was a modern erection of brick and concrete built round a court over shops. The influence of buildings was never more clearly shown for this hostel always showed an alertness, a vigour and a sense of community which the other could never rival. The third hostel rambled through some old buildings, and was the reported abode of Jains who must not eat after dark. The new hostel seemed to attract the more alert youths from New Delhi or the Punjab; the other the rustics. There were a group of Jats from Rohtak to whom education was still relatively new and some of whose fathers had had to be fetched back from their villages to which they had fled because of the strangeness of city life. In the twenties they were fast becoming sophisticated but they would still seek leave two or three times a term to fetch *ghee* (clarified butter) from the purer air of the countryside. This they would pour down their throats in a continuous stream without spoon or ladle before admiring groups. They were the strong men of the college and also the butts of much popular humour. Stories would begin "a Brahmin met a Jat", or "a Jat met a Brahmin", both being certain preludes to Jat discomfiture in a battle of wits. The Jats had an extraordinary loyalty to their homeland, flat, dusty and parched as it usually was. To them there was no place like Rohtak, a country town forty miles from Delhi dignified only by some earth mounds of possibly the Kushan period. Their eyes would gleam and their faces shine at its mention; Calcutta and Bombay had nothing in their eyes to compare with it.

Life in these hostels was intimate and the interchange of influence between superintendent and students continuous. Amongst the students themselves they formed crucibles of social pressure for they were too small to break up into cliques while too large for the communal groups to dissolve into individuals. Two vital elements in the process were the throwing of communities into intimate personal contract and the effects of interdining. The hostels were unusually cosmopolitan, even for India, because of the diverse elements which made up the official class in New Delhi and the middle class in the city and the Punjab. There were city and Punjabi Muslims, a Bengali group from New Delhi, men from Uttar Pradesh, Marathas from Bombay, southerners from Madras, a hillman or two and an occasional Rajput. These were divided between two messes, vegetarian and non-vegetarian. This simple division was itself at that time regarded as almost revolutionary. For it involved the mingling of several castes in the vegetarian mess and of Muslims and Christians with Hindus in the non-vegetarian. Neither Hindus nor Muslims of the middle class of northern India at this time commonly objected to eating with Christians; but it was otherwise with each other. These messes, with all their petty disputes and perplexities, were really educative in promoting mutual understanding and public spirit. Of course the students were in advance of their elders and were mostly for "no distinction in caste, colour, creed or sex". The social environment too often cooled their ardour in later days, but it was devices such as these which gave an impulse to Indian society whose results are visible today. In the vegetarian mess there were special refinements of distinction. There was often controversy as to whether onion should be served at table. Tolerance suggested their sitting at one end of the table so that sensitive noses could take refuge at the other end, but from time to time there would be a walk-out and a rival non-onion mess established. Stricter spirits still objected to any article suggestive of blood, so that the ruddy beetroot would become a centre of argument. On the whole there was progress through continuing tension. The one group who could not be got to cooperate was the Jains, who were not only strict non-onion, non-beetroot vegetarians, but had to dine before sunset, lest in the dark they should unwittingly consume insects and so take life. The coming of electric light had not then changed their traditional scruple.

The college dining life was crowned by the institution of a monthly college dinner held in the college hall. It was a bold and imaginative step taken by the Indian principal and it proved a great success. The whole college was invited and up to three quarters of them attended at a time. In fact only the little Jain community were permanent absentees. Vegetarian and non-vegetarian food was served on opposite sides of the hall where all sat down as they pleased. The staff attended with their wives (in the case of the Christians). The Principal opened the proceedings with a sonorous and heartfelt grace 'Lord Good, bless our food and fellowship together'. The custom was unique in northern India and had a perceptible effect on public opinion. Indians dearly love a social occasion and found this one hard to resist. A curious distinction was often made between tea parties and other meals. People of all groups amongst the public as well as in the college, would cheerfully meet together for tea functions when they would have misgivings about any other meal. The factor of cooked food was not decisive for they would happily eat European cakes and Indian sweetmeats about the caste of whose cooks they had no knowledge and (if they thought at all about it) would have had the gravest misgivings. This was a great help in entertaining students, for your class tea party was a never failing success. In contrast to a staunch Hindu professor who went to the leading restaurant of the day and demanded "vegetarian" cakes (without eggs) I could point to a whole series of conversions to the cult of chocolate cake, eggs, chocolate and all.

The classes were at first a problem for a new arrival. The students varied greatly in age and I soon found that they resembled exactly no comparable English group in school or university. I next discovered that anyone who was clear and knew what he wanted to say was listened to. "High teachings" were respected for their highness, and anything philosophic met an immediate response. One lecturer who adopted this method had a class where you could hear a pin drop. The lecturer's greatest ally was the instinctive respect for learning and teaching in India. If the teacher was felt to be a real teacher or *guru*, whatever his subject, the students behaved as *chelas* or disciples. On the other hand haziness or lack of grasp would soon cause the chalk to fly and disciplinary roars then would only cause it to fly the faster. Indian students were as fond of a joke and a riot as any other. One young English lecturer believed in the conversational method and his class would buzz like a human beehive. His loose Indian slippers (it was the hot weather) would be abstracted from his feet as they dangled from the dais to be returned at the end of the lecture. One broiling day in June he returned barefooted, heatsore and indignant to his quarters. It was not, he complained, that he minded their taking his shoes during the class but that they had forgotten to return them at the end. One lecturer was muddled and stumbling with quick results. A student left the class, bought an egg at the nearby "tuck shop" and threw it at a comrade. It broke over the wrong comrade who then arose from the class and did likewise. It was only at the second discharge that the lecturer noticed something unusual. For another a booby trap was prepared; a form was arranged which would collapse when a stooge in the class who had been sent out returned and sat on it. but the noise from the class had already reached the ears of the Principal, who came in at the back and sat on the form to observe the proceedings. The device worked and that was the end of that class's diversions for some time to come.

The college staff was a microcosm of the India of the day. The Principal was a brilliant Indian Christian who had taken a Wrangler's degree at Cambridge. He came of one of those Bengali families who were attracted to north India by service opportunities. With the help of his Punjabi wife he united Punjabi vigour with Bengali intellect and charm. There were some half dozen Englishmen who shared the work with Punjabis and north Indians, men of Bengal and the South and Muslims. The Professor of Arabic was a Muslim *maulana* of overpowering dignity and courtesy. He understood but did not speak English; he was a master of Urdu speech so that he could at will move the simplest to gusts of laughter or be so "high flown" or elegant that no student could understand him. There was the young southerner whose English accent aroused the mirth of the northerners but who was quite prepared to tell his English colleagues how to speak English. There was the young philosopher who sat in the staff room apparently immersed in meditation and when asked what he was thinking about would reply, 'Trying to think of nothing'. There was a much loved senior professor who taught all his classes sitting in a chair and smoking a cheroot. His English was so mixed with Hindustani and his Hindustani with English that it was often difficult to understand what he meant. His stories in this style of the Brahmin and the Jat (who always got the worst of it) were favorites at any gathering. He did not read much but his skill as a teacher was supreme. He taught more philosophy to more people with fewer books than any man in his generation.

In spite of these diversities of race, community and temperament the staff in general got on well together. There was a notable friendship between a Bengali so sensitive that the smell of cooked meat affected him with nausea and a Muslim who loved his beef and his whisky and who would remark casually at times of communal tension in the city, 'I think I will sacrifice a cow'. He reserved his enmity for another Muslim who belonged to the other principal division of Islam in India. This kind of enmity was a well known feature of north Indian life, making progress within the Muslim community difficult. Similar inter-communal friendships were widely spread. Their existence showed that it was not inevitable that either enmity or friendship and understanding should flow in strictly communal channels. For me contact with these men was a revelation and an education. Intercourse between Indian and European was freer than almost anywhere else in India at that time. Here was an entry to the contemporary Indian mind without inhibitions and restrictions. Indians sat not only on the staff committees but on the Governing Body as well. We were colleagues on the same level in college, in the University and in the city. And these contacts were public as well as personal. A previous Indian Principal had been a close friend of Mahatma Gandhi and other nationalists; C.F. Andrews with his Gandhian and Tagore connections had worked for ten years in the college and had left his legend behind him; a Bengali member was in the Tagore circle and had translated some of his poems. A Muslim member had connections both with the Muslim nationalists and the traditionalists. These contacts, along with our own connections with the British official world, gave us one of the most comprehensive views of modern Indian society available at that time. Our defect was that, although we visited the countryside and thought we knew something about it, we were insufficiently aware of the great weight of traditional Indian society.

Our students like the staff, were a representative collection. We had a strong contingent of Muslims from both the city and Punjab because there was no government college in the city and many preferred a Christian institution to one of the two Hindu colleges. In a choice of evils the absence of idolatry and a reputation for good teaching turned the scale. Next in prominence were the Bengalis. They were numerous because of the Bengali families working with the Government of India. With their flowing *dhotis* their vivacity and their chatter they made a picturesque group. They were prominent because of the rather brittle brilliance of many of them and their tendency to flock together in groups. While the Muslims were conspicuous on the playing field, the Bengalis sustained the college cultural activities. It use to be said that where two Muslims were gathered together there would be a feast, where two Jats, a quarrel and two Bengalis, a Bengali club. Their other characteristic was clannishness. With a few conspicuous exceptions a Bengali would usually be found with other Bengalis. They were tenacious of their own culture and way of life, their dress, their diet, their clothes, their music, literature and art. They were leaders in things cultural, especially in anything dramatic or anything to do with Tagore. Thus Shakespeare qualified as a poet and dramatist, like Tagore, and Wordsworth as a nature mystic, like Tagore. But this same Bengali consciousness also kept them rather apart from the rest of the college to whom their enthusiasms implied a shade of cultural disdain for other traditions. As a group they were therefore charming, stimulating, provocative but rather apart; they were never very popular in the college society as a whole.

Many Bengali students came from families temporarily stationed in Delhi on government service, the Delhi-Simla community as they were called. But another section came from the city of Delhi itself and belonged to the remarkable Bengali migration of the nineteenth century. As Bengalis led in western education they also led in the new western skills. When the demand for these arose up-country only Bengalis were at first available. For all their alleged timidity and lack of enterprise they went in thousands throughout the north as far as Peshawar on the frontier. They came as school masters, college lecturers, railway officials, as telegraphists and minor officials and above all as doctors and lawyers. In every sizeable town there was a Bengali colony, with of course a Bengali club. The *dhoti* was spread, as it were, from the Hughli to the Indus. In my time many of these families were in their third generation and many had acquired the local culture without losing their hereditary one. Our Principal was a Bengali of the second generation, our college lawyer another who built himself a city house where his son followed him. Every Indian city had its Dr Sens, often combining private practice with free dispensaries in the crowded city centre, its legal Mittra Babus and its retinue of pedagogues. So numerous were these that in many colleges there were Bengali "parties" which strove with the local *Kayasth* or professional caste for the control of college policy. This was an intricate and absorbing occupation, involving much sitting in the staff room and many serious conclaves elsewhere, but only producing much result if leadership was weak or local councils divided. It was, in general, the summer lightning of Indian collegiate society.

Next came the city boys, both Hindu and Muslim. The Mughal tradition still gave them some feeling in common. One of these was an aversion to Punjabis, who in their eyes were uncouth, boisterous and semi-barbaric. Barbarians traditionally came from the north and had left an indelible mark on the Punjab. Many were the sighs at the Punjabi invasion attracted by the rapid development of the city. Another common link was the Urdu language, spoken by both communities, and its related Persian. Persian, the cultural life-blood of the Mughal regime, was regarded as French or Latin might be in England, and was still studied widely by Hindus as well as Muslims. It was common for an undergraduate to take Persian along with History or Economics as his optional subjects for the B.A. degree in addition to compulsory English. In the poetical gatherings or *mushairas*, for which Delhi was famous, Hindu and Muslim poets would impartially declaim their poems in Urdu or Persian. Some of the charm and dignity of the old Mughal world lingered down to the Second World War. This did not prevent, however, communal tension and occasional severe riots.

The most active Delhi group was the *Kayasths*, the writer caste who commonly held administrative posts and had spread into modern commercial activity and retail trade. Through long association with the Mughal government they had acquired some Muslim habits. Some were vegetarians, some were not; some would change this habit every few years. They took easily to European ways and diet, and had a taste for wines and spirits. They liked company and led the way in inter-dining. They were a practical, hard-headed, cheerful down-to-earth sort of people. They were go-betweens by habit and moderates by instinct. They were apt to be a little misleading because their easiness of manner and approach tempted one to regard them as typical Hindus which they were not. Next in prominence were the *bania* or merchant community. He sought education to obtain government service not from custom like the *Kayasth*, but for status or *izzat*. It would raise his prestige in his brethren's eyes. Thus one brother would go in for education with a view to government service, perhaps becoming deeply imbued with a love of culture in the process, while another brother took care of the family business. College education was often a salutary experience for this group, for they tended to be unusually specialised and isolated from their fellows both by caste and habit of mind. Many were kind and humorous and most were highly intelligent but they were certainly financially centred. College life pulled them out of themselves, gave them larger vistas and some sense of personal relations. They came to look on their fellow students as people, and not merely borrowers or lenders, payers or receivers. For some the old pull remained strong. I well remember the chagrin of the Principal when one student who had worked his way through college with the help of full-fee grants on the ground of poverty forthwith took ship for England to continue his studies at his own expense.

In addition to these groups we had representatives from nearly every part of India. We had one or two Rajputs, handsome well-mannered and proud, no intellectuals but shrewd and ready to lead.

India has a great reservoir of leadership in the Rajputs if only they would cast aside their restricting customs and inhibiting habits of thought. Crisis came to one of them when, agreeing to play a Roman in *Julius Caesar*, his approval of Roman nobility was sadly damped when he found that his leg must be uncovered at the knee. The march of progress continued eventually but only after a severe struggle. We had a few from the South, slim, intelligent, fastidious and gentle, one or two from Malabar who were intelligent, pushing and insensitive. They were noted in general for their aggressive temper even in the North, hardened to Pathans and swaggering frontiersmen. The south Indian students got on with the northerners well enough, but not so the south Indian professors. Their pride of knowledge, and rather tactless display of it, their set habits of mind, and (to the northern ear) their peculiar accent grated the nerves of the northerners. They felt an irresistible urge to rag them; mimicry of and jokes about them were endless. We had one or two Marathas who kept us in mind of Shivaji and his glorious fight for freedom (against Muslims) and one or two Parsis from Bombay. There were also a few hillmen who had to skip the summer term because they could not bear the heat. Finally there was our contingent of Sikhs, mostly from New Delhi and belonging to the new rich class of contractors. Nearly all were handsome, some were fat from good living and some were dissipated as well. Some had cast aside the manners of the East without acquiring those of the west and the result was more money than manners and more sensuality than sense. Their presence was often a difficulty and their integration a problem. But all had high spirits and some had fine qualities. I think on the whole the college did a good job for them as the later careers of some of them testify.

It was a curious fact that though the students of the college were three parts Hindu the leadership was often Muslim. In my first year the two contenders for the medal for general distinction were Muslims and Muslims continued to be prominent all my time. This was not because the two groups came from different levels of social strata. The Muslims seemed, in college as well as in society, to throw up a few people of great ability and powers of leadership. Then came a gap, followed by a large proletariat. The Hindus, on the other hand, had fewer outstanding figures but a large class just below of capable and competent people. This could be explained historically on the ground the under the Mughals the Muslims occupied most of the top posts while the Hindus supplied the middling or ministerial ones. The able Muslims were promoted to the top cadre, but once there, would employ Hindu assistants who cold work efficiently rather than Muslims who couldn't. This can be seen on a national scale when we compare the almost faultless leadership of Jinnah with the lack of a middle class competent to carry on the state he created. This explanation may be good for the Muslims but it is not so easy to understand why the Hindus did not produce such outstanding figures among themselves. the Muslims would answer with the single word "caste", but could it not have been Muslim domination itself? Since the Hindus have had their own national movement they have not lacked vigorous and outstanding leadership.

Our college was part of the University of Delhi. During most of my time this was largely a phantom institution. It was said to have been founded as a political job to placate a liberal or moderate lawyer in the early days of the reforms. In its infancy it nearly expired under the Inchcape axe and thereafter was mercilessly starved for funds. It was the educational Cinderella of the Government of India until the magic glass slipper was supplied by the good fairy in the surprising form of the federal Chief Justice of India, Sir Maurice Gwyer. Looking back, it is difficult to understand why it was not abolished altogether, except perhaps that it would be even more disgraceful for the capital of India to have no university at all than only a phantom one.

The University started in a hired hostel built in a cross of Moorish and Indo-Gothic styles and dignified with the name of Curzon House. Then it migrated to the temporary secretariat when the government moved to New Delhi and only in the early thirties found a permanent home in the old Viceregal estate where the British forces had encamped during the siege of Delhi at the Mutiny. It was organised grandiloquently as a federal university with constituent colleges of which there were four. The federal part consisted of a Vice-Chancellor who was a lawyer hoping for a title, a Registrar and later a Reader in Economics[3] and two Readers in Science[4]. The Registrar[5] or the economist could each have ruled the University had they been so inclined, but the one was a sensitive Bengali very open to the shafts of insensitive Sindhis, and not very energetic, while the other was a Sindhi who so enjoyed acting as a gadfly to the academic herd that he forgot to arrange the combinations necessary for control. I liked Chablani. Besides what many considered to be his factiousness and delight in stirring up trouble, he had a certain love of battle, a sense of humour and a staunchness which were attractive. He was one of those people who enjoy opposition and who grow more unreasonable the more they are deferred to, largely, I believe, through unconscious irritation at being deprived of an argument. I found this out early with a battle over the syllabus of Indian history in the B.A. course. With his goatee beard, his keen acquiline face and rather watery bespectacled eyes crowned by a light black cylindrical hat—a Turkish hat without the fur—his jaunty walk and quizzical air, he made a highly individual figure. Alas! after a few years he died of the effects of a mastoid operation.

The university was then little more than an academic ghost and what little life it had was provided by the collegiate members of the various academic bodies. We had titles but no salaries, votes but, in many cases, no liberty to use them because members had to do what their Principals told them. We all had free voices, however, so many made up for the lack of frees votes by an excess of free speech. Meetings were numerous and interminable, usually three hours at a time and ended by virtual exhaustion. The wise Chairman put the most important items at the end of the agenda, because five or six items were commonly taken in the last five minutes in a fever of exhaustion and frustration. At that time social life in the academic world was still very feeble. Caste restrictive habits if not prejudices inhibited many contacts and these meetings were among the chief occasions when many of the members could meet people of their own world outside their own colleges. Arguing across a table was a kind of social function for them, and enjoyed accordingly.

If the University's first defect was the lack of the corporeal blood of finance, its second was of the chronic conflicts of its constituent colleges. The inward-looking tendency of the Indian caste system appeared at once in the federal structure of the University. Each college was jealous of its privileges, suspicious of its neighbours and insistent on its rights to a degree which made any corporate action or cooperation almost impossible. In this, afraid, my own college was no exception. University life became largely a collegiate struggle led by the principals of the two chief colleges. In my corner this was happily mitigated by my friendship with the History Professor at the Hindu College. He had lived in the Oxford mission hostel at Calcutta and studied at Oxford. Though a thorough Bengali in his taste and fastidiousness he was unusually balanced and almost prosaic, free from fears and suspicions as well as naturally friendly. We worked a system of intercollegiate lectures for Honours and graduate students for years together through which I came to know many students from the Hindu College as well as my own. It did my college nothing but good, but few of my colleagues saw this. I always knew of his visits beforehand because he had a wooden leg which gave a characteristic squeak when he worked the joint. When he was Principal of his own college for some years the University enjoyed unwonted peace. Even the Muslim students of his college, keen critics in these matters, agreed that they had a fair deal from him. He died from overwork before he was fifty.

In the University there was always a good time coming, and expectation took the form of endless discussion with the government of India. But in my time it was neither a place of aspiration nor inspiration. It examined and gave degrees and that was about all that could be said for—or against—it.

The Citizen

Our college tradition, and actual practice of close contact with students and the Indian staff led naturally to contacts with the city. We inherited the work of our predecessors who were regarded as part of the city life. The college itself had been founded to fill a gap caused by the closure of the old government Delhi College which dated back long before the Mutiny. It had the blessing of leading citizens including the surviving head of the Mughal imperial family. For nearly twenty years it stood alone in the city. In those days missionaries, if imaginative and able, could be powerful public forces. It was said that what Allnutt and Thomas agreed upon would be accepted by the citizens of Delhi. Allnutt was the first Principal of the College and for many years head of the High Anglican Cambridge Brotherhood; Thomas the forceful head of the Baptist Mission, originally founded by a disciple of the great William Carey of Serampore. High Anglican and Baptist was an unusual combination in Victorian and Edwardian days but these two understood and respected each other rand together created a legend. I think that this readiness to receive the foreigner into Indian society was unusual if not unique at that time. Close contacts of Europeans with Indian students and staff may seem an obvious cliché today, but it was by no means obvious forty yours ago. 1924 was the year of the publication of *A Passage to India*. In government colleges the Europeans were regarded and sometimes behaved as semi-government officials. Contact with other teachers was hindered by questions of status and with students by their numbers and entanglement in the European social round. In Christian colleges the question of Christian and non-Christian occurred. Though the non-Christians were no longer the damned, they had still to be saved. Though Indian culture should certainly be studied, it was dangerous to appreciate it too much. In our case the influence of Allnutt in the city, the close friendship of C.F. Andrews with the first Indian Principal Rudra (appointed in 1906) and the outlook he spread of "Christianity the crown of Hinduism" helped to get over these barriers. While all sorts of opinions, including anti-Indian ones, existed in our circle, it was possible to enter freely into Indian life and thought without anguished searchings of heart or incurring suspicions of heresy.

The centre of the city was reached from Kashmere Gate by a long and winding footbridge across the railway marshalling yard. It led to an open space known as Queen's garden and now as Gandhi park, once a Mughal garden. It was used for meetings and was otherwise by day a dormitory of great bats who unlimbered and flew off with sinister lurches at dusk, and a playground for monkeys. These had a regular route to Kashmere Gate and one troupe could be identified year after year by a one-legged monkey who, perhaps understandably, had a very bad temper. Across the garden you came to the Chandni Chowk. Designed by Shah Jahan as a processional way to his palace it was broad and nearly a mile long. Once a canal had run down its centre, but this had long been covered over. There were no impressive buildings; its only features were two lines of jaded looking *neem* trees, as if distraught by the incessant clamour and two sets of tramlines close to the pavements, along which trams crept noisily clanging from their way wandering cows and beggars and unwary pedestrians.

The Chowk was the hub of the city. By day it was wracked in unending din and appeared to be a permanent chaos of trams, cars, tongas, bullock wagons, camel carts, bicycles and cattle, each making noise after their kind and finding their way on the halma principle of zig-zags and jumps rather than by any rule of the road. The people were a cross-section of all the races of India with a sprinkling of Europeans and a Greek chorus, as it were, of coolies with baskets seeking customers, and beggars. The infirm, many of whom where probably lepers, would sit against walls holding out stumps of arms and legs. In the narrow *Dariba* running towards the Great Mosque there were rows of silversmith's shops. The wares of the Chowk were less obvious, but much more varied and valuable. In some the finest cloth of Kashmir, India and China could be bought as you sat on a rickety tin chair on the pavement. In others you could pick up, along with the latest ivory novelties designed for the tourist, genuine Mughal miniatures for a few rupees. At the far end of the street was a great mosque (Fatehpuri Masjid) and the shops of Muslim merchants. Behind the unimpressive shop fronts lay family mansions of unexpected dimensions. On the one side were Jain and *bania* merchants and bankers, some amongst the richest men in India, but of the simplest habits and dress and the humblest manners. On the other side in separate blocks, were the old town houses of the Mughal nobility, one block now mostly occupied by the enterprising *Kayasth*s and the other by Muslim merchants or aristocratic relics. These houses were reached through lanes known as *kucha*s or *gali*s and without were undistinguished. But with-in they spread out into court after court with open verandahs and *neem* trees. From the roof of one of them the old city looked like a garden city.

By day the dust, the noise and the glare of the sun played havoc with one's notions of the romantic east. But at night the scene changed. There was no deep roar of traffic to cease, but the hubbub of the streets, the innumerable sounds more tiring by their stridency than penetrating by their volumes were stilled. The crowds had departed and the shoddy aspect of the ordinary buildings was veiled by a merciful darkness little relieved by dim lamps. The moonlight would emphasise the contours of the domes and minarets of the mosques and would make even the shops and booths look mysterious. You could wander down the *galis* and *kuchas* to meet only an occasional passer by, or a stray sweet vendor sitting hopefully on his platform by the light of a primus gas lamp. Delhi then was tranquil, withdrawn and mysterious.

A very pleasant part of my life was the study of the Delhi monuments. It is these, more than anything else, which make Delhi unique among the cities of northern India. Agra has the Taj and Jampur, its unique mosques, but in each case these monuments belong to a particular period and the cities themselves are unplanned. Delhi has a tradition going back three thousand years and copious monuments stretching over nine centuries and illustrating successive dynasties. It provides a history of medieval and modern northern India in stone. So often thought of as a place of vain regrets and lost glories, in fact with New Delhi it pointed to the future as well. These long bare roads of the twenties with their rows of trellised brick circles concealing newly planted saplings were symbolic of the sprouting nationalism which was to overspread the land within a generation. Within the city the central features were the great mosque and the Red Fort or Mughal Palace. The mosque was a magnificent object from any angle and in any light, but it was irritating to visit because of the mingled cupidity and fanaticism of its janitors. It was number one on the tourists' list and they were, I suppose, regarded as legitimate business. It was not so much prayer as prey that you found there. After one had mastered the plan of the fort and its sites of its vanished buildings, had admired the classic proportions of the Halls of Public and Private Audience—great tents frozen into stone and marble—I was oppressed with its air of melancholy and foreboding. Barracks which were caves in winter and furnaces in summer, stood on each side on the former quarters of the bazaar, the imperial *Zenana* and the places of detention of the junior members of the royal house with their immense and untold burden of misery and despair. Over the buildings that survived, clean and well-maintained as they were, hung an air of decay and one could well understand the survivor of the imperial house who once a year was said to mount the throne of the *Diwan-i-Am* and recite with lamentation the former glories of his race. The palace had been mainly occupied by the court in the declining days of the empire, and that was why, perhaps, for all its beauty the prevailing air within was one of sadness. The palace brooded, as if absorbed in past disaster, and mindful also perhaps of calamities yet to come.

But the city contained much more, both large and small, than these show pieces. It was delightful to wander though the lanes and streets, picking out mosques, mansions and *sarai*s, nearly all with some historical association attached. The Sikh temple in the Chandni Chowk, being laboriously rebuilt by New Delhi contractors with exactly the same Jaipur red stone as was used for the new secretariat, marked the spot where a Sikh *guru* or religious leader had been executed by the Emperor Aurangzeb. This was a main occasion for the bitter and fatal break between the Sikhs and the Mughals. The graceful if sometimes anaemic forms of the eighteenth century buildings gave me a taste for late Mughal architecture which I have always wanted to follow up. The people who produced such symmetry and design could not have been wholly corrupt. There were the beautiful collegiate buildings or Ghazi-ad-din, (now the Delhi College) and later still, the classical town houses of the Begam Samru with its Mughal marble bathroom suite. She married a German adventurer, became a Catholic and later ruled a principality near Delhi for many years complete with palace, cathedral and specially appointed bishop, by name Julius Caesar. The walls contained Mutiny memories. You could walk down one street and know that behind nearly every door lived members of the imperial family. You could go into a section near the great mosque and see stalwart Muslims constructing their *tazia*s or symbolic cloth and paper hearses decked with tinsel and bright colours for the mourning procession of the *Mohurram* festival. Or you could watch the mingled fair and ritual of the *Dassehra* festival celebrated by the Hindus. Here (if internal dissensions did not suspend the proceedings) processions led by bands, jugglers and acrobats, and consisting of the chief characters of the great Hindu epic, wound through the streets ten days running to a fair ground outside the walls. There, on the final day, giant paper figures of Ravan and the chief villains went up with loud bangs in a blaze of fireworks.

The plains of Delhi were littered with monuments for some ten miles south and several miles to the north of the old city. Here the successive imperial cities could be traced and the development of style studied. But when this had been done something further remained. One returned, but not to measure angles or read inscriptions. Some of the buildings, in fact, were gaunt and austere, and many were tumble down and ruinous. Nor was it mere antiquarian sentiment with its oriental expression "the spider weaves its web in the palace of Afrasiab". Except for some focal spots like the Qutab Minar, Humayun's Tomb and the palace of Feroz Shah, there was little evocation of historical scenes. Rather, I think, they acted as focal points of grace and meaning from which to enjoy the North Indian countryside. The monument provided the object and convent *milieu* for the excursion. The pleasure was no doubt enhanced by the buildings but came mainly from nature, the sun and blue sky, the crisp dry air, the spreading trees with their grateful shade, the gambols of squirrels and the chattering of parrots. Tombs were frequent targets, but in no sense gloomy ones. They were, at their best, stately domed buildings with large enclosures laid out as gardens. The form and colours of these buildings with the reddish stonework, white marble domes and excellent proportions were neither macabre or even funereal; rather they formed convenient backgrounds for a grouping of trees and lawns and an assembly of wild life. My favourite was Humayun's Tomb, the finest of all the Mughal tombs after the Taj. It contained several smaller tombs within its enclosure, was nearly a quarter of a mile long on each side, and was well studded with trees. Its garden was large enough for crowds to visit the tomb without invading the privacy of those strolling or sitting on the lawns. There one could enjoy nature, fine architecture and the flow of local life at will, and as it were, without involvement. The tomb of Feroz Shah was another favourite and was unique of its kind. It was a pre-Mughal (fourteenth century) monument and stood in no enclosure of its own. But lawns had been laid out round it and linking it with a large collegiate building which stood at the corner of the great irrigation tank or lake, now dried up. This was described by the conqueror Taimur as so wide, that a man could not shoot an arrow across it. Thought dry the bed of the tank was fertile and green with crops in the cold weather. The buildings gave dignity, calm and repose, the raised bank a sense of space and perspective and the crops life and colour. In the clear but mellow evening light of the north Indian winter it seemed an otherworldly haven of peace.

As some tombs had no enclosures, some enclosures had no tombs. These were a Mughal gift to India, enclosed gardens pure and simple, formerly devoted to flowers, fruit trees and fountains. The British added the inevitable green grass with its adjuncts of space and repose. These enclosures were even quieter than those with tombs, but they lacked, paradoxically enough, a certain sense of life. The British added to these remains by landscaping some areas containing groups of tombs and turning them into parks. The Willingdon Park in New Delhi was one of these. In some cases like the Talkatora Gardens in New Delhi and the Qudsia Bagh in the old city they enlarged on old Mughal Garden with lawns and flower beds. Flowers, flowering shrubs and trees combined to produce a blaze of colour during the winter months which the trees prolonged into April and May. For all their beauty, however, these were gardens to visit and view rather than to pass a day in. They were often thronged; they had blazing colour without repose or that sense of oneness with nature to be found elsewhere.

The climate and the scene found social expression in the picnic. In the cold weather they could be leisurely all-day affairs centered on some garden or tomb, and diversified by exploratory walks to neighbouring ruins. Delhi was so rich in remains that it was harder to miss them than to find them. Even the golf course had the graceful mausoleum of a Mughal princess. The first airfield was named after a nobleman's tomb and was lighted from its walls. These days in the fresh air and bright sunlight were one of the elements which gave the Delhi scene and the life there its special flavour among Indian cities. In the hot weather there was the vogue of the moonlight picnic. The days were far too hot for such ventures; the night air was refreshing and the moon could be relied upon to shine. The one hazard was the dust storm, which would spring up suddenly in a matter of minutes, with violent gusts choking the air with suffocating dust and often end with a few drops of rain, promising relief from the heat without providing it. They did not usually last long; they were short and sharp rather than tempestuous, though one I witnessed from a shop in the Chandni Chowk overturned cars and twisted lamp posts. But they always broke up the party; from shock if not from physical discomfort, it was impossible to settle down again. On these occasion parties would assemble on lawns or on the flat roof of some building (fewer mosquitoes up there). The sound of voices was accompanied by the grinding of icecream machines, the chirping of the crickets, and the coming and going of bearers. Two philosophers we knew would sit back to back (for mutual support) and each discourse to the air in front of them, the one on Plotinus and the other on Spinoza. The argument would get more and more confused as each failed to catch the other's meaning until either icecream came to cool their faculties or a dust storm to blow them away.

Another interest of mine was the development of New Delhi. When I arrived the secretariat and Viceroy's House were still a-building. These buildings were five miles from Kashmere Gate and one of my first journeys was cycling to see the still shapeless masses of brick and stone with the long lines of "coolie" men and women carrying materials on their heads to the tune of dirge-like chants. At that time, in 1924, only one or two avenues, like Asoka Road, where inhabited and had grown trees. The monotonous effect of the American grid pattern was avoided by the system of radiating roads from a number of circles which were the forerunners of the roundabouts of today. A minor drawback was the frequent radiation of five instead of four roads from a centre with resultant confusion when trying to fulfil a dinner engagement in the dark. The confusion on the return journey was often even greater. A feature of the roads was their vistas. Both the great mosque and the Old Fort, amongst others, could be seen from a variety of angles so that one was never oppressed by the feeling of being lost in a sea of modernity. Another effect of the planning was its variety and frequent surprises. The straightness of the roads indeed was oppressive before the trees grew up, so that we would feel impelled at times to drive down Sonehri Bagh road, which had a curve and old trees because it was a fragment of an old main road. One would come unexpectedly not only on new vistas but also on old buildings "over run" as it were in the new town plan. Thus the "Jantar Mantar", the giant observatory of the Rajput Raja Jai Singh, stood out suddenly by Parliament street, while the ruined tomb of a late Mughal chief stood out in the middle of Kingsway. In the spaciousness, the vistas and the leafiness of New Delhi Lutyens served posterity well. It will take many years of encroachment to convert the whole into a bureaucratic slum. The bungalows were more impressive for their spacious compounds than themselves. The fatal measure was taken to build "types" according to status. So it came about at the beginning of World War II, when communication became important, that one road had a telephone in each house while its neighbour had none. It was only when kings began to build palaces and private people their own houses that the buildings themselves became interesting.

The Viceroy moved into his "House" at an inauspicious moment when Gandhi's great civil disobedience movement was at its height. It was just in time for the Mahatma to take his famous walks up Kingsway before the Gandhi-Irwin truce. From that moment, I think, New Delhi became a city with a personality of its own, for it then had a place in every Indian, as well as every British, mind. The other two stages in its growth to maturity were the opening of the circular Parliament House which brought to it leading figures from all over India and the development of the shopping centre in Connaught Place. This was a great double circle of collonaded shops with cinemas, restaurants and hotels nearby. Thither the Kashmere Gate shops migrated in the early thirties, to be joined by branches of the great city stores, the branches in turn becoming principals. New Delhi in those years was a pleasant and spacious place to live in or visit. It was occupied but not crowded; it was busy but not fevered; it was growing but not out of control. It was filled with fresh young trees, and interspersed with parks and gardens. In the hot weather it was still dead but in the cold season it was a busy centre ablaze with the colours of gaudy flowers, of flamboyant creepers and flowering trees. The government centre was impressive though not quite classic. The double ranged secretariat stood out boldly on a slope but its classic features with oriental details seemed just to fall short of greatness. But the inner courts, where the architect had not to think of effect, had charm and beauty as well as convenience. The Viceroy's House itself, thought set back too far to dominate the whole composition—the occasion of the famous Lutyen-Baker dispute—had on it, as it seems to me, the hallmark of greatness. Its simplicity, its purity of line, its sense of repose and proportion and its single dome breaking the skyline make a whole which both impresses at the time and lingers in the memory.

In the twenties in Delhi there was little social life amongst the Indians in our sense of the term. Society was divided into sections by caste and community, and within those sections to a large extent there was still segregation between men and women. The chief social occasions in the traditional society still strong in the city were weddings when numbers gathered for the *barat* or procession and the group meals which followed. This involved a gathering of family groups rather than a mixture of them. Then there were the great festivals, always with a religious background whether Hindu or Muslim. These had both a private and public aspect. In public there were processions and fairs, with an atmosphere rather like that of a bank-holiday. The most attractive of these was *Diwali*, (described elsewhere), when crowds of all classes thronged the streets in holiday mood buying sweets and toys for the children. Some were solemn such as the mourning procession of the Muslim *Mohurram* or the *Id*s which began with congregational prayers in the city mosques. Then the great mosque would be filled with ten thousand worshippers, men only, standing in orderly and serried lines, with an overspill on the open space outside of twice as many. The other mosques would be filled in proportion. Privately there would be occasions for feasting and family reunions. But again the linkage was within family and social groups and not across them. The Muslims added the *Urs* or religious fair which consisted of trips to the spring of some *pir* or saintsage where prayers would be offered and amusements enjoyed. They were, I believe, frowned on by the orthodox, but they were highly popular especially among the less well-to-do. Gaily dressed parties would career along the roads in small rickety two-wheeled traps endangering the traffic with their races, and without a thought for the lean ponies relentlessly whipped up by tattered drivers.

Because of the lack of social intermixture, public life was turned into a kind of social occasion. I am sure that many committee meetings and the like where needlessly prolonged because the members of various communities enjoyed meeting each other and had few opportunities of doing so. This applied to the Municipal

Committee and the Hardinge Public Library where books were divided up among committee members and recovered from their houses by the librarian on requisition by a reader. When a member of the committee I essayed reform and proposed new rules. All went well at first. Each proposed rule was agreed to with alacrity until we came to the one charging a fee for late return. Then silence fell. There were difficulties, it appeared, there were doubts about the wisdom of such a thing. The new rules unlike the books were shelved. Professional associations afforded some means of communication. The Bengalis had their club, which cut across their own castes but insulated themselves from the rest of the city. The chief activities of such clubs were reading and talking. On gala nights (which I had the privilege of attending more than once) there would be what may be called a swirl of *dhotis* whose owners would consume some wonderful curry to background sounds of Tagore songs and dances to the strains of the stringed *dil ruba* and *Vina*. The Bengalis were certainly the most cultured single group in Delhi, but their culture was strictly provincial. The most active of these professional groups was the Bar Association, which also provided the best cross-section of Delhi society. Here men both from the different provinces of India and the various communities of Delhi met and exchanged ideas. The Bar associations up and down the country were generating houses of political ideas and as such were viewed with suspicion by the authorities. They would have closed them if they could. But they were a direct offshoot of British institutions. They reflected both in their achievement and level of activity, the nature and limitations of the British impact on the country. In disparaging and disdaining them the British officials where really criticizing themselves.

Apart from these groups the main social "mixers" were the "mixed" clubs and the tea party. Bungalow dinner parties were still for the officials in their Shangri-la of New Delhi or the scattered Europeans with some Indian friends in the civil lines. Delhi had a mixed club in the Roshanara, mixed in the triple sense of being open to Europeans and Indians, Hindus and Muslims, men and women. Only well-to-do Indians could afford to belong and these attended in numbers both from the city and official classes. Here they met the local European official and business community; there was a good deal of fellowship and some real friendships. Perhaps inevitably in the circumstances club activity tended to drinking, dancing and card playing which meant that only the less sensitive and more westernized Indians would take part. The Roshanara was colourful and useful but not typical. The tea party on the other hand, had become an established institution throughout the middle class. Through the cold weather, rising to a crescendo in March, these parties would be held in the grounds or compound of some well-to-do man. There would be a central awning or *shamiana* where a few great ones would sit awkwardly on great settees and easychairs spread like pieces of artillery on carpets which hid the green and perfectly dry grass. Around were scattered small tables loaded with European cakes and sandwiches and Indian sweets and savouries. Gaily uniformed men brought round tea. The quantities provided amounted to a main meal per head; the quantities left over must have meant a fortune for the caterers. But you could not provide less or you would lose face. Here all classes could come. Tea not being known to Manu, was non-caste; Hindus and Muslims could sit together at a table here and sip tea which they would not do together anywhere else. By some curious convention the food as well as the tea seemed to be exempt from caste protocol. Under the blue sky and warm sun of Delhi with the varied costumes of the guests and the flaming colours of the flowers these occasions were colourful and cheerful. They had an ethos of their own even though conversation was often a strain owing to the distance of the mental worlds of the speakers from each other. These were the more formal parties with fifty to a hundred guests or more. Others were less so. A man would send round a *chaprasi* or messenger with a list of names summoning you to a party in two days time or perhaps the next day or same afternoon. You would find your name, tick it, return the list to the messenger and then consider whether you would go or not. This procedure had its advantages. There was no need to invent excuses for declining or offence given if you did not go. You had done your part apparently by making that little tick and the host was happy in the thought that he had done his duty for another year.

Delhi in those days was a highly conservative city, and the new life of New Delhi had hardly yet impinged upon it. Hardly any

Muslim women appeared in public except in the shapeless cotton sack with a woven eye-grill known as a *burqa*. Hindu women were not so restricted but still lived mainly at home. A Muslim girl student would drive to the college wearing a *burqa* to be discarded on arrival; their girls' schools were in strict seclusion. There was some stirring among the Hindu community. But it was not until I had been in Delhi for several years that the first women's arts college was started in a city already approaching the half-million mark. The Muslims were still so ingrown that the feeling against western education as something infidel or *Kafir* still widely existed. A conservative city meant absorption in traditional interests, so that internal factions were more important than national issues. The rivalries of *Kayasth* and Bengali, Hindu and Muslim, *bania* and butcher were more absorbing than Congress campaigns. Delhi had produce two Muslim leaders of national rank, and was to produce another but that did not prevent the mass of Muslims from being communal rather than national in sentiment. Anti-government feeling among Muslims fed on Mutiny memories rather than national hopes. Their positive sentiment was pan-Islamic, soured it is true by Turkey's abolition of the Caliphate and now finding expression mainly in distrust of the Hindus. The extremism and provocation of the proselytizing *Arya Samaj* found its counterpart in Muslim organizations and journals. Each side had its martyr and these were of greater concern to the masses in the city than the fasts or the spinning wheel of Gandhi. National politics at that time provided a sort of background to the current competition. Its leaders were divinities to whom homage was paid on certain national festivals but were otherwise regarded as remote and not very relevant. The only secular occasion on which I saw the Muslims really moved was that of a visit by the Nizam of Hyderabad. When he visited the great mosque they turned out in greater numbers than for one of the great annual festivals. For them he was still the representative of the great Mughal. Had not his ancestor been promoted by Aurangzeb? The Muslims did not mind the petrol famine caused by his transport demands but they were bitterly disappointed by his mean appearance, his shabby clothes, his lack of dignity. And when he attempted to play the part of Harun el-Rashid by visiting a famous sweet shop in the Chandni Chowk incognito, he spoilt the effect by haggling over the price. The word went round that the Mughal had become a *bania.*

This was the state of affairs in the twenties—disillusion, absorption in small concerns and petty disputes. The first example of sectionalism I remember occurred in a plague outbreak soon after my arrival in 1924. Infectious rats were trapped in large numbers and dumped outside the city gates ready to be drowned in the river in the morning. Good Jains arose by night to achieve merit by releasing them and so saving life. The next instance was graver. Within six months Delhi was rocked by severe communal riots causing much loss of life. They proved to be historic for they provoked the first of Gandhi's famous three week fasts. The city was hushed while he lay in a Delhi suburb and there is no doubt that, whatever talk went on about eccentricity, it struck responsive chords in the Indian mind. There is a deep seated belief in the efficacy of suffering, not only for purification, but as a sort of dynamo of spiritual power. After the fast he was not only a holier man in their eyes but a more powerful one as well.

Even a lethal riot can have its lighter moments. It happened that, unaware of what was happening in the centre of the city a friend and I were wandering around the outskirts. On entering a main street of a suburb we heard the dull roar of human voices. There, at a slow trot, came a crowed of Muslim rioters shouting slogans and waving knives. Fifty yards behind at an equally stately pace (but as fast as it could go) came a tram full of police and clanging its bell loudly. Behind again, on a high built Ford two-seater, looking rather like a mobile dog-cart, came the Police Commissioner immaculately dressed in well-pressed khaki shorts, a sun helmet and an eyeglass. All kept their distance; the Faith, law and order and decorum were alike vindicated—until the end of the tramline when they called it a day and dispersed to their homes.

These riots would spring from a state of tension and would start from any one of several provocative acts. A dead pig in a mosque, music played provocatively before a mosque, beef hurled into a temple or a cow killed in public are examples. Or a brawl might break out in which someone was killed and the cry for revenge raise. The Muslims were apt to be first off the mark for they had a standing task force in the butchers. Once roused they would raise the cry of *"Din! Din!"* (the faith) and *"maro! maro!"* (kill! kill!) and were as ready to cut human as animal throats in the name of God. The Hindu citizens were less warlike; they would retreat to their houses and await reinforcements. But they were not without resources. I heard an almond eyed student member of the mercantile class remark on one of these occasions: 'We are collecting stones and sulphuric acid'. 'What for?', I innocently asked. 'We keep them on our roofs to throw on the passers by', was the reply.

The real answer to the butchers and the Pathans were the Jats from the countryside. These sturdy Hindu champions liked a fight now and then and had long memories of old scores to pay off. Ahmad Shah the Afghan of two centuries earlier and Timur more than three centuries before that, were still real figures to them. At the news of trouble they would flock into the city with their iron tipped staves. Sometimes they were imported as a precaution so that if an unusual number seemed to be about, one knew that trouble was in the wind.

This public death-in-life persisted through the twenties. It was brought to an end by the great civil disobedience movement of 1930–31. The first stirring was the arrival of the Simon Commission, but this did little more in Delhi than afford the young an opportunity to wave black flags and shout, 'Simon go back' at New Delhi station. Simon himself did not make matters better by sitting up stiffly in his saloon studying his papers with elaborate unconcern and pretending not to hear the shouts which were deafening. But with the movement itself the city awoke to life. Early in May, I saw a great procession of protest filing past our college house in a happy mood and exchanged friendly greetings with them. Half an hour later its mood changed when, I believe, a car tried to force its way through them. The police charged in the rough Indian police way on the unarmed crowd. There were casualties. The atmosphere became electric and remained so for months. Most of the Muslims looked on but the Hindus were united as never before. Students went to prison as *satyagrahis* and we would attend their trials and supply them with books. The most dramatic feature was the emergence of the Hindu women. They marched the Streets singing patriotic songs. They picketed liquor and foreign goods shops, they addressed meetings and organised rallies. One was the local Congress leader for some months until she too was arrested. The uprush of national emotion swept over the barriers of caste, seclusion and sectionalism with such force that they could never be wholly replaced. Delhi returned apparently to its doldrums in the early thirties with the repressive measures but with a difference. The calm and stagnation were on the surface but deep currents were moving in underneath. The non-cooperation movement of 1920–21 was really a clarion call to nationalism, which those who answered hardly understood. It was the civil disobedience movement ten years later which turned an option into a state of mind, an aspiration into a settled purpose. It made the national movement national. And Gandhi did it with salt.

The Missionary

My college was a part of the Cambridge Mission to Delhi and this body again was closely connected with one of the major British Anglican missionary societies. They remained separate in theory but it was said of a certain Head of the Mission that only he and God knew where one began and the other ended. For a time only God knew. But this became too great a burden and the two bodies are now merged into a "diocese". In practice in Delhi the two bodies formed one group and there were enough members to form a separate community. You could not work in a mission institution without taking some part in mission life, without feeling its ethos and being influenced by its attitudes. The mission society stretched out on one side to the Indian Christian community, on the educational side to the westernised non-Christian society, and had contacts with the European official and non-official groups. But it was a compact unit in itself which could not be disregarded.

The Cambridge Mission was founded by the famous Bishop Westcott in 1877 with the declared object, "to interpret the faith of the West to the East, and bring back to us new illustrations of the one infinite and eternal Gospel". Missions in the nineteenth century were mostly the ecclesiastical form of colonialism. Their object was to collect converts as imperialists collected subjects and they were as convinced of the inferiority of other world religions as imperialists were of other civilisations. This declaration was therefore something of a landmark, for it suggested that the West might learn from as well as teach the East. A religion of which this could be done could not be wholly bad. At the back of Westcott's mind was the conviction that there was an affinity between the Johannine gospel and the Upanishadic philosophy which might one day form a basis of understanding. He never worked out this belief and his followers in India came largely to forget it. But I think that this approach left the Mission as a whole with a respect for things Indian and an interest in Indians as persons rather than as potential converts which distinguished it from most of the other societies working in India. It tended to attract more liberal minded people so that it was regarded by many missionaries as almost heretical and by many officials as almost seditious. This was specially the case after the Amritsar massacre in 1919 when many of the mission signed in mistake a manifesto of protest intended only for the local heads of missions. This little body with its ill-assorted members and confused ideas was perhaps the only one in India where C.F. Andrews, the friend of Tagore and Gandhi, could have found at that time (1904) a launching site for his propulsion into Indian society. No other society, I think, would have borne with him for ten years, or he them, nor would they have parted amicably and remained friends. The Delhi of the early nineteenth century under the rule of the Metcalfes had an atmosphere and tone unique in British India. I like to think that the same city bred the Christian counterpart to the Metcalfe "Kingdom" in the late nineteenth and early twentieth centuries.

The College as a Christian institution set itself to provide a sound education in a Christian framework. It hoped for and welcomed converts, but it did not set out specifically to make them. In this it differed from some others where desire to justify activity by results tended to turn education into a series of soul traps for the unwary. This view was neither absent nor silent in Delhi but fortunately never prevailed in the college. The college view was that the period of education was a time for sowing the seed; results should come after. So while there was formal religious teaching for all classes every day of term, there was an equal emphasis on the infiltration of Christian ideas and ideals through personal contacts. Persons are the germ carriers of ideas. Rather more than half the college staff were Christian, Indian and English. It was these who in social and cultural societies, in sport and in hostels and in the tutorial class, exercised the vital influence on the students. It was this attitude and these teachers who were responsible for the impact made by the college on its *alumni*. After an old student had recalled the cricketing prowess of Andrews or the disciplinary rigour of Wright—'Downright we used to call him'—he would go on to this or that professor whom he had grown to admire and love. Never did I hear econiums passed on our religious teaching as such. So far as the college influenced Indian society, it was through the cultural germ carrying activities of the staff.

This question of the direct or indirect method of exercising Christian influence has been one of the basic issues of all Christian activity in non-Christian countries. The ecclesiast feels that a visible church should reward his efforts; without it those who are influenced will "backslide". The nationalist calls this spiritual imperialism, an attempt to capture the souls as well as the bodies of its victims. The western sceptic labels it cultural aggression. 'Are not most missionaries apostles of the west as much as of Christ?' On the other hand the believers in sowing the seed secretly, in influence rather than argument, in example rather than precept, are subject to the charge of ineffectiveness, of milk and water Christianity. Both methods have their place. But a way of assessing their relative value is to look at the results of Christian endeavour as a whole after a century and a half of Protestant missionary activity on a relatively large scale. We see a small body of Christians, two per cent of the total population. These are turn divided into all the sects of the Western world. These bodies are moving towards unity among themselves but they are also tending to turn inwards for self protection rather than outwards towards evangelisation. There remains the great mass of non-Christian India. But how non-Christian is it? The most revolutionary moment in modern Asian history was when the British under Lord William Bentick deliberately introduced English education and western institutions into India in the eighteen thirties. With this went the basic ideas of the Christian west, to be propagated, often quite unconsciously, by officials, technicians, agnostic educationalists as well as educational missionaries. The second great moment was the educational "explosion" from about 1870 onwards when Indians themselves took up Western education in a big way. One has only to compare the India of today with that of 1800 to realise the immense transformation that has taken place, the immense influence that the Christian west has had on the mind of modern India. And in spreading that influence in India no agent has been more fruitful than the mission college.

The mission society had its twin hearts in the Brotherhood and the Community. Then men who came out as the result of Westcott's call formed a Brotherhood with an elastic kind of rule. They had a house in the city where for many years they exercised a great influence. The highlight was perhaps the occasion when the then head, Lefroy, was invited to address the assembled Muslims in the Jama Masjid or cathedral mosque of Delhi, rather like inviting a Muslim divine to preach in St Paul's Cathedral. After the World War I they sold this house at a great profit and moved to a bungalow in the miniature garden city to the north of the old city, called the Civil Lines. The bungalow they purchased dissolved at the touch of the contractor and when I arrived they were building a new one. They lived rather uncomfortably with the college men whom some of them thought frivolous. Their head was a liberal mined and philosophical mathematician with a taste for bridge and a liking for the expletive "oh the devil". He would have been more at home in the college or university but eventually found satisfaction in drafting the constitution of the independent Anglican Indian church. His silences were famous and so were his sick visits which began with, 'Hullo, how are you?' continued with the perusal of the nearest book to hand and ended with, 'Oh the devil, I must be getting along'. He loved to distinguish the issues and was constantly "betwixt and between". But though one of the ablest men in Delhi he lacked pomp or pride; he was well loved, not least at such moments as when he suddenly said in a meeting to a senior woman missionary, a lady of great force and dignity, 'But my dear girl you can't do that'. His successor was a little man with an eager and wistful personality, giving and receiving much affection, filled with ideals and generous plans and dogged by loneliness and a sense of frustration. It fell to him to try to weld this loose clerical group together in the stresses of the post-war world and the labour nearly broke his heart. The brethren had their fine new house in a beautiful setting but they could not find contentment or unity among themselves. Perhaps they had somehow lost a sense of direction, perhaps they had left Bishop Westcott's ideals behind in the city house they sold so well. The tension in the thirties was something that could be felt on entering the house. On occasion they would ask you to dinner and after a strained meal retire each to his own room leaving the guests to find their way out. Later they decided that the way out was to have a much stricter rule of life and they now, so I am told, have services in Latin and recite the 119th Psalm, all the hundred and seventy six verses, every day.

The penumbra to the Brotherhood, as it were, was the married missionaries maintained by the S.P.G. When I arrived, one of these was an architect[6] who had built several dignified churches and a number of substantial schools. He maintained the Victorian Anglican formality; he wore a clerical frock coat and still expected formal calls from his younger colleagues before he took notice of them. But he had done the very un-Victorian thing of marrying an Indian lady, which somewhat isolated him even in Delhi and gave occasion for other missionaries to say, 'you see what becomes of being liberal.' These men were in charge of churches in the city and the neighbourhood and with their domestic surroundings provided points of human contact not available in the Brotherhood. They helped to bridge the social and human gap between the mission and the Christian community.

The other heart of the mission was the "Community", the Sisterhood of Anglican women who ran the women's hospital, taught in and ran schools and worked in the city parishes and the villages. They had virtually two centres, the "Home", a comfortable bungalow in the civil lines adjacent to two schools and an orphanage, and the hospital, close to the old city wall. In 1924 there were perhaps thirty of them in all and one would go far to meet a more colourful collection of forceful women. They were then just emerging from the stricter school of Victorian deportment and there was the usual tension between old and young. To wear a bonnet or a veil was a crucial question, and if a bonnet, strings or no strings. One member told me of a severe reprimand from one of the old school for omitting strings to her bonnet. It was next door to revolution. They all wore grey and were known as the grey ladies, and could be divided into right and left wings by the sign of the bonnet and the veil. Hats, I believe, were a kind of red danger signal of the thirties, when all standards were crumbling.

The Community had its personal problems too, but nevertheless these women formed the real social centre of our group. Though they were less in touch than the Brothers with modern Indian sentiment, they were far closer to the people of the city. In the nineties it was the Anglican Allnutt and the Baptist Thomas who knew the mind of the city; in the twenties the grey ladies. Again, though they were more old-fashioned in their views than the Brethren they were far more humane in their attitudes. As a result the Home and the Hospital were social centres where one always received a welcome and found friendliness. People complained that they were un-Indian or even anti-Indian, but to a newcomer specially they were havens of fellowship. They had their Sunday at-homes, their periodic dinner parties, very simple but pleasant, warm hearted and often genial and above all the Christmas party. Then the mission members and its Indian friends gathered and Queen Victoria was forgotten in a medley of charades, skits and local mission squibs. Those who imagine that all missionaries were pompous and dull, and the women in particular prim and repressed, should have attended one of these gatherings. (All very non-U no doubt but genuine and enjoyable nevertheless.)

In the inter-war years, the age of the long term male missionaries seemed to be passing. The men who ruled their kingdoms for forty years with devoted but oppressive benevolence, disappeared and left no successors. But with the women the cult was still in full swing. There were those who refused to retire, or, if they did, retired in Delhi. They not only refused to retire; they were tireless. One lady retired to England for several years ad then returned at nearly the normal retiring age to stay on until here late eighties. An adopted son grew up to be ordained, live out his ministerial life and die while she still tramped the dusty miles of the north Indian villages on a plateful of porridge per morning. We once met her at a viceregal garden party when in her late sixties. I must look out, said she, for the mission doctor, because she said, 'I was too ill to come out today.' In a moment she was bounding away having caught sight of her enemy in the distance. When World War II broke out she was about to return to India and was advised to cancel her passage by the Society. 'I don't care tuppence for the S.P.G.', said she in a deep booming voice and proceeded on her voyage, allegedly in someone else's cabin.

In one respect the women had an advantage over the men, in that pioneering was still possible. For the men the inhibitions of custom, of finance and mental convention were now too strong for much originality to find expression; in the women's world much that was new in India could be attempted without violating accepted canons. One such pioneer came to Delhi in the time of Lord Curzon (1904) and was still working there at the time of writing. She was tall, handsome, conventional in outlook and impressive in presence. She had a will of iron and allowed nothing to come in the way of any purpose once formed. She was utterly disregardful of her own comforts and would live cheerfully in one room or less to provide more space for her institutions, living on any diet which happened to be available. But never for a moment did she lose her dignity or drop any of the claims of etiquette. When a group of missionaries were asked by the wife of a member of the Viceroy's Council to meet other officials and their wives, it was she rather than the honourable member's wife, who was soon holding court of the officials. No situation was too much for her. I went to tea at her school in my early days and mentioned that I had just seen Mahatma Gandhi after his twenty-one day's Delhi fast. 'Did you shoot him?' asked a Major who until then had been speechless. Miss X[7] treated him as Queen Elizabeth might have an interrupter to one of her speeches. With a word of disapproval and an air of disdain which could be felt without being expressed, she passed to the next subject. It was enough that she was not amused for the Major to regain his speechlessness. The Bishop of the diocese, a powerful man in those days, once expressed his disapproval of a very special project of hers and said he would stop it. 'Really,' remarked Miss X, 'the Bishop can't stop a thing like this. Of course it will have to go through'—and it did. When, not for the last time, it was thought to be time for her to retire, matters went as far as selecting a principal to succeed her. But Miss X did not wish to retire from this particular post just then. She remained imperturbable and after a few weeks announced quite casually, 'Quite a surprise you know, Miss so and so has suddenly decided to marry and to leave us.' As Miss X was one of the principal matchmakers for the educated Indian Christian community no one had much doubt as to whose decision it was. On one occasion she had arranged for the Vicereine to give away the prizes at one of her schools. The Vicereine was unwell and sent the Viceroy to represent her (all Delhiwallahs will know who he was). When the prizes were presented the Viceroy, according to custom, got up to make suitable remarks, 'No, no,' called out Miss X, 'we're having no speeches today, please sit down'. The Viceroy obeyed and commented to his lady that never before in India had he been told not to make a speech. Miss X's genius lay in the fact that not only did she do these things but that she got away with them.

Her first pioneering feat was to be the first Englishwoman to ride a cycle into the old city. This she did wearing long skirts and holding a parasol. Lord Curzon in his *howdah* on an elephant and Miss X on her cycle beneath her parasol, and there was no doubt as to which of the two was more regal. Perhaps she did not realise that an umbrella was a sign of royalty, and perhaps that was why in a city where at that time no respectable woman went unveiled and few even went on foot, she was never molested but treated with wonder and respect. Some year later she founded, against the advice and without the help of the Mission, a High School for non-Christian girls. It has just celebrated its jubilee and is now a leading Delhi school. Years later her health would not stand the hot weather, so she went to Simla for the summer. Here she started a school for the daughters of officials who came up with the Government of India every year. Soon a New Delhi branch appeared for the same girls in the cold weather. Then the school outgrew peripatetic officialdom and became anchored in New Delhi in its own right. The object of episcopal frowns, it is now a leading school in New Delhi. Miss X was a strict disciplinarian and was once reported in the press as telling a meeting of advanced educationalists that she had always found corporal punishment very useful. But her pupils loved her and would record with glee years later their pleasure at being corrected by her. From this school she went to junior schools and kindergartens, always founding a blazing trail until she was to be found living in a vestry and starting a nursery school for Christian children in a cantonment.

The women of the mission contrived on a mere subsistence pittance which was even less than that of the Brothers' and all that most of them had. The rule was not strict, a sort of compromise between the freedom of a social worker and the restrictions of a religious order. Sometimes this led to the difficulty of not quite knowing where one stood and there was the inevitable tension between the "strict" and the "lax" as well as the social tension between the bonnets and the veils and hats. But on the whole their rule suited the circumstances of their work and one would go far to find a more harmonious or more constructive body of women. An annual wonder was the exodus of these slender-resourced and hard worked people for their summer vacation. Many would go to Kashmir where they would live in tents or huts; others would take long hikes in the mountains, carrying their provisions with them. They were fearless and indefatigable with the gift of the widow's never-failing cruse of oil.

The Mission in the inter-war years was almost wholly European so that one might well ask where liaison with India came in. There were one or two married Indian clergy, in responsible positions, but they did not solve the problem. They tended to be regarded as show pieces on the one hand and so inflated, and to be thought unsound on the other if they took an independent line. Their shortcomings, such as they were, were different to those of their European colleagues, being related to their own Indian setting. But they were judged on European standards which made neither for harmony nor understanding. Celibacy was an obstacle to their entering both Brotherhood and Sisterhood, for most of the sexes married and married young. The only real mixing of Indian and English colleagues on equal terms was in institutions, some in the schools, a beginning in the Hospital, and most in the College. There we had an Indian Christian principal of great distinction and several Indian Christian teachers of ability and character.

Beyond the mission lay the Indian Christian community which was itself the soul-child as it were, of the mission. It was organised into a well-to-do church and a poor church in the city, and a mixed congregation in New Delhi. Later a great church which became a cathedral, was built by the efforts of Lord Halifax and there was St James in Kashmir where Europeans Anglo-Indians and Indian Christians attended impartially. Outside there were a number of village congregations. These were not by any means the only Christians to be found for there were Roman Catholic, Baptist and Methodist Episcopal churches as well, border groups of Seventh Day Adventists, Jehovah's Witnesses and possibly others. This recital in itself may be considered an indictment of Christian activity in India, but I would say it indicts the method of procedure rather than the fact of approach. On matters of principle you cannot represents yourself to be anything other than you are, but you can encourage others to be themselves and not replicas of yourself. This replica idea was a trap into which the early missionaries fell so that Anglicans would call themselves S.P.G. and C.N.S. Christians and the use or otherwise of Hymns Ancient and Modern could become almost an article of faith.

This community was of the most varied kind and far from completely integrated. In fact it provided a subject ripe for the sociologists, of which subject our little group was unfortunately quite innocent. The principles of social psychology, I felt, would have been of more value in understanding them and meeting their needs than the canons of pastoral theology. But this was what they got—as applied to that peculiar sub-species of mankind, the homo Britannicus. The oldest established Christian families were perhaps in the fourth generation but most of them were in the second or third. At the top came a small group of highly educated people, mostly belonging to the upper castes (you could tell them by their names). These were the descendants of the *Brahmin* and *Kayasth* converts of the mid and late nineteenth century and o *Khattri*s from the Punjab. Some were Bengalis settled in Delhi and some may have come from Duff's Christians in the eighteen thirties when there was a high caste movement towards Christianity in Calcutta. These people would intermarry amongst each other but caste feeling came out if a marriage with a family of low caste origin was suggested. They were the aristocracy o the community and often held high positions in government or society. The trouble was that beyond this small group there was no established middle class. The rest of the body had been recruited from two "outcast" groups in the city and surrounding districts, the sweepers and the leather workers. For them Christianity was a liberation, social and economic as well as spiritual, though their caste superiors, specially in the villages, saw to it that the former kind was as restricted as possible. In the city, education followed conversion and opportunity education. The opportunity was heightened by the rapid expansion of the city after it became the new capital. So in the course of a generation or two the brighter converts climbed into positions of responsibility and modest prosperity. A few became outstanding. These people became a middle class in the economic sense, but they were new men, they were *arrivistes*. They were not fully recognised by the small upper class—the attitude I think was a mixture of disdain, jealousy and fear, and they were not sure of themselves. They had still to develop their own taboos and conventions in this new position. They were therefore very difficult to handle, though often very charming to meet. They were unwilling to submit to each other and thought it a mark of their new position not to submit to others. Their problem was a social or sociological one, but the missionaries would treat it as a moral one. So they were constantly firing at targets over the heads of the offenders and being surprised that the objects of their endeavours remained quite unaffected.

I have said that the problem of these people was mainly a sociological one; in fact there were a whole series of such problems. Among the unlettered or outcaste town Christians there was an acute economic problem of employment. Those of the leather worker caste formerly made Hindustani slippers, but these were rapidly being replaced in the towns by European style shoes made by the enterprising Bata. The occupation in itself was a craft, but it lacked respect and opportunity to practice it. So even if you got over the status objection to the craft, you still had not got a craft to practice.

The other main section of the "outcaste" Christians was the sweepers who had every reason to hope for a change of employment. But what were they to do? There were enough labourers for the building works already, sturdy villagers who came in with their families (who also worked) camping in huts called coolie lines. There were the cotton mills, and here I think was an opportunity. There was a demand for labour; the pay meager though it provided a livelihood, and having houses already these people would not have been condemned to the appalling conditions of the many who came straight from the countryside. This might have sufficed until by education both groups had been enabled to climb higher. But the missionary answer was to encourage them to become domestic servants, "bearers" and cooks. In doing this, they forgot that the service of Europeans and westernized Indians was a profession nearly two centuries old with standards and techniques of its own. The profession itself was a useful outlet and at that time an expanding market, but successful entry into it required training and careful selection. Nothing of this kind was done with the result that while a few made good like our own cook, many wandered in to slip quickly to the bottom rung and to give the whole community a "bad name" by their incompetence and lack of standards. Why blame them for lacking standards which no one even tried to give them? If you asked for a domestic servant the tendency was to send along a member of a family judged most to need help. He would arrive innocent of the right end of a fork or spoon and blame would be meted out when he was judged unsuitable. 'Not kind to Christians' was the missionary verdict. But philanthropy at the expense of the customer did much harm to these people; it gave them no employment and discouraged them, it exasperated the public and gave them an unduly adverse view of Christian servants. The missionaries concentrated on moral faults when they should have been finding these people purposeful employment. This would have given them a sense of self respect and belonging in a new situation instead of merely not-belonging in an old one.

The problems of the rising middle class and the small upper class were of course different, but they were essentially social and ideological rather than moral. The new middle class had employment and some status; they had a place in society but not yet an assured place. They had not yet defined their position both with the rest of Christian society and with society at large. The oil of the social machine, convention and habit, the sense of limits and the permissible, in short social values, was lacking. I don't think there was or is any easy solution for people in their situation. It called for endless patience from those who dealt with them and ingenuity in directing their energies into socially constructive channels which would draw out these great latent creative abilities. The problems of the top class were the most complicated of all. They had for the most part adopted western values as well as Christian doctrines. But now they found themselves being overrun, as it were, by the great westernizing movement within Indian society. The point of crisis was where the *Erlhing* of nationalism threatened to engulf its victim. They were blamed for their association with the imperialists, they were reproached for being denationalised (Edwardian Indian ladies had gone to the length of discarding the sari) and by some they were threatened with dire consequences when "freedom came". They were but a drop in the ocean of Indian life, and who could blame them for nervousness and anxiety. The missionaries on their side blamed them for liking the glitter of the west too much, or for worldliness, (seeking government posts not mission service). They retaliated by demanding self-government within the church and charging the missionaries with imperialism. Their dilemma was that if Hinduism was all evil, a favoured missionary stance, how could they compound with nationalism, which was closely bound up with it? And if they became nationalists, could they remain good Christians? And if they held aloof from it all what was to become of them in the new world which was clearly coming? Men like C.F. Andrews and S.K. Rudra, who combined Christian principles with fervent nationalism, were a great help, but they were a minority and Andrews was regarded by most missionaries as next door to a heretic. Their dilemma was real and painful; small wonder that in the tension of World War II many of them were much more bitter towards the British than Congressmen. In the end their best friend turned out to be Jawaharlal Nehru, for his secular nationalism and openly western cultural sympathies, enabled them to settle happily into the society of the new India.

How the community will develop is anyone's guess; most Indian aspects at present seem to be the least sophisticated. Then Christian fairs resembling the Hindu *mela* and the Muslim *Urs*, have caught on; so has the *Prem Sabha* or devotional meeting which has affiliations with the Vaishnavite *Sankirtan* and often lasts all night. Processions, long services and rituals also appeal. All that one can say, perhaps, is that when the Christians find a real means of self-expression it will be much closer to Indian practice than to the semi-western now in vogue.

The Householder

When my wife and I set up house together Sibbu was our *khansamah* or cook factotum. We secured a modern bungalow opposite the old Mughal Qudsia Bagh (from which the Kashmir bastion had been bombarded in the Mutiny) and just off a road running down to the river then known as Asmanpur road. This delightful title—sky or heavenly road—was in fact a mistake for Usmanpur, the village of Usman across the river towards which the road ran. But no one minded until independence came when some one noticed that Usman was a Muslim name. Then the road came down to earth and water as Jumna road. We obtained the house through the good offices of a *Kayasth* group connected with the college. Some members of this group owned this plot of land, given after the mutiny as a reward for services of the *munshi* or Indian secretary of the Residency. A college colleague of this caste told me of this proposed house at the last moment. I surveyed the foundations, wired the owner and secured it. The house was to be ready in October but one of Delhi's double monsoons occurred that year so that when we arrived we found the walls, a deep pit in front of the house and the workers, men and women, prostrated by malaria. Eventually the house was finished, though not without the usual incidents. The pit was due to the architect building the house to the height of the road opposite, forgetful of the fact that the land sloped three or four feet from the road to the house. This turned to our advantage, because earth was brought to make up the drive to and round the house, giving us a charming sunken lawn in front and an impressive bank to the south, later adorned with Mughal brickwork. The owner, the architect and the engineer were all members of the same clan; the incident caused a good deal of mirth amongst the clan members as well as a little annoyance to the owner who had to pay the extra. The kitchen was forgotten and improvised out of two old sheds. The back verandah was omitted to save expense. We eventually move in with one side of the house completed and witnessed the final episode. There were stairs to the flat roof and the upper flight had still to be completed. Work began from both ends with great energy. It seemed clear that they would not meet but no one, engineer, foreman or workmen would take any notice, till the tow sets met but did not fit. Then with equal energy and good humour the hammers were wielded, the concrete was broken up and the stairs relaid, this time correctly.

Eventually all was finished and very neat and convenient was the result. The front of the house consisted of a deep verandah with two classical pillars and a small room on each corner. In the centre were the stairs and a passage which proved invaluable in providing a through draught. On one side was a lounge and dining room, opening to a pantry later added and on the other side two bedrooms with attached bathrooms and a small verandah between. Altogether it was as handsome and convenient a small bungalow as could be found in Delhi. It could always be flushed with fresh air and totally lacked that stuffiness in the hot weather and gloominess in the cold with darkness at all times so common in the traditional type of north Indian bungalow.

Sibbu was a Christian of unknown origin. He was never known to have been married; his relatives were utterly unlike him in appearance; even his place of origin seemed to be uncertain. He was of medium height and well-made, with a chestnut complexion. He had a dignified carriage and his features were more those of a Rajput or some types of Bengali Brahmin rather than of the humble caste from which most of his class of Christians came. He loved the baggy Punjabi trousers and flamboyant Punjabi turban and looked magnificent thus attired with the Mughal descended *achkan* or long coat buttoned up to the neck. He originally appeared in the college community as a boy engaged by a young Englishman on the staff before World war I. When the Englishman married, Sibbu asked leave to resign. He was persuaded to stay on and became devoted both to the *memsahib* and the four children who followed. He followed the fortunes of this family until they returned to England not long before we were married. He was then in middle life and took over as to the manner born. He had formerly been a bearer or a house servant but now he showed himself apparently without any training or previous experience, to be a skilful cook. His dinners where excellent and when such incidents occurred as the loss of the sweet on the kitchen floor in the dim light of an oil lamp (before electricity found its way into the kitchen) he was always equal to the occasion. So he was when, having lent the icecream machine to a neighbouring cook, the orders were changed and icecream was asked for that evening. It always appeared, if necessary from another neighbour's icecream machine.

If Sibbu had a fault, it was an inability, in spite of his general diplomatic talents, to deal with the *dhobi* or washerman. He was magnificent in clean clothes, but the clothes were not always clean; he did wonders in the dark little place called a kitchen, but the kitchen was sometimes fuller of dark substances than it need have been. Eventually a compromise was worked out. The kitchen was inspected each morning when cleanliness was insisted upon; when his dress was insufficiently fresh he was asked if the *dhobi* was late that week. This never failed to produce the desired effect. Sibbu was a practitioner of Micawber finance. He always lived up to his income and whenever his needy relatives appealed to his generous heart he borrowed. He borrowed first from us, but this did not always meet his needs. Then from time to time we would see a towering Pathan lounging at the garden gate and Sibbu would become very thoughtful. No amount of exhortation ever quite cured him of this habit but he always managed by some means or other to send him off for a time.

Financial embarrassment did not disturb his relations with us for there was never a more honest or open hearted man. He kept all his bazaar accounts in his head and when some detail occasionally escaped him he would as cheerfully give a figure below as above the market rates. He took careful account of our financial position and would seriously warn my wife that such and such a thing was too expensive at that time of year. When we went into government service during the war he knew the financial position almost before we did ourselves. Wages went up, but not the kitchen charges beyond the bazaar rate. As promotion came he would think allowable certain "luxuries" like fish from Karachi, which he had frowned on before.

Sibbu had the strangest assortment of relatives, for whom, like an Indian Burke, he had untiring affection and solicitude. One, said to be a half-brother, was the most lugubrious booking man I have ever seen. He was hard-working and honest and would very occasionally take too much when he would look sadder than ever. A younger man was claimed to be a full-brother—a promising youth who was clouded by a weakness for drugs and drink. He started as our bearer, but alas, on Christmas Day he celebrated so early that he was missing for the Christmas dinner. Though reprieved that time he had later to be banished from the compound. Sibbu pleaded for him as in duty bound, and when told he could not come back, was downcast until the rider was added, 'But his children and wife many come in'. His face brightened and there was never a further word spoken. His brother was twice married and had three children who in turn married. Sibbu regarded all these as his own. He would receive them in his kitchen, walk between two and three miles every night and morning (he had never learnt to cycle in spite of several attempts), in order to be with them. He would tend them in illness, plead for them and arrange their marriages. These were his special concern, but all children were his parish. They would gather round the kitchen door and rarely went away empty. A special treat was a share of the icecream on a hot weather night. I remember, one very hot night, when the guests finished the supply, my wife happened to go to the pantry and saw three pairs of big dark eyes looking up in expectation. Just then the bearer came and told them there was no icecream. Their faces fell and they stole silently away. Thereafter we arranged that we would never come down to scraping the barrel again.

When we returned after an absence o two years, his delight was affecting to see. He had been released late by the colleague to whom his services had been lent, and when he saw on arrival that we were already in the house he ran so fast that he stumbled and almost fell. Nearly six years later the time came for our return at the end of the war. We dreaded telling him the news and our fears were justified. The deed was done some four months before the event. Sibbu broke down in tears and ran from the room. Thereafter, when my wife took the daily *hissab* or account and gave the daily orders the interview would usually end with a groan and a cry, 'But Memsahib, you are going away.' The tears welled up and there would be a hurried retreat. When the final scene actually came there were no dry eyes.

There was, however, a happy ending to this story. We did our best to fix him up in another household, but he would not stay for long. However, he married a Christian *ayah* who lived with an Indian family nearby. With Indian warmheartedness, they treated him as one of their family and there he lived till his death sixteen years later. He became a government *chaprasi* or messenger and must have looked very ornamental on some verandah outside a *burra-sahib's* door. He could not have walked very far, but that is usually left to the young *chaprasi*. Every year we wrote him for Christmas and received in due course a letter from a professional writer expressing gratitude and affection, and praying for our return. When the last scene came, the *mali* or gardener, of whom I am about to write, visited him in his hut; and then called on the neighbours to bid them to the Christian funeral. At the funeral itself, forgetful of his caste feelings, he helped to carry the bier to the grave.

The *khansamah* in small households in northern India was generally regarded as the head servant, the *sardar* or chief. The *khidmatgar* or head bearer, lost the position because there was only one bearer. At any rate, this was the situation in our household. In this sphere Sibbu found a filed for his diplomatic talents. Our staff consisted, besides Sibbu, of a bearer, a *mali* and a sweeper. There was also a visiting *dhobi*. His weekly visit was an occasion, when he would arrive with a bundle of spotless clothes on his head. There were occasional lapses, which he treated with great presence of mind. Once a yellow dress arrived bright green. With artless calm the *dhobi* remarked that it had been accidentally left in the rain and turned that colour. They all came from different classes and they all possessed character. Though a Christian dealing mainly with Hindus, Sibbu kept the peace among them and their families. Harmony and quiet was the general rule and I do not remember having to deal with any serious strife in twelve years. Indeed, he came to be increasingly looked up to, so that the others would go to him to arbitrate their disputes.

At first we had in addition a *chokidar* or watchman. We were told that living on the outskirts of the city, with members of the so-called criminal tribes just across the river, we ought to have one. The usual procedure was to employ one of these people themselves on the principle of an insurance cover. Our *chokidar* proved a jovial though not very energetic soul. He was a good sleeper and when a cow got into the garden on a cold night could hardly be aroused to drive it out of the gate he had forgotten to shut. With the *chokidar* came a cow which was to supply us with milk. But as the hot weather drew on the milk seemed to become increasingly anaemic until one day our cat took a few sips from its saucer of milk to leave nothing but water behind. The *chokidar* was summoned to explain this enormity and told he must go. Then Sibbu stepped in. The *chokidar* was not a bad man he explained. He was short of milk owing to the hot weather shortage of fodder and he had made "a mistake". He should be given another chance. This inevitable compromise followed. The *chokidar* was allowed to say; it was the cow that was dismissed. This was really most unfair to the cow, for she had done her best. But perhaps she gained in the end through not being expected to provide an impossible amount of milk to too many customers. There was a sad end to this story, as so often in India. Our merry *chokidar* was not there to greet us when we came back from the hills that summer; he had died of cholera. We never had another and we never had a theft.

Our bearer was another Christian. He was useful and efficient but self righteous and taciturn with a turn of bad temper. He could drive a car and was very much aware of his position. Sibbu kept the peace between him and the rest of the staff and on occasion between him and his family. Next came the *mali*, by name Buddha Ram. He came from a village near Agra and was a member of a cultivating caste from which *mali*s where commonly drawn. He was a little man with only one eye but like "Ranjit Singh" of the Punjab and Odin in Norse mythology he made up for his optical deficiency by the keeness of his vision and the sharpness of his intellect. To these he added a strong will, a great willingness to be helpful and a capacity for hard work. An uncle was the *mali* of a neighbour's garden, and a brother worked in another, so that the Indian system of exchange of garden products was in full swing and worked very much in our favour. There was little to be spent on seeds or plants; these came and went in the *mali*s exchange market. Our chief expenses were earth and flower pots. The *mali*'s delight was flowers and his ambition to grow the best and most numerous chrysanthemums in Delhi. X sahib, he would say discontentedly, had fifteen hundred pots and Y sahib over a thousand whereas ours did not even approach four figures. The chrysanthemums were all grown on single stems, and with good soil and the favourable climate, would produce wonderful blooms.

The *mali* loved flowers; not merely because they added to his *izzat* or prestige, but for their own sake. But we insisted upon some vegetables as well, and this, with his strong will and clear cut views, made for a tussle. When he came he was very young; he seemed hardly more than a boy and he never seemed to get older with the years although he often reminded us that he was now grown up. When crossed in some desire he would explode in temper which he would work off by brushing the lawn and sometimes end the incident by falling asleep on the lawn itself. He passed through the phases of rebellion, when it was a question as to who should plan and control the garden; through respect, when he realised that my wife knew more about English flowers and their lay-out than he did and his own knowledge grew; to affection when, without any loss of self-respect and independence, he worked willingly in partnership. For partnership it became since he always had his own ideas to contribute to the pool and his knowledge of soils and of climatic conditions was considerable. He then attached himself to the family, regarding its welfare as his own, and considering the garden as the outward expression of its prosperity.

When the war came and prices rose and with them wages, he was a well-established *mali* and could easily have earned more elsewhere. But he remained with us, content with a wage he considered suitable to our circumstances. He had a brother of equal energy but much less intelligence; him he attached to a wealthy neighbour, acting as consultant in the background for which no doubt he received a suitable fee in the form of his brother's wages. The brother was younger and his earnings were controlled by the elder; an excellent arrangement, since we had the *mali* we wanted and he had the money he thought right.

Thus the *mali* blossomed out into what might be called a general outside bearer and handyman. His choice of tasks and relations with the other servants were interesting to watch, based as they were upon the nicest gradation of caste etiquette. He would do no bearer's or sweeper's work in the house, nor prepare hot water for the bath. But any new activity, not yet covered by tradition or caste rule, aroused his interest. Thus he would happily mend electric faults and deal with fuses, apparently impervious to the smart electric shocks he often brought upon himself. The telephone was not caste bound and was useful as well, so we found that he would not only answer it, but use it on his own account. But he never took advantage of this facility. Outside the house he would clean the car while he would clean nothing else. This might have been considered sweeper's work, but this too, apparently, was above caste. He would go on errands (on my wife's bicycle) more usually performed by sweepers. But not any errand. He would fetch ice in the hot weather from the ice factory three miles away (before we had a refrigerator). He would go to the post office for parcels, registrations and stamps, keeping all the accounts in his head. This, we thought, was because it was a kind of clerical work and all writing has a slightly sacred ethos in traditional Hindu society. Professional pride entered into the taking of flowers to the hospital or friends; notes went along with them and then often without the flowers. These visits enabled him to comment upon the recipients' floral shows, which did not always increase his or our popularity in those quarters. He would also buy English bread and fetch goods from European shops. But he would not go to the bazaar to do normal Indian shopping.

He took a great interest in the World War. Wile he could not take up arms himself, on grounds of both religion and relative importance, he could send a few men from his village if we wanted them. With the fall of France rumours abounded. Was it true, he asked, that King George had taken refuge in India and was now sailing up the Jumna? He would be quite safe in Agra Fort.

With the rest of the staff his relations were equally varied. They were all recognised as part of the family, though I am sure he thought some o them very peculiar parts of it. Between him and Sibbu there was a surface flow of banter with an undercurrent of respect and affection. Sibbu would affect to think little of his vegetables; his potatoes were small, his cabbages pale, his lettuce dry. The *mali* would imply that Sibbu knew nothing about flowers, hardly one end of the stem from the other. But each would look after the other; they kept in touch with each other, as I have just related, during the sixteen years that Sibbu survived after our departure.

With the bearer, who could drive our car but would not clean it, relations were correct rather than cordial. With one young sweeper, on the other hand, he struck up a real friendship. In spare moments they would sit on a step talking and laughing together. But they never touched each other, nor could they eat together.

I remember three sweepers during those twelve years. One, a surly boy, has been described elsewhere. He was removed by a corporate act when we were on leave one year. Another, who was the headman of his group in a village, was a middle aged man of singular grace and dignity. He was tall, handsome and fair-complexioned. Alas, his other duties called him away all too soon. The third was the young lad who was the *mali*'s friend. He was sturdy in build, good-looking, intelligent, active and willing. He stayed with us until called back to his village in our last few months. Months after our return to England a pathetic letter reached us asking to return because he was now free to take service again. I am certain that great potentialities lie within this much repressed Indian social group. Two of our three would have done credit to any social unit for intelligence, industry and integrity.

Our house stood in an enclave of land bordering the Qudsia Bagh and the Jumna riverside, occupied by a number of related Indian families. They lived in western or semi-western style; that is to say they had western type bungalows, and maintained gardens of which they were proud; their public rooms were furnished in western style, and their menfolk wore western dress in public; they would cheerfully eat western food, and even more cheerfully drink western wines and spirits—though most cheerfully in private. But the furnishing of the private portion of the houses was Indian (so far as they were furnished at all), the normal diet was Indian and so was the dress when at ease and specially in the hot weather. The ladies always wore Indian dress. Traditional social customs and ceremonies relating to birth, marriage and death were maintained. Language was very mixed, individuals often breaking into English but more often expressing themselves in conversational and slurred Urdu interlarded with English words. These often seemed to be used for greater emphasis, an underlining as it were. Someone would remark, '*yeh bahut* wonderful *hai* (This is very remarkable), the available Urdu word in this connection being considered less emphatic.' At other times the English word would be used merely because it was better known or came into the mind quicker.

These families were considered advanced. The boys went through school and on to college if possible; the girls stopped at the school stage when I first went to Delhi. Twenty years before, many of them would not have gone to school at all, and twenty years later many went on to college as well. The difference between those families where only the men had been educated and those where both men and women had at least reached the high school stage was most marked. Westernisation, or modernisation as they would have called it, was for the former a public thing not to be maintained at home and perhaps a private possession to be cherished secretly. For the latter it was a shared possession which could be passed on to the children and expressed at home and in private as well as in public life. It by no means meant that the essential Indian values had to be discarded; it could and often did mean that the traditional social shackles for the women could be thrown off. Some, for example, had a keen relish for English literature without losing their taste for Urdu poetry. Western-educated couples found it much easier to disregard the stricter caste restrictions on interdining and social intercourse and the finer points of the marriage rules than those where only one partner had such notions. At once the oft quoted excuse of, 'of course I would but my wife, or mother objects', was countered.

Our relations with these families were cordial and the atmosphere of friendliness was delightful. Nearly all of them were *Kayasths* related to each other. There was one Bengali family who later moved away and during the war a retired Punjabi policeman rented a new bungalow. Our *Kayasth* friends soon lamented their folly in making that let but, they sadly explained, it was now impossible to move him for he would be able to make things very uncomfortable for them. Their feelings were an example, in *parvo*, of the general Delhi attitude to Punjabis. We too had experience of the Punjabi attitude to *Delhiwallahs*. For the supply of canal water which used to come to our garden monthly via the Punjabi's bungalow, and was quite an occasion with much talking and splashing and gurgling, grew less and less and finally vanished altogether. The Punjabi had need of it. Opposite in another new bungalow lived for a time a German insurance manager who, in the intervals of Nazi propaganda, would listen to Mozart in the moonlight. He disappeared before the war and was replaced by a secluded Muslim household and then by an American businessman, who rode camels round his lawn by day and held noisy parties at night. Both these were disapproved of by everyone.

At the end of the road the head of the family still maintained a joint family with two prosperous middle-aged sons living under the parental roof and the next generation coming along. The head was a patriarchal figure who had been a keen lawyer and had mellowed with the years. The other families were all related in some degree. We attended their family gatherings at festivals like *Diwali*, were invited to their wedding celebrations and other special occasions. Great care was taken to warn us when the *barat* or procession from the bridegroom's house, a noisy occasion involving loud drums and blaring trumpets, would arrive so that we could be away if we wanted, the time of the actual ceremony and so on. At *Diwali* we would look at their light decorations on their houses and tell them which should be improved next year. At our gatherings there would be reminiscences of the early college days. 'In the time of Canon Allnutt' (1880–1909), was to speak of a legendary past, while C.F. Andrews was referred to with almost as much reverence and affection as Gandhi himself. It was in this atmosphere and with these neighbours that we came to feel at one with the Indian people.

The World War

When World War II broke out, we were on a small passenger ship in the Mediterranean. We had started ten days before as the crisis was just boiling up. We had found Gibraltar crowded with shipping, most of which was diverted round the Cape. We rather hoped to share their fate, but with one other ship we were sent into the Mediterranean. Our captain compensated for the slowness of his ship by a certain impetuosity in harbour which nearly led him into a newly laid minefield of which he was unaware. Shouts and whistles and hoots restrained him just in time.

We were not very popular in Gibraltar and were glad to creep along the north African coast. When war was announced, we were between Malta and Tunis. We did not know it Italy had come in too. The captain called the passengers together and announced that he had orders to call at Bizerta. But his rich Scotch brogue reached the back rows of passengers in the form, 'We are now going to desert her'. After the passengers had recovered from this shock, it was the turn of the French officials. Our officers were politely welcomed and asked a politely why they had done Bizerta the honour of calling there. On being told that they had orders to do so in the event of war with Germany, they professed ignorance and astonishment at any such thing. They had heard nothing from Paris. So we brought the war to Bizerta.

We now made our way to Malta, where a young man in a launch told us in an affected voice through a megaphone, 'We have no orders for you whatever'. The ship had been torpedoed in World War I outside Malta harbour. The captain thought she deserved better treatment. He ascended the bridge in dudgeon, put on what he called his rompers, and was no more seen until we arrived at Port Said. There was reason for his annoyance and anxiety. The frugal Scotch company would not get rid of the ship because its engines where good and refused to wear out. The ship was so slow that a submarine could overtake it. From Malta to Port Said we followed a majestic zig-zag course, a sitting target for any stray submarine. But there were none and at Port Said we discovered the reason for our Mediterranean meanderings. From the hold came a number of Bren gun carriers for Wavell's Army of Egypt.

On arriving at Bombay, we took out our Austin and proceeded to drive to Delhi. The journey was uneventful except for one incident. On arriving late one evening at a posting house (dak-bungalow) in a village o a small central Indian state we were told that the manager (*khansamah*) had gone to the bazaar. While a message was sent to him we examined the bungalow and found that it had marble bathrooms but no water. The *khansamah* took some time and when he arrived it was with a police inspector and a posse of constables. You, they said politely, are runaway German spies and we are going to arrest you. The showing of passports did not help much for they could not read English. But a little Hindustani and our general acquaintance with the country did. After a time our passports were solemnly scrutinized again (upside down) and magisterially pronounced to be *achcha*. Relations became very friendly and the upholders of the law did not disdain a trifle for their pains before departing. In act some Germans from neighbouring Indore had not yet been located and we seemed to be the providential rams caught in a thicket.

When we had settled in again in Delhi, we soon found the war was very remote to India during the "phoney" period. It was little more than a splendid talking point for most people. Business was little affected except perhaps for the better; there was not even large scale recruiting. It was said, I think with truth, that the Army advised the Government of India that this war would be a mechanized one. The Indian army was not mechanized in any serious sense; therefore there was no point in expanding it. The real public interest was in the resignation of the Congress ministries as a protest against the government's announcement that India was at war with Germany without consulting the people's representatives, and what would Gandhi do next? Some Europeans joined volunteer organisations and some took Red Cross courses. Others contented themselves with occasional visits to the Chief Commissioner who assured them that the government at present had no need of their services. In Calcutta European businessmen said that the government was "weak".

So the cold weather passed. When the storm burst on Norway we were in the hills below Simla reading examination papers. While two cuckoos, our own and one with a charming double note sang, the land was dazzling with light and the bright spring green, and the air hummed with the comings and goings of busy birds, we heard of the fall of Norway. Back in Delhi the news became graver and faces grew solemn. We had no radio and a friend used to send us messages. These were always bad and I have a nightmare memory of a cyclist appearing through the tense dust-laden air heavy with heat, with a "chit" which announced in turn, 'Holland has fallen, Belgium has fallen, Dunkirk has fallen, Paris has fallen, and France has fallen'. The public became alarmed and anxious and the somewhat native but very natural satisfaction at seeing Britain, recently bestriding India with such evident self-confidence, in real difficulties, gave way to real concern. After all, no one really wanted Hitler's *gauleiters* and concentration camps, not even the young Bengali followers of Subhash Bose who went about in very artistic black shirts. With the fall of France there was a real loss of confidence. I was now giving daily five-minute radio commentaries on the news. When Paris fell I had to write three. The first was before the news came; the second was judged too sad and likely to cause alarm; only the third, the most colourless of the three, got on the air. When France fell rupees disappeared for a time into hoards underground, dacoits (robber gangs) appeared on some of the roads; rumours went round the villages that King George was taking refuge in India; and some clever Brahmins in the south were said to be learning German to be ready for the forthcoming takeover. When it was realised that England had rallied behind Churchill and defied Hitler, panic declined and the Battle of Britain ended it for good. The moral effect of this stand was tremendous; even hard bitten anti-Britishers could scarce forbear to cheer their declared enemy Churchill as he stood on the beaches hurling defiance at the "Narzees". The Indians are a generous people.

With the fall of France, the government seemed to realise that a war was going on. The army began to expand, India was declared a base for the supply of the Middle East, the Viceroy began to study files of production instead of interviewing the hundred and one politicians who were said to represent the various segments of Indian society. There was little more visible result from the one than the other, but at least we knew that he was busily occupied. Even a little publicity about the war and its conduct was thought desirable. The appropriate office in the Home Department, so it was said, declined to do this on the ground that it might be regarded as a breach of its professed impartiality in political affairs. So a high official was entitled Director-General of Information and told to collect information about the war. The only group ready to do this was the information section of the Army intelligence which ran a newspaper called *Fauj-i-Akhbar* (Army News) for the Indian troops. So it came about that a haphazard group of colonels and captains became responsible for informing India about the war. The flesh was indeed willing but the brain and the knowledge were weak. So a wandering journalist was appointed, adding literary style and a beard to the outfit. Another was appointed when it became clear, after several months, that the war still continued. Then it was discovered that the enemy possessed radio and was actually broadcasting wrong information and "bad thoughts" to the country. So a monitoring section was started to find out just how bad they were. Then France fell; things were getting quite serious, the time seemed ripe for another appointment.

This was how I came into the picture. Not to appear too hasty and extravagant the appointment was delayed for six weeks in case Hitler should surrender after the Battle of Britain and it should prove to be unnecessary. Then it was made in Simla with one week to go for the move to Delhi so that the government had the expense of carting us down the hills.

By the autumn there was an air of activity in Delhi. Many Europeans were absorbed in the new offices and the wives of officers found welcome employment in such jobs as ciphering, censoring and monitoring. But I don't think the country was much moved except for industrialists with increased orders for Middle Eastern supplies, and surplus young villagers with a new avenue of employment in the army. The army offices still kept to pre-war ways, when officers returned after lunch in mufti, preparatory to the real business of the afternoon on tennis court or golf course. When General Auchinleck became Commander-in-Chief early in 1941 (in the middle of the blitz on Britain) his first measure was a decree that officers should attend their offices in uniform throughout the day. Then faces grew long and expressions serious. The war had indeed come to India.

My wife and I both joined this office, she as a librarian and I as a journalist, and spent our first few months with it in the Nizam of Hyderabad's palace in New Delhi. We were in the charge of a colonel who was full of zeal but nearly as puzzled as us about publicity and propaganda. He was kept from active service by an old wound and made up for his chagrin by tenseness of purpose. Holidays or leave were not to be thought of—how could you with the men dying "out there"?—Matters of pay and allowances were mercenary, unsuited to the gravity of the hour. A somewhat difficult man at times—as when he vetoed a library catalogue scheme put forward in favour of one of his own inventions, only to discover that it was completely unworkable. But he was a large hearted man for all that and had a saving sense of humour. We were all more or less in on room; we would hear him tell his colleagues over the telephone that he was in charge of "a bloody bunch o civilians". When the Armistice Day silence came round, he boomed on through the two minutes until the closing gun was fired when he exclaimed through the shocked silence. 'What's that damned gun going off for?' On one occasion his bell began to ring continuously. 'Who's ringing that damned bell?' shouted the colonel, 'see to it'. We ran hither and thither ringing all the other bells, turning handles and banging doors, looking under tables to find the evil genii. Still the noise went on. The colonel rose in fury. 'Can't anyone do anything?', he shouted. At that instant the sound ceased; he had been pressing the bell with his elbow all the time. One day in Simla he met his match. A journalist just back from China arrived and asked to see him. He called me in and eyed the young man doubtfully, 'And what can I do for you', he said. In a perfect Oxford accented drawl came the reply. 'I have been visiting China and graving impressions on my mind. World you please grave some impressions on my mind?' 'God bless my soul', said the colonel and choked.

When Russia was attacked, I helped him to put up the new wall maps. These are hardly worth putting up he said, they'll not be wanted after three weeks. This was the current Indian army opinion. We all liked him and were sorry when shortly after, he left to join the new army publicity department. He had hoped to be its head, but to his horror found himself placed under a Bombay journalist with the rank of Brigadier who knew well that a brigadier can say what he likes to a colonel and a colonel can't answer back. It was a cruel fate and we all sympathised with him.

Two years after the war had started, the Government of India created a Ministry of Information and Broadcasting. Our "bunch o civilians" became the Counter-Propaganda Directorate, the whole institution being usually described as the misinformation department. Monitoring now went on in a big way in Simla, where reception was good. Those in charge had to deal with delicate personal problems such as the housing of Chinese and Japanese monitors under the same roof, and coping with orthodox Muslim Arabs who insisted on praying five times a day whether or not the Axis radio was on the air. Then there were the very free French whose most volcanic feelings were reserved for the not-so free French, but most of all for each other. Then came the refugees from Singapore, from the British Ministry of Information there. They set up a Far Eastern Bureau of their own complete with a monitoring unit. As they had no one in particular to inform, they informed themselves about us and then us about the way the war should be run. Many of them had tragic tales to tell which aroused one's sympathy. In Delhi they felt boxed up and out of tune with the decorous officials of the capital and the absorption in local politics. (Malaya had virtually none at that time). They resented their fate and the criticism of Singapore and Burma, which they felt rather than heard. They had little to do except plan for a hypothetical future and so they naturally turned to criticism. What would we have done in the same situation anyway? This did not make for easy bedfellowship.

In the main office we produced weekly summaries of world affairs and background commentaries on events along with a stream of pamphlets on special aspects of the war. All these went out to the press. It was amusing to see bits of them appear, especially in the Congress press. Impecunious papers would often print a commentary and occasionally our leading article on some war topic would be favoured by some leading Congress journal. Then there was joy in the camp. Our rebuttals of Axis propaganda may have been futile and our title may have been laughable, but I think our steady stream of informed comment about the war which went out to the press and was used by All India Radio, was worthwhile and had its effect.

The psychological crisis of the war for India came in 1942. Pearl Harbour followed almost immediately by the loss of the *Repulse* and the *Renown*, sent an electric shock of alarm through the country. India had got used to the war as "noises off", with specially interesting noises coming from the Middle East where Indian troops were involved. The stand made by Russia had made people feel that the result was no longer a foregone conclusion—Axis victory or stalemate. After Pearl Harbour the significance of America's entry was at first missed; it was the Japanese menace which was sensed. When in quick succession Hong Kong, Malaya and Singapore fell, followed by the loss of Burma, the sinking of an aircraft carrier off Ceylon and the bombing of Madras, morale fell to a low ebb. It seemed that the British, successful for so long, could do nothing right. It was not that Indians looked forward to the Japanese with any more pleasure than to the Germans, rather the reverse. The "German Brahmins" or Madras were indeed said now be learning

Japanese, but this was only a cultural *sauve qui pevt.* Nor did anyone outside a small group relish the thought of falling under the Japanese sponsored Subash Chandra Bose with his Indian National Army raised from the Singapore prisoners as an alternative to working on the Siam-Burma railway. 'Better the devil we know than…', was a fairly general attitude. But the devil they knew seemed to have lost his once potent black magic; and as long as he continued to thwart the general desire for self-government no one felt inclined to replace it for him. And were not their leaders all in prison?

Distressing to us as well as alarming was the collapse of European morale. At first little notice was taken of the Japanese. The Americans were in and that settled the issue. When Singapore fell and Burma followed suit, when the Indian army's own general had been sent to retrieve the situation and had been removed, when stories of massacres and hair breadth escapes, of refugees hardships, of incompetence and bewilderment began to trickle through, complacency turned to alarm and then to despondency. Strong men spent much time propping hotel bars and explaining to a chorus of tinkling cocktail glasses that nothing could prevent the Japanese from marching from end to end of India. The despondency was such that if they could have landed an army in Bengal at the moment they might have been able to do so. The Viceroy, as stiff and formal as ever, was dumb and gave no lead. One felt that he would have met the Japanese on the steps of the Viceroy's House with an office file in one hand and a declaration of what he could do towards the realisation of a Co-Prosperity sphere *after the war* in the other. The only figure which remained stolid and apparently unperturbed was General Wavell, then back in India after the collapse of the east Indies theatre. But only a few attended the press conference on his return from Singapore and he made no public impact.

At this moment came the Cripps Mission, at the end of March 1942. I attended the crowded press conference at which the proposals were announced and sensed the air of excitement and hope. The general outline of events is well known—the wish of leaders like Nehru and Rajagopalachari to accept the opposition of Gandhi, and final negative outcome. What is not so generally known was the attitude of the Indian public in general. The average middle class westernised Indian fervently hoped that the proposals would be accepted. The Indian bourgeois was peacefully inclined, and as he hoped to avoid the struggle of 1930, he hoped for acceptance now. Those against, were the forward wing of Congress, the same groups who had been so influential in the thirties, and whom Gandhi had had such trouble to manage. They had no faith in British intentions and were disappointed when fights were called off, as Gandhi repeatedly did so. This time Gandhi was on their side so negation won the day. The highest degree of hope at the start was matched by the depth of gloom at the failure of the talks. The average man was bewildered and exasperated. It was a Congress achievement and specially Gandhi's that he turned this exasperation against the government. The average man was pitiably divided between desire to take part in what he now regarded, since American entry into the war, as a crusade for freedom and resentment that apparently everyone in the world could be free except the Indians. For them it was to be jam tomorrow add jam yesterday but never jam today, under the formula "after the war". Gandhi's discovery that the way to keep the Japanese out of India was to tell the British to go out first raised no enthusiasm in itself. The prospect it offered was bleak enough. But at least it was something to do. It was a call to action. And it had the usual Gandhian suggestion that they were not as other men were, that they breathed a purer air because they lived nearer the stars. The sequel to the swift arrest of the leaders after the passing of the Quit India resolution in August 1942 exactly expressed the general feelings. A substantial section of the Congress membership, released from Gandhi's restraining hand, took to violence as they might have done at any time in the previous twelve years but for his subtle management. They caused considerable disruption, specially in Bihar and the United Provinces (Uttar Pradesh). But it was the worst possible moment for such a move since there were larger forces than ever before armed with a war time resolution for victory. They were repressed with vigour and bitterness remained. But not the bitterness which would have occurred if the rising had been sanctioned or led by the national leaders. What happened when the country was exasperated and Gandhi was removed is my case for the claim that Gandhi in fact stood between the Government and an attempt at violent revolution in the late twenties and thirties. Gandhi's non-violent tactics were directed as much against the revolutionaries as against the British. He smothered revolution with the featherbed of satyagraha, non-resistance.

The substantial majority, which included the people one knew and met in business or socially, stood sullenly by to see what would happen. When the rising ended they resigned themselves to a stalemate until the end of the war. It was this apathy, suspicion and resentment which helped to make negotiations so difficult after the war. In common with most officers, I found one morning a notice typewritten in a government office (probably one's own) headed "Quit India". Sentiment was unanimous against the government. The government could do nothing right and was as much blamed by those who wished to be arrested but were not, as on account of those who had actually gone to prison. A prison sentence conferred a status at that time much sought after—a sort of pass with distinction in the Congress ranks, and a passport for promotion in the coming Congress raj.

After a few weeks, however, everyone settled down again. It was still Britain's was but it was recognised that for the moment Britain (with American backing) was in overpowering strength. A number of factors contributed to the restoration of confidence, European as well as Indian. The first, which I remember vividly, was the arrival of the Americans about April 1942. At that time neither Indians nor British had many reservations about them. To the Indians they were friends of liberty, to the British enemies of the Japanese. They were fresh, they were confident. They had immense resources. They brought with them a wave of hope. It was true that rumours soon went round that they had rejected all government office supplies which were being flown from America down to silver inkstands. Their Indian popularity did not last but the effect of their arrival was great. The second factor was the failure of the Japanese to appear after the rains in 1942. Probably quite wrongly, at that time, this was thought to argue allied strength. The third was the setting up of the South-East Asia Command. The presence of a large number of officers determined to get on with things, and above all the electric presence of Lord Mountbatten himself, had a tonic effect. People everywhere turned from contemplating their own miseries and grievances and began to find contentment in constructive work.

There was one more electric moment when Gandhi went on a twenty-one day fast in the early months of 1943. The viceroy refused to release him. As the crisis approached, the tension in the secretariat was immense. It was widely thought at the time that the crisis was surmounted by nourishment. If Gandhi had died then the public would certainly have been profoundly moved. But it was widely felt that the occasion of this fast was too trivial to risk such a life. It was, in fact, his last fast under the British.

Indians were now fully involved in the war situation. From the beginning of 1943 they experienced a price rise which upset all the old values in a few months and led on to the Bengal famine. Bengal was the grave of Lord Linlithgow's reputation. His refusal to interfere or to visit Calcutta seemed heartless and callous. Long trains of grain could be seen passing from the Punjab to Bengal which we knew would never reach the starving thousands in the Calcutta streets. But the Viceroy, it seemed, only studied his files. Lord Wavell endeared himself at one stroke by visiting Calcutta and giving the army the job of distributing food. By imposing rationing on all towns be did much to revive a belief in a British sense of justice. The rationing system was clumsy and shot through with abuses but it did give the masses something to eat which otherwise they would not have got. It was unpopular; our gardener would point sourly at monsoon clouds which refused to rain and murmur, "control hai". But he and others did not realise from what Bengali horrors it was saving them.

At the beginning of 1943, I found myself in the main secretariat in New Delhi as a deputy-secretary in the Information Department. It was interesting and intriguing to work with the targets of all unofficial shafts in India, the I.C.S. the thrice born, the sun-dried bureaucrats, the emasculators of India were now one's colleagues and superiors. It was interesting to be at the receiving end o these shafts, to know the real nature of the target, and on occasion to feel the impact oneself. One's first impression was of an alert and active band of men generally of marked ability. Next, I think, that their minds tended to run in grooves, with a certain lack of the large imaginative sweep. They would contrive and improvise with the greatest skill.

They would never let any situation get the better of them. They were industrious and level headed, but they lacked the political touch, and they could never catch the imagination of the people. In method and drive I thought they compared favourably with the British civil service, who came out with S.E.A.C. They had more energy, more resource; if they could not do a thing one way they would do it another.

The next point of interest was the relations of the British and Indian members of the I.C.S. and Political Service. As I saw them these were very good and they confirmed my view that if Britain had Indianised the service earlier and more generously the whole development of the country, and the type of independence which emerged, might have been different. These relations rested on the fact that Indians are very susceptible to leadership, and have stores of devotion which are easily moved to personal loyalty. They admire courage and integrity; their sensitive souls demand respect and courtesy. The union of these qualities with consideration provides the tap to release the reservoirs of devotion which then flow out in the form of loyal and disinterested service. The Indian joint secretary openly admired the British secretary under whom he had served in the Punjab, and so it went on. British officers who treated their Indian juniors with confidence and candour were richly rewarded thereafter by admiration and emulation. There were many other types of officials within the secretariat; no doubt rivalries and intrigues were rampant, but these in general were personal and careerist, not racial.

Part of my job was to supervise the various attached offices which conducted the government war propaganda. The most colourful of these was the War Exhibition which moved about the country as a morale booster and recruiting agency. On the whole it was a great success; its only drawback from my point of view was a disinclination to keep accounts. But as the Exhibition was always on tour, I only occasionally saw a few irate officers demanding pay which some clerk had failed to pay or more modestly explaining away the absence of receipts or account books. I had a closer association with the Ministry's film unit which made propaganda "shorts" depicting the war effort which were compulsorily shown in Indian cinemas. Its director was a sensitive Indian Jew who found the ways of bureaucrats hard, who in turn considered him hopelessly unbusinesslike. So I became a sort of buffer to take the shocks or Abraham's bosom on which to rest his head after his periodical buffetings next door. The "shorts" improved until they included expositions of industrial development, and of the arts, crafts, and beauties of India. But the war did not go on long enough to get a sundriet Walt Disney cartoon going. A vexed question with cinemas was the supply of raw film. Indian films lasted four to five hours; there was not enough to go round so there had to be rationing. This gave the government its chance. Supplies for three feature films were given to producers provided they undertook to give one of them a war publicity twist. The producers in Bombay liked neither the war nor rationing nor government. They could not evade the condition but did their best to evade its fulfilment. It was my job to examine and pass the scripts of these thirds. Some of the scripts were deliberately farcical, and there followed interviews with wily and suspicious film agents. But after a time we established friendly relations. When they found that they were not expected to scarify the Congress, that war publicity could embrace social and moral uplift as well as recruiting they changed. We would sit down and revamp scripts, in, as I would explain, the higher interests of India. As a result a lot of forced publicity which could only have done harm was avoided and some films were perhaps a little better than they might otherwise have been. A sideline was the Russian desire to show war films in the government's official time. This led to contacts with their agent, an energetic Armenian who entertained generously and imported the best Moscow vodka (so he said) in film cylinders. It was certainly good vodka.

Then there was the poetic department. A well know Punjabi pet agreed tot write and publicise martial songs for general morale. He was called Director of Song Publicity. His method was to recite his poems at the great poetical gatherings known as *mushairas*. Then he would teach them to professional singes who undertook to sing them at weddings, festivals and social gatherings, where they were commonly employed. He also had the songs recorded and put on sale. Anyone would listen to Hafiz reciting his poems, but whether they preferred his war songs to his others, or whether the singers sang the songs he had taught them, no one ever really knew. So a pale cast of doubt overshadowed his proceedings and aroused misgivings in bureaucratic minds. The secretary who had thought up the scheme thought it necessary to keep him up to the mark for his own reputation's sake. So I became a second buffer and provided another bosom when the distraught poet would unburden himself after each secretarial interview. This treatment he seemed to enjoy, for his visits grew more frequent and longer and his manner more affectionate.

An unexpected assignment was to become the government whip during the three sessions of the Legislative Assembly in 1943. This gave me a glimpse of the working of Indian politics and of Indian politicians. The full strength o the Assembly was 144 members of which about twenty were nominated officials and another dozen nominated non-officials. The Congress members were absent at first, but began to trickle back later in the year. The chief party was the Muslim League, twentyfive strong and then there were about a dozen Hindu nationalists, a dozen Independents and ten Europeans representing commerce. The League and the Nationalists were usually in opposition so that it needed both Independent and European support to be sure of a government majority. The position was not a sinecure, for the Europeans were often touchy and the Independents were more independent of themselves than of anyone else. The League made the running in the opposition and their game was to line up the Nationalists, and Independents. Our reply was to exploit the Independents' independence and the European's willingness to wound but fear to strike to keep a majority. With the aid of "sleepers" in the lobbies ready to be roused and other devices we usually succeeded, but there was one occasion when the League managed to adjourn the House just after lunch for want of a quorum. Some of our sleepers had not started their naps, being still at lunch upstairs and so out of call. The quorum was only twenty but in the attenuated house of about ninety this meant more than half of the regular government forces.

The principal Congress leaders were absent but there were still a number of interesting personalities. The greatest was Mr Jinnah but he rarely visited the house, and when he did, passed silent and brooding through the lobbies where the conversation hushed to whispers. His lieutenant Liaqat was active and genial. His speeches were clear, loudly delivered in a flat tone. Just then he was embarrassed as a result of getting mixed up with a Hindu group in Delhi University politics. He purged himself by a root and branch opposition to the Delhi University bill, intended to be a non-controversial measure, on communal grounds. The line of attack gave us Hindu Nationalist support but sent cold shivers down the government's Muslim supporters. One member of council in particular found it difficult to find the diversion lobby. For a time it was touch and go, and it kept the whole monsoon session lively. The League whip was a mild mannered Malabari Muslim whom it was difficult to envisage forcibly converting Hindus, as the Moplahs are said to do. He was frank and friendly and we had many jokes and tussles together. Among the Nationalists was the fiery Bengali, K.C. Neogy. Whenever he disapproved of a ruling of the President, an elderly Muslim lawyer, he would bound out of the chamber with great strides as though he had springs on his feet. Half an hour later he would appear, very calm and dignified, with a gleam in his eye to warn us all that we had been deceived in supposing that he had lost his temper a few minutes before. He later joined the Nehru Cabinet, but found the Prime Minister as unbearable there as the Assembly President had formerly been. So he bounded away into retirement. There was the little Muslim Leaguer with a scraggy beard who was always asking supplementary questions. The President could not bear him and after one or two would jump up and growl, 'the honourable member is arguing'.

Relations with the British officials seemed generally friendly. At this time of tense feeling the way in which members distinguished between personal qualities and political opinions was remarkable. The Home Member had been responsible for the suppression of the "Congress rebellion". He was regarded as a die-hard; he was angular and unimaginative. Yet he was regarded with affection everywhere and there was real regret when he retired. In their eyes his sincerity and integrity outweighed his political faults. One of the secretaries sat behind the Leader of the House to give him advice on procedure. He was a plain spoken man who liked to utter forthright opinions. This he did during the proceedings in a *sotto voce* voice which could be heard all over the chamber. Phrases like “perfect nonsense”, “fool”, “utter idiot” would punctuate members’ speeches specially if the speaker was of the more tiresome sort. But he was liked; the President never heard these interjections; the members loved them and never protested.

The Assembly at this time was certainly a miniature, perhaps a Lilliputian parliament. The politics played there did not matter very much, but the year’s membership was an interesting experience. The atmosphere which prevailed there at one of the most tense moments in Indo-British relations helps to explain why Lord Mountbatten was so quickly able to restore cordiality. The quarrel was essentially a surface one and never bit too deep into people’s hearts. Apart from religion, Indians are bad haters, and always they are good friends.

Concluding Reflections

I left India seventeen years ago but India has never left me. No one can tell beforehand how anyone will react to India. There are some who take an instant dislike to the whole scene and are restless and unhappy until they can leave. They will then become normal and balanced again and live happily ever after. If you find yourself in that class when you get there (you cannot tell beforehand), the sooner your leave it the better, for you will do no good to yourself or the inhabitants as long as you stay. Half a lifetime's residence will make no difference to your attitude or feelings; you will only seem to others to be more and more difficult and crusty. Then there are those on whom the country just seems to make no impression at all. They will do their work, they will adjust themselves to the conditions, they will make friends and inspire affection and respect in their circle, whether English or Indian. But all the time their souls, as it were, will be somewhere else, so that when the time comes to depart they will slough off the Indian experience as if it had never been. They will return to English life as a duck returns to water and you would soon never know that they had been there. None of the vain regrets for them that the Indian expatriate is supposed to feel. These people lack neither imagination, goodwill nor ability. It is just that the Indian scene seems to strike no responsive chord in their hearts and kindles no fire while the soul muses. An occultist would say that they have no pre-connection with India. And then there are those who, once they have settled in the country, find that there is something which draws them and holds them, something from which there is no escape. Approval in itself is no key to this state of mind; abuses fascinate even while they are condemned and horrors grip while they horrify. Still less have political opinions anything to do with it. It may affect the sternest die-hard as the other states of mind may afflict the most convinced supporter of Indian liberty. It is, in fact, a state of mind and neither a condition of opinion nor a phase of feeling. For it will continue however your opinions may change, and haunt you whatever your state of feeling. I would call it some sort of affinity in the soul, which once realised can never be discarded because it is a part of you. The phrase "I have been here before" might be used, but I think the words "I am part of this new scene around me and it is part of me" might express it more clearly.

It was this experience that overtook me before I had been long in India. The how and the when I cannot say exactly. Perhaps those long talks cataloguing the library on hot-weather afternoons were a start. Then there were the hills, which once seen were always part of my consciousness. The Buddhas at Taxila were an initiation into the deeper side of Indian life. I have not seen many Buddhas, or known many Buddhists, but I can never see a figure of the Enlightened One without being moved. But perhaps the most vital factor in the process was the close contact with the students, who themselves represented most of the communities in India. Four hours a day of teaching classes or supervising small groups of two or three, with the constant social contacts besides, seemed to build up a sense of oneness without one's knowing it. Whether it was this, or the visits to the monuments on fresh, sunny, cold weather days, the frowning battlements of Tughlakabad or the graceful Qutab Minar, the sunsets by the river or the haunting cry of the peasant as he drew water from the deep wells with his ox, I know not. I only know that the magic worked, so that while in India I thought of England, while in England I thought of India. At will I can scent the musty odour which arises from the dusty earth with the first monsoon rains, or hear the moan of the dust laden "loo" or the roar of the city bazaar with the cries of its vendors or see the monsoon clouds climbing up the hillside and sliding through the lowest gap, a warning of the deluge to come.

Everyone I suppose has their kinks, their interest or taste for which there is no rational explanation. In my case it was the Mughals. Babur and Akbar, yes, they were fascinating personalities on any reckoning. But why the rather grisly and later religiose Aurangzeb, and why, on any reckoning, the later Mughals, whom no one could call impressive? But there it was. Not only their buildings (and to make matters worse their later ones) but their dress, their habits, their fortunes, even their genealogies would come into my head whether I wanted them or not. Indian friends would say that this reflected a previous Mughal incarnation; it was certainly a Mughal invasion and a very successful one.

This intuitive sympathy, unsought and undeserved as it was, was of great value in seeking to understand Indian history. When one was so aware of the reality of Indian life and the Indian past, one could not help asking what does it all mean in relation to the present and in relation to the west? If you are so bemused with India and its history, what lessons do you drew from it? As soon as one reflected on this question one could not help being faced with a whole series of glaring contrasts. Here was a country claiming a high civilisation sunk in dire poverty; a country claiming spirituality in contrast to the materialistic west showing apathy and indifference to massive suffering and social abuses; a country claiming freedom as the right of all people whose society was parcelled out into exclusive and separatist groups. If light came from the east was it not hidden in the east itself?

Such thoughts inevitably led one to examine the past, to look for clues for what had gone wrong. The usual answer is caste, an institution which is almost unique in the world and quite so in its Indian range and depth. It is the first talking point of every reformer, religious or otherwise, and the ready reckoner for historians adding up causes for decline. So much so is this that it is assumed that if you are looking for the ills of India it is only necessary to consider the state of the caste system and if you analyse the forces working against it you are contributing to Indian progress. In fact the word caste is used as a convenient cloak for a whole series of other problems which we do not want to mention for fear of offending Indian susceptibilities. A restraint we never exercised in the past in the name of good feeling is now enforced in the interests of good trade. As soon as you look at caste you find that it is by no means the whole explanation of India's ills. In the first place caste in its social sense is only an exaggerated form, reinforced by religious sanctions and instinctive taboos, of class distinctions to be found everywhere. When Hindus become Christians they carry over the instinctive taboos without the religious overtones and the result is not easy to distinguish from social snobberies and colour feeling elsewhere. The different castes will meet and mix together for business purposes freely but only reluctantly for social ones. There remains social disdain and separateness without actual aversion and refusal of contact. There is reluctance to intermarry between people of high and low caste origin without actual prohibition. That something which distinguishes caste from class feeling would therefore seem to have been provided by religion. Again, when the modern Indian throws off most of the shackles of caste, where does he begin? He begins with the ideas underlying it. Either he doubts the theistic basis of Hinduism and proceeds from philosophic doubt to social agnosticism or, as I think is more common today, he accepts (whether overtly or not does not matter) certain assumptions from the west such as the equality of man or the equal worth of all personalities and then finds they are in conflict with the traditional structure of society. Like the Indian Christian he does not emerge into a state of pure brotherliness, but exchanges class for caste feeling. His class is a new sort of class which, like the Indian Christians, has still to find regular rules. But though confused and ill-defined it is certainly there. The caste emancipated Brahmin may consider all men his brothers, but he would add (privately at least) that some brothers are more brotherly than others. It is a case of two cheers for fraternity.

This something that separates class from caste would seem then to be its religious element. This comes from the Brahmins, the twenty-five millions or so at the top of the caste-system. Brahmins are not merely a hereditary in-marrying group. Their influence depends, and has depended through the ages, on the ideas which their group has retained and enforced on Indian society as a whole. Brahmin philosophers received them and Brahmin teachers and priests expounded them; the other castes, often with reluctance and protests—have come to accept them. In times of crisis such as large scale barbarian invasion or the internal Buddhist movement the Brahmins have often made large concessions, but by and large they succeeded in impressing their pattern of society upon India as a whole. It has been the greatest *tour-de-force* in the historical period.

To my mind it has been Brahminism, not caste, which has been the Indian evil genius. Brahminism justified a society split up into separatist ingrowing exclusive units. This society is organised on a hierarchical plan, not excusing injustice on the ground of sin of human frailty but justifying it as part of the order of the universe. They converted the functional arrangement of society in four orders into some two thousand mutually repelling groups and they invented the outcaste concept to justify economic and social slavery. They used the concepts of *Karma* (cause and effect) and rebirth or reincarnation to capture the minds of their victims, and to pin them down, as it were, into their various caste groups. Their victory was not an outer one of physical force, but an inner one of mind, a mental displacement, as it were, with Brahminical concepts. By the same subtle mean they fastened the domination of men over women. Convince a woman that her husband is her divine lord on earth and the lordship on man, the harshness of Hindu widowhood and even *suttee* can find specious justification. Every wrong incidental to the system can be explained by the manipulation of the doctrine of *Karma* and rebirth. You suffer for former sins by low-caste birth and enjoy the rewards of former virtues—by being Brahmins. And where is right and wrong in this system? There is no right and wrong. By a masterpiece of obliquity the Brahmin system provided a *dharma* or moral duty for each caste, differing in each case. Thus the emergence of a single law of God and duty of man to his neighbour has been stifled at birth. One knows very well that there exists the ancient wisdom with its ways of release or realisation. The India of the philosophies and the Gita, of the sages and the Buddha—these were tolerated by the Brahmins only when they led away from the world and not to it. Transformation was banned so escape was the only way out. The Brahmins smothered the Ancient Wisdom with the pillow of dialecticism. It was embalmed in the caste system and the Laws of Manu were its coffin.

The ills of India, in my opinions, should be traced to Brahminism rather than to caste. Without it caste would break down into class; without it variety would not have grown into division; without it the underlying cultural unity of India would have found a political and national expression. Indian history would have been as continuous as the Chinese, with no British period. The situation would no doubt have not been ideal for there would have been strongly marked classes. Apart from the binding power of Brahminism one cannot help noticing its absorptive capacity. Wave after wave of invaders, some barbarian and some as civilised as the Indians have either been absorbed into the system or sealed off in separate compartments like an unwelcome visitor in a beehive. Nomadic tribes were broken up into classes and collected again into castes. More advanced groups found their gods welcomed into the Hindu pantheon while their minds were bemused with metaphysics. Exclusive cults like Islam or Christianity were sealed off intellectually, tolerated practically and slowly undermined on the social level. The inference of this was that you could not hope for any radical change in India so long as Brahminism remained secure in its citadel. The attack must not be on Hindu practice which was largely customary, but on Brahminism which provided the life blood of custom. This was why much propaganda, whether Muslim or Christian, was ineffective, because it was directed against things like idolatry which were only the outer face of something much deeper and less tangible. The system was such that those who attacked it were as much subject to *maya* or illusion as those who were its victims.

It was for this reason that nothing seriously challenged Brahminism until the British introduced western education and the English language in the nineteenth century. Then, for the first time in millennia, it was challenged at the roots, in the realm of the mind from which its dominion sprang. The Muslim challenge had been a root and branch, an all or nothing attack, and so was the orthodox

Christian one. But the challenge brought by western education was one of ideas, which worked secretly without any immediate outward manifestation. The first real sign of its effectiveness was what has been called the western educational "explosion" of the latter years of the nineteenth century which took the form of the creation of numbers of colleges through private effect. The proof of the magnitude of the change going on was the "explosion" of universities and technical institutional of all kinds which followed independence in 1947. No sooner had Indians a wholly free choice than they went west with a vengeance. What would have happened to India if the Greeks had controlled northern India for a century and had been able to institute some such system of education?

What then of the future? If Brahminism is being undermined, and I think there is no doubt that it is, what is to take its place? I think it can be confidently declared that some coherent set of ideas and values must take its place, or in due time it will rise again in perhaps a different guise. The forms of Shiva are endless. Here I think a distinction may be made between basic concepts of Indian thought such as *karma*, *maya*, rebirth and self-realisation and certain developments of it such as the Brahminical system of hierarchy and the turning away from the world. There seems no prospect of these basic ideas disappearing in the foreseeable future, and in consequence, no prospect of a wholesale changeover to orthodox Christianity. But there is evidence of an intrusion into Hinduism, or acceptance by Hindus, of certain human values from the west, which in my view are basically Christian. These may be briefly described as the equal value of all personalities, their value in society and the consequent obligation of man to be his brother's keeper and of society to foster the general welfare. The view that all individuals have potentially equal rights and duties is surging into India with the mass of Western literature she imbibes, and the view that the world is a real place of relevance to all is an assumption of all the science she now assiduously cultivates. That nature is real, and human beings equal and real as a part of nature is the burden of this message.

These ideas seem to be taking root though it cannot be said that they have yet been integrated in the Indian intellectual consciousness. That is the task of the next generation of Indian philosophers. But we can mark some of the signposts which give ground for hope. Recent Indian sages and reform movements have stressed the reality of the world as a scene of action and the importance of service for the realisation of the individual. They have, as it were, led Hinduism back to the world of man and rediscovered man. So we have Ram Mohun Roy with his *Precepts of Jesus* and his Brahmo Samaj. Too westernised you may say. Very well, there is the very Hindu Arya Samaj with its very definite emphasis on social reform and equality. We are all Aryas is its message. The seers Ramakrishna and Vivekananda with their Ramakrishna Mission of good works, the great Sri Aurobindo, re-interpreter of the Upanishads, preached activity and action in this world. And Tilak, in his influential commentary on the *Gita*, maintained that action for one's fellowmen and not for oneself only, was essential. Action included political action, of course, but this did not affect the core of the argument. All those except Ramakrishna, who was a mystic, may be called intellectuals with a limited appeal.

But then came Gandhi, a man of the people, a non-Brahmin who appealed to the people. His message was to the heart, his intellectual acrobatics were reserved for the politicians. I for one accept his general bona fides without thinking of him as superhuman or a spiritual *avatar* or divine teacher. As I see it, non-violence began with him as an experiment, developed as a political tactic and ended as an over-riding principle. In the thirties it might be said that he played with the principle but in the end the divine play was with him. It led him on his missions of mercy in Bengal and Bihar, to his mission of justice in Delhi and his assassination. He who had resisted to the last the division of India at Muslim insistence died for his insistence on their rights in India. Such a record may cover inconsistency and even trickiness at times but not shallow insincerity.

Apart from this ethic of non-violence or *ahimsa*, the burden of Gandhi's teaching was, 'Thou shalt love thy neighbour as thyself'. This principle inspired his "Untouchable" campaign, his various reform movements, and his doctrine of soul-force itself. It was behind his disregard of caste taboos (though not of caste distinction itself). Some see in Gandhi a subtle reactionary because of his recognition of caste in general; but I think it is nearer the truth to call him a social revolutionary (no doubt subtle also) because he sought to transmute the basis of caste from hierarchy (higher and lower) to function (service to the community). The sum total of Gandhi's work, as I see it, was to bring back into the Hindu fold the value of service to one's fellowmen. In so doing, if his work proves enduring, he laid the foundation for a welfare-conscious Indian society. His work has been to imbibe values in his youth not visible within the Hindu fold, to naturalise them as it were, and to stamp them with the mark of his authority. Gandhi was a good Hindu, said the people; what does it matter if some of his inspiration came from elsewhere? And what matters in the ultimate, it may be added, the name that a society attaches to a truth, so long as that truth is accepted? Christians will claim, and I think rightly, that much of his inspiration came from Christian sources. It may be that India, having taken, as it were, their re-vitalising injection from outside, will develop in time its own version of Christianity, as the Roman did with the original Jewish version. But it will certainly be in her own way as well as her own time.

One of the most distressing as well as pressing problems which strike the observer of India is her poverty. Two hundred years ago India was no poorer than most parts of Europe. Today the contrast with the west is so glaring as to be the major impression made on the average European observer. The usual answer to this problem, and the one favoured by Mr Nehru's government, is industrialisation. Western Europe had a long start in this respect, both because it was the seat of the necessary technical progress and because of the slowness of the British Indian government in introducing industrialism itself or encouraging others to do so. But something was done which serves to underline the problem with which that of poverty is closely linked. Various checks on population growth (famine, disease, war) were reduced and the resulting increased population was fed a little better than before and given rather more security. The result is a population problem on top of a poverty problem. The population approximately tripled between 1800 and independence, when people talked of the "four hundred millions". It has been growing still faster since so, in spite of the loss of Pakistan with its then seventy-five millions, people are again speaking of "four hundred million" Indians. If the attempt to raise the Indian standard of living is not to end in a horrible famine and revolution, the population "explosion" must be controlled. At present the Indian government is making strenuous efforts to increase production but only taking tentative steps towards population control. This population overspill is the most ominous present threat to India's future.

Linked with these questions is that of education. I see this as perhaps the key question of the whole series. Population control has to encounter religious resistance, both Hindu and Muslim. These taboos are in the mind and the only force which can loosen them must come from the mind too. Education with its widening mental vistas and its implanting of new desires and new ideas of living provides both the necessary mental freedom and additional objects of spending. The educated middle classes already practice birth-control on an appreciable scale; if the masses are to be persuaded to do likewise they must have education also. Then they must also have practical means both effective and simple. Mass education will also provide the answer to the problem of working democratic institutions and dealing with Brahminism. Mr Maurice Zinkin thinks that universal suffrage will suffice because under it the Brahmin had to solicit votes from the *sudra* and the untouchables. But without education the voter will have neither the knowledge nor the self-confidence to make judgements of his own. Whether he votes for Brahmin or anti-Brahmin he will be a victim and a dupe. Without mass education the women of India as a whole will never be able to overcome orthodox opposition to their taking their proper place in Indian society. There would continue to be, as at present, a brilliant elite which would advertise Indian womanhood round the world and help them to forget the great mass of their sisters confined to the cooking pot, a husband's worship and the widow's veil. If mass education is central to Indian development, we have grounds for apprehension here also. Fifty-two years ago the nationalist leader G.K. Gokhale produced a plan for mass education and denounced the then top-heavy structure. Today, fifteen years after independence, there are about fifty universities (double the number under the British) but only about 25% of the population are barely literate. Mr Nehru has a greater responsibility for keeping the masses of India ignorant during his long rule than for allowing the Chinese to occupy a few thousand square miles of rock and stone on the borders of Tibet.

What, if anything, has India to offer the modern world? Poverty, fine buildings and smooth words many would say. A sociological museum, a field for planners, an avenue of escapism. To the claim that India is more spiritual than the west, the west retorts with charges of apathy, cruelty, self-righteousness. Such charges get nowhere and I cannot think that they begin to answer the question. Indians are not more spiritual than Europeans but they have a greater potentiality for spiritual awareness. Even those who disagree with this view would admit this great sensitivity. I am not conscious of being any better for living in India, but I am certain that I am more aware of the spiritual values. It is this heightened consciousness, the sense of living *sub specie acternitatis*, which India has to offer to the west. It is this sense which could give meaning to the "materialism" of the west, by reducing it from the status of a thing-in-itself, to making it a means to an end of good living. Materialism as a means to a social and spiritual end can be beneficent while as an end-in-itself it is deadly. With this sense we could escape from the dreary round of having more and more of what we want less and less into a world of having enough of what we need. If India can provide an antidote to aimless materialism it can also provide a technique for the adjustment of the mind to modern stresses. This is the science of meditation which India has practised longer and knows more about than any other group in the world. Recollection and the entry into the silence is a way of finding meaning in ceaseless activity, calm in anxiety, and balance in times of stress. Our modern prayers and services serve as anodynes for the few, and formal occasions for the many; their failure to provide a meaning to life is shown by modern man's general abstention from attendance. Here is a need which the churches, if they would, could meet.

I have often asked, 'what have your years in India meant to you personally', and have found it very difficult to find an answer. Apart from the Indians themselves about whom I have written already, I think I would mention again this sense of the spiritual. Whether it is the air, the sun, the heat, or the nature of the people, the fact remains that this sense pervades one's mind. It is very difficult for anyone to be wholly agnostic or materialistic in India, though there is much mystery and much materialism both squalid and gross. Allied to this was a sense of the Oversoul. Perhaps a physical reason can be found for this impression like the vastness of the great plains with their canopy of blue, the immense scale of the hills and rivers in the north, the luxuriance of nature and teeming life in the tropics and the relative puniness of man. For myself I think there is something more and it is that something which has stirred the Indian imagination into such concepts as the great god Shiva and the brooding god Brahma. It was easy in England to confine one's sense of the real to Sunday observance and the reading of books on Platonism, but in the Indian air it became insistent and would not let you go.

Have I any regrets for the twenty-one years spent in India, without any visible result in terms of career or financial reward at the end? Was not most of one's energy spend in building academic sand castles already engulfed by the tide of time? The answer is, none at all. The intangibles we carried home were far greater than the tangibles we left behind. There was the rich store of experience provided by the intimate contact with India and its people, with all the widening of horizons which it involved. There were the rich pastures of Indian history and thought which have been nourishing me ever since. And there has been the deep satisfaction of having, as I believe, helped in some degree in introducing the real values of the west to the Indian mind and seeing some small part of that process by which they may be incorporated into a new synthesis significant for both east and west. Those values I would call chiefly the Christian personal and social ethic, the positive idea that spiritual values are properly expressed in material and social forms; and the scientific ethic of objective inquiry and weighing of results, of precision and patience and of devotion to the truth. India will reward anyone who goes to her with an open mind. But full understanding is granted to no one. For those who seek there are rewarding glimpses of 'The gorgeous palaces, the cloud capp'd towers', but always '*Delhi dur ast*', the Delhi of full knowledge is far off.

دلی دور است

Part Two

Verandah Viewpoint

From a verandah in an Indian house was reflected as in a mirror, the life around. Owing to the heat the rooms inside were usually closed in and dark, but the verandah was bathed in light and was a never failing source of interest in observing the everyday drama of human life set in a framework of flowers and trees, birds and animals. Sometimes while sitting watching the birds, so tame, gay and varied in their colouring and song, I would be aware of the honk, honk, of the coppersmith, with his little red cap plainly discernible in the large fig tree across the road. My eyes would be caught by the sight of the golden woodpecker hammering away at an old tree stump, on the lawn in front of me were the hoopoos, with their unique tawny colouring, black and white wings, long beak and lovely crest which rose and fell as they uttered plaintively their soft cry of "hoopoo", "hoopoo" while they dug into the ground to find their food. They are said to be the legendary birds which carried messages between King Solomon and the Queen of Sheba, and they certainly look the part.

My attention was then diverted by an approaching figure on a bicycle to which was attached a big bundle. With a cheery smile and a courtesy perhaps unparalleled anywhere, a Chinese pedlar deposited his wares at my feet with a, 'you look memsahib, I have plenty lovely things'. It was never any use but to look, for the Chinese were not easily put off, and their good humour never seemed to fail, even when sent away empty handed. For my part I must say I always enjoyed seeing the contents of that bundle on account of the exquisite and beautifully wrought workmanship, mostly done on silk. The Chinese pedlar was often followed quite closely by the Kashmiri merchant on foot, who I think kept a wary eye on him. He was quite a different personality. Usually tall and handsome, he would *salaam* with great dignity and removing his bundle from his head, would lay it before me. Here also were hand embroidered bedspreads and table mats in lovely colourings and designs; the motifs most loved were those of the lotus, the chamar tree, and kingfishers, all characteristic of the beautiful vale of Kashmir from which they came. I noticed that in every design there would be some flaw somewhere and one day I asked why this was. The Kashmiri looked at me thoughtfully as he replied, 'God is the creator of all; we are but his creation; we would not try to rival God by making every design perfect'.

A vendor I always liked to watch pass by was the Bengali sweet (*mitthai*) *wallah*. On his head he carried a basket covered with a spotless white cloth, inside of which I knew were delicious and most succulent Bengali sweets. He gave warning of his arrival by intoning in dulcet tones the three words, "Bengali sweet *wallah*", but so musically was it rendered and so clear the voice that intoned it that one never became tired of hearing it. Another itinerant vendor carrying baskets of fresh fruit was a most familiar figure, and a smiling one too, for in such a hot and dusty country, he did not find it difficult to empty his basket. The most unhappy sight amongst these salesmen were the chicken and bird sellers. The chickens were cooped up tightly together in a kind of net-like basket slung across their shoulders and thus paraded along in the boiling heat; they were scarcely more than skin and bone. No more pleasant was the sight of all the little birds that had been trapped and were hawked around in far too small cages to be sold as pets. These little birds I noticed sometimes appeared to have unusually brilliant colouring—which later turned out to be but an imitation of nature, and which often, in a few days, gradually faded out revealing perhaps a little brown sparrow.

One bright morning, when all was still and quiet, I settled myself down to writes some letters. I was soon interrupted by loud shriekings all around me. On looking up I saw that my cat had caught one of the "Seven Sisters" a name given to brownish, rather heavy looking birds, who always went about in "sevens" and talked and scolded incessantly, especially if annoyed. The hue and cry they raised now was really quite alarming; I hastened to the rescue and managed to retrieve the bird who was quite unhurt and return him to the flock, whose indignation was still so great that it was a long time before peace was restored. I think even the cat herself was frightened for she came and sat very close to me while assuming an air of utter innocence. A mongoose too who lived in a hole in the wall opposite, looked out of his hiding place and then moved swiftly across to see what it was all about; finding a saucer of milk nearby, emptied it with great satisfaction and then stole silently away. At this moment I became aware of a different kind of interruption in the form of a figure sitting on the wall of the garden. Unfortunately he too was a familiar, but not a welcome sight. With a gay and buccaneer air, this tall and handsome son of the Frontier, with his white baggy trousers, smartly tied turban and velvet waistcoat was, I regret to say, lying in wait for my cook, who was always (however much we tried to clear him) in his debt. These men were moneylenders and were able to make their living all too easily by getting into their clutches those who could not resist their offers, especially when wedding and funeral expenses took more than their little all. He looked at me with a provocative smile, while swinging his legs and dangling the little cane he carried. My cook was safe just as long as I remained on the verandah for he would not come in while I was there. Turning my gaze from him, I saw a totally different person standing before me. So silently had he come that I had not noticed his approach. He was India's "holy man" wearing but a loin cloth, covered with ashes and complete with begging bowl. Uttering somewhat strange incantations he held out the bowl to me. These wandering "holy men" run into their millions and were to be seen everywhere. Among them were those who could perform incredible feats of endurance and phenomena and also those who were real *sadhus* in search of Truth; but the faking majority lived on the credulity and alms of a people who have always held in respect and reverence those who say they seek the spiritual. No sooner had he turned away than a Sikh approached, with carefully oiled beard and hair rolled up inside a gaily coloured turban, though the rest of his outfit was European. He was an astrologer and had come to tell my fortune. I did not care for the rather evil leer in his eyes, and decided it was time I sought shelter inside, but he was very persistent and tried to follow me in. I immediately called my gardener who was quite near and asked him to send the Sikh away. The gardener, though only half his size, was nothing loth, and more than made up for lack of stature in the volubility of his language which I suspected was by no means complimentary, judging by the quick exit of this teller of fortunes. Another visitor, and one too frequent for my liking was the snake charmer. Unfortunately there was no protection against him. Snakes were to be reckoned with as we all knew well. His arrival was heralded by music as he played a kind of bagpipe with long drawn out notes. Then he would seat himself quite happily on the verandah and far too close to me for my liking and produce from a large round basket he carried first one cobra then another, and while he charmed them with his music, they would encircle his arms and climb around his shoulders and neck. Sometimes they would turn, look at me and strike out as if they intended to dart towards me, but he would recall them, just in time. As quickly as possible I would congratulate him on his performance and offer him some money upon which he would very slowly replace the snakes in their basket and happily set off to intimidate the next victim. Only once on these occasions did a cobra get out of hand and make swiftly for me and my exit from the verandah then must have been the quickest I ever made.

Two sorry sights that often appeared were the performing bears who had been captured in the hills and now were dragged round on a chain looking shabby and unhappy and very reluctant to perform any tricks. Monkeys too, dressed up in little brightly coloured jackets passed by, often sitting on their captor's shoulders, grimacing and full of mischief. There was one visit I always looked forward to every week and that was the Postman's. He was a Moslem, a small man, clad in khaki, very conscientious and reliable. The great day of the week for us, and the most arduous for him, was Saturday morning, when the sea mail was due from England. In those days there was little if any air mail. How I used to love to see him appear with a bulky packet which he carefully drew out of his bag and handed to me. He then sat himself down while I scrutinised the mail. He knew we received letters from home that day and he would often ask me if I had heard from my Father and Mother and were they well and did I feel lonely so far from my home across the black water. They must be good people and fond of me, he continued, to write every week and would I tell them it gave him great pleasure to bring news of them to me, even though sometimes the load on Saturdays was very heavy. When the cold weather came he suffered from chilblains and I was brought in as consultant. His foot was held out for my inspection, the socks and shoes carefully removed and my advice anxiously sought for his livelihood depended on his walking and chilblains can be very crippling. Fortunately I hit on some ointment that seemed to work wonders and forever after he was a very good friend. I for my part always had the precious ointment available. The postmen were indeed rather a wonderful community, for although most of them could not read or write English, every letter seemed to quite unfailingly find its destination.

The garden was looking exceptionally beautiful one morning. The various shades of bougainvillaea were in full flower, mauve, flame, and pink. The large rose bed was alight with blooms of every hue and their perfume filled the air. Around the sunken front lawn was displayed a mass of flowers of all colours, sizes and shapes, all intermingling into a mosaic of harmony. From their petals the brilliant tiny sunbirds in their metallic gleaming feathers of blue and green were sipping the nectar. On a creeper in the verandah a tailer bird was making its nest, neatly sewing the leaves together to make a perfect cradle for its offspring. The numerous sparrows, never to be daunted, were building their nests on narrow window ledges and chattering all the time. It was a most unsuitable place, for they were always falling down and the floor beneath was usually strewn with sticks and straw. Eggs and even tiny birds fell down and had to be rescued.

Suddenly I saw two people standing and *salaam*ing me. So noiselessly had they approached that I had been quite unaware of their arrival. One I recognised as the sweeper's mother and with her was a young woman, whom she introduced as the sweeper's bride. She was a gorgeous and picturesque figure, attired in her wedding finery. Her wide ballet like skirt was of a bright yellow trimmed with a deeper golden braid, her blouse of a glowing pink and her headdress and shawl an emerald green; her ankles and arms were covered with wide heavy bracelets and she wore a number of necklaces. Her shawl was drawn well over her face (according to custom) but after I had duly admired the bridal clothes, she allowed me to see her face. She was attractive and very vivacious and was quite plainly a young girl of great personality and charm, and I felt sorry for her when I remembered how dull and bad tempered was Kishan, our sweeper. They both then sat down on the verandah steps for a chat. I was very fond of the old mother who had been an *ayah* and could just string a few disjointed sentences in English together. When I had fever she would steal into my bedroom and so gently massage my forehead, till all the ache seemed to melt away. Now we had just returned from a furlough and her conversation went something like this—'when sahib and memsahib away, we very sad, compound very quiet, Sibbu (our cook) he sad, we sad, all sad; when sahib and memsahib return, we all very glad, we happy be, our Father and Mother have come back; we thank God, they are happy and well and we all glad again'.

After a little more conversation in the same vein and I had been informed that the bride's name was Beeg Bo, that she came from a village and did not like leaving it but had to be married and that Kishan was the family choice, they withdrew. I did not see much of the bride again for awhile, though sometimes I would catch a glimpse of her (shorn now of her wedding finery) fetching water from the tap in the garden or squatting down and cooking outside her quarters. Occasionally she walked round to the verandah and would smile at me and *salaam*. But one day, about a year later, they both appeared again and I was told Beeg Bo was expecting a baby and I was asked to send her to the Mission hospital where she would be well looked after. So to the hospital she went. That same day Kishan gave me no peace and refused to work but just sat himself down by the verandah and kept worrying me to phone the hospital and find out if the child was born. Such concern seemed deeply touching at the time, and I promised I would let him know and in the meantime it would be better for him to occupy himself, a piece of advice of which he took no notice. In the evening I learnt that Beeg Bo had a baby girl and I called Kishan and told him. Never shall I forget his cry of rage when he heard it was a girl. He turned away in utter disgust. A few days later I saw a trap drive up, bringing Beeg Bo and the baby back; I also heard voices raised in anger; going to look I saw Kishan, his face livid with rage shouting at Beeg Bo and then seize a stick, evidently to strike her with. She still held the child in her arms and was remonstrating with him. I thought it was time I intervened and summoned Kishan to me; very sulkily he threw down the stick and came. I ordered him to clean all the windows in the bungalow, which I knew should keep him occupied for some time, during which I hoped his anger would subside. In the meanwhile, Beeg Bo came sobbing to me, holding the little bundle very closely in her arms and sat herself down on the verandah. I asked her what the trouble was. She took the tiny baby and held it out to me. 'Memsahib', she said, 'it's a girl and Kishan wants a boy, but I can't help it, I did not make her, God made her'. I tried to comfort her and being young and full of spirit she soon recovered and began to take an interest in the life entrusted to her, saying she would love her and look after her well, and added that Kishan would not be allowed to touch her. That was the birth of one child, a first child, a baby girl born to a young strong village girl still endowed with plenty of personality and spirit.

I also witnessed the reception of the birth of another child, also a girl. When Josephine, our bearer's wife, came to live in the compound, she already had four children, all under seven and she looked very worn and anaemic. When her fifth child was due. I sent her in good time to the hospital where the baby was born. About a week later I heard a commotion and shouting going on by the kitchen and went to see what it was. Josephine had just arrived back and her husband, Daulat, on hearing the baby was a girl was shouting at her. Her four other children had gathered motionless around her. I entered the scene just as Daulat, losing his temper altogether, slapped her. I ordered him very firmly to go. By this time, all the other servants were standing round. Our cook, who loved all children, shook his head sadly and Josephine herself, looking utterly worn out and sobbing audibly, sat herself down on the verandah steps while her children clung to her; the two elder ones, a boy and girl, stood with their heads bowed and the two little ones, the youngest being only just two, clung to her skirts, their little faces frightened and troubled. Suddenly the youngest, a little boy, burst into tears, crying mam, mam, and turned his face in her lap. Josephine herself took no notice, her humiliation was too great; she might have been a figure of tragedy carved in stone; the little child she held at her breast never stirred either. Our cook came forward, spoke gently to her and lightly touched the baby's head; there was no response; he then fetched some sweets and gave them to the children; they remained in their hot sticky little hands quickly melting away. After a while, Josephine wearily got up, and without a word and followed by her children, walked slowly but with great dignity towards her quarters. She named that baby Usha, meaning the dawn, but Usha did not stay long with us; a sudden chill a few months later and that little life flitted away.

Illness too could strike very suddenly in the compound. I remember one morning sitting on the verandah watching the great black buffalo who belonged to the Indian family just beyond us come ambling down the road, endeavouring by any means she could to enter any garden gate that was open en route. She was on her way to the river for her daily bath and was a magnificent creature, but being somewhat adventurous by nature had always to be carefully watched as the straight and narrow path did not appeal to her. Suddenly there was a woman's shriek from the back of the house and I ran to see what was the matter. When I arrived, I saw the cook's wife holding in her arms her little boy of about 2 years. Her husband was by her and they were both crying "Ram", "Ram", (God, God) in utter despair. I thought for a moment a snake had bitten the child—but was told it was fever. The little boy was immediately thrust into my arms. Never have I felt so hot a child, and never one who looked so near death. I called quickly for some ice and applied it to his forehead.

His head fell back and for a moment I thought he had gone, but to my great surprise and joy the dark heavy eyes opened and looked up at me. Without wasting any time, I got out the car and took him and his mother to the hospital—where an injection of quinine was immediately given—and I learnt he was suffering from malignant malaria and his temperature was 107 degrees. In a couple of days we welcomed him back again with us, laughing and shouting and running about.

One another morning, a Sunday, when my husband and I were drinking tea on the verandah, the bearer brought the car round for us. As this was usually the gardener's job, we asked where he was and were told he had gone to the bazaar to get some medicine for his wife. We took little notice of this, for very good herbal medicines were often obtained by our servants thus and we then went out for a drive. On coming back, though, at lunch time, our cook seemed very agitated and asked to speak to us. He then informed us that the gardener's wife had cholera and furthermore that she had been suffering with it all night and was now nearly dead. Cholera is of course most infections—strikes suddenly and quickly and is one of the most feared of all diseases. We knew it was about, for a neighbour just across the way had lost their cook and his whole family just the day before and now we were faced with the fact that for sixteen hours this woman had been in close contact with the other servants and their families and had been staggering to and fro from the water closet used by all. It was not a pleasant situation and was not made any better by it being a Sunday, when all disinfectant departments seemed to be closed and the Isolation hospital said they could not admit anyone. In despair we rang the Mission hospital; they replied that in such an emergency they would send an ambulance and isolate the patient until they could get her into hospital. Never have I felt more thankful in my life for their so kindly coming to the rescue. While we were negotiating with the hospital, the gardener himself came in and said that he could not allow the woman to go anywhere for this would "break his caste". We firmly overruled this, however, and the dying woman was taken away to the hospital where a quick injection of saline brought her miraculously back to life. That night was one of great suspense and we could see the fear in our servant's faces for cholera when it strikes, strikes swiftly and they all knew that. We tried to appear as unconcerned as we could, but as the dawn came I listened anxiously for the usual sounds of life in the compound and how great was our relief when the bearer, as silently as ever, appeared with the early morning tea, and quietly said to me, 'We are all well memsahib, all well, thanks to God'. A little later the gardener asked if he might return thanks for the recovery of his wife by allowing his pandits and priests to come and say prayers and purify the compound. It had already been well and thoroughly disinfected. So they came, these holy ones, and sat in a circle, intoned many prayers and afterwards walked round sprinkling water in every direction.

On another morning an entirely different incident occurred. I had been watching the black and white flycatchers dart from bush to bush, and the bee eaters, perching on the telegraph wires, giving a beautiful display of their long tails and copper and green plumage glinting in the sun. The pigeons were cooing softly and lovingly and the black and white striped squirrels were chasing each other up and down the trees in a never ending game. Suddenly the whole compound was in an uproar. I saw the servants, usually so quiet, rushing about with great sticks and the *chokidar*, or watchman, brandishing his *lathi* (copper headed staff). For a moment I failed to see the object of all this chase and called to them, but they did not hear and finally I caught sight of a great snake in the grass trying to escape from them. They caught up with it though and battered it to death. As we all gazed down at the lifeless fangs, the gardener who had not been in the chase and who was an orthodox Hindu and did not believe in taking life, came up to the group and said, 'this is only a great grass snake and quite harmless. But at the back of the compound there has always lived a deadly cobra. Why not kill him?' This was the first I had heard about the cobra and I asked for more information as it was there that the children played. I was quietly told that the cobra was quite harmless, he had come when the house was built (we were the first residents) and therefore he was the guardian of our house and brought good luck; he was given milk every day and was quite alright. Remonstrance was useless—I left it at that.

Two Villages

My first sight of an Indian village was under flood conditions. It was soon after my arrival in Delhi, when the monsoon had been one of the heaviest for years. In consequence some of the villages near the river Jumna, which were built on low lying ground, had been almost washed away as the river had overflowed its bank and seeped into the land around. The village I visited had been adopted for flood relief work by St Stephen's College and every day some of the staff and students went out there to render help with food, medicines, blankets, etc. This village was situated some five miles from Delhi and one afternoon a party, in which I was included, set off on bicycles. As we proceeded, the road became worse and worse and finally reached a point where it had been washed away in the aftermath of the floods. The last lap had to be done on foot where we waded through a slippery muddy track with pools of water everywhere. The fields around us were still under water. At the entrance to the village the villagers were awaiting us, some squatting patiently in the mud, others shrouded in blankets and lying on string beds, and most of them suffering from malaria. We were welcomed by the village headman, a small man, but evidently of great importance who reminded me of a little Napoleon in charge of operations. At the moment he was, I thought, quite naturally concerned with obtaining in the future a better site for the village higher up than the place at which it now was where as a matter of fact it used to originally stand, but had been removed by the Government which required the site for other purposes.

We proceeded through the village accompanied by some children, the leader amongst them being the headman's son who guided us on our tour while he proudly carried a large bottle of liquid quinine we had brought with us. Another child fortunately carried an equally large packet of sugar as an antidote to the bitter taste of the quinine much disliked by our patients.

The scene before us could be summed up as one of devastation and misery. The village houses, which for the most part were built of mud and covered with thatch were almost washed away, so that many of the people had no shelter at all, except for a kind of tent that had been provided by the College. In addition, all the stagnant muddy water lying about was a fine breeding place for mosquitoes. Files abounded everywhere and the dung cakes made by the women and used for cooking were all wet and smoky. The villagers themselves looked desperately poor, ill and miserable. Much of their clothing was in rags, and the children, wearing for the most part one short little shirt, revealed more plainly their emaciated bodies and pot bellies. The village itself was divided into various sections, according to caste and occupation. There was a Brahmin quarter, a shepherds quarter and a quarter that housed a mixed community which worked on the land. The outcaste quarter stood right on the outskirts of the village. Around us were cows, buffaloes and goats, all painfully thin; lying or standing about, they gazed mournfully at us, but did not move. Some of the cows were being milked, but it looked as if it might have been easier to extract blood from a stone; pariah dogs too lay about licking their sores. The dumb suffering of all these animals was indeed eloquent, for while man was short of food, the animals were in an even worse plight.

Most of the villagers were suffering from malaria. Some were trying to suckle their babies, though they had high temperatures themselves. Never shall I forget the plight of these women and children. Overcoming their shyness of a stranger and a foreigner too, they came especially to me because I was the only woman among the party of helpers. I saw how disappointed they must have been with me, for I had only just recently arrived in Delhi and their language was practically unknown to me. Still by signs, gestures and smiles and a great willingness on both sides to be helped and help we established some kind of communication whereupon they began to show me the ulcers on their legs, boils on their necks, and allowed me to register their temperatures and pulse. They were nearly all suffering from malaria, bad colds and coughs. They were for the most part young women, for India's average life span is only thirty years or so, but the hardship of their lives had left its ravages on their patient, gentle faces and on their physical and mental make up. Some of them brought their children too, tiny ones in their arms, and tried to make me understand what was the matter with them. I saw their little bodies which, when touched, were burning hot, and beautiful dark eyes covered with sores and tormented with files. Most of them had coughs, colds, bronchitis, malaria and very likely a mixture of all. I sat in the makeshift shelters which were full of smoke and rubbed these children's chests with camphorated oil and dosed them with cough mixture and quinine which they protested against and choked over and I cleaned, anointed and bound up sores and ulcers. I could do nothing for their sore eyes, nor the plague of flies. The women's gratitude for such inadequate help was disarming and almost as if by a miracle these children by degrees and with many rubbings of camphorated oil and innumerable does of cough mixture and quinine got better and I had the joy of seeing the little faces smile at me and feel cool little bodies once more. On once occasion I had to bandage a very sick baby who had bad sores on its body and a boil on its head. A doctor had come and lanced the boil the day before and saved its life, for otherwise meningitis would have set in. The mother, who was in *purdah* and completely enveloped in a dirty *burqa*, brought the baby to me. She sat on the ground so I had to kneel down to attend to the child, who seemed almost lifeless.

I unbandaged the head and proceeded to wash the sore clean and disinfect it, and I was just putting some clean lint on when one tiny leg kicked out and one piece fell in the mud, whereupon the mother in her ignorance and in her wish to help me picked it up immediately and would have placed it, covered with dirty, on the open sore had I not seized it quickly. While this was going on, I heard the sound of wailing in another part of the village and asked what it meant. I was told someone's wife had died and they were wailing in consequence. Two incidents always come before my mind when I think of that village. One is of a young girl who always stood on the periphery of the crowd of children and was invariably sick whenever she even saw the bottle of quinine. The other is of a Bengali student clothed in a spotlessly white dhoti, kneeling in the mud, and with a look of great compassion on his youthful face, binding up the wounds of a village man, who was covered with sores from head to foot.

Before we left the village each time food was distributed in the form of grain. Amidst all the suffering and hardship endured it was such a joy to see the worn and tired faces light up at the prospect of some much needed food. The children, especially, laughed and clapped their hands. Such a pleasing contrast to the horrid quinine we brought which they had taken so bravely! Indian children are very sensitive and respond quickly to kindness and they also possess great courage. Despite all the adverse conditions under which they lived, their gentle smiles soon broke through while their delicately formed features and their beautiful serious brown eyes distinguished them from all other children. The Indian parents too showed great fondness for their young ones who never appeared to be cowed down by harsh words or beatings.

I shall never indeed forget the courage, patience and endurance of these Indian villagers in circumstances which would have challenged the morale of the bravest. Before we finally stopped visiting the area, when the people were for the most part better again; when their land was drying off and their huts were being rebuilt and they were beginning to stand on their own feet once more, with true Indian hospitality, these people so poor, in the material sense, invited us to a dinner with them which they served with dignity and grace, as a token of their gratitude for the little we had been able to do for them.

How lovely was that Indian evening with the children laughing and playing, the cows and buffaloes sitting as quietly in our midst as always and the people animated and happy, while the setting sun lit up the sky with a crimson glow and made more clear the tiny crescent moon, guarded by a beautiful evening star, under which we sat and shared in the happiness of a village which we had been privileged to help and which seemed now to be imbued with new life and self respect. Many were the *salaams*, many the farewells, many the smiles and many the garlands given to us as we left and always I shall hear the shrill cries of the children as they shouted their own special greetings and waved and waved till we could see them no more.

Another village that I visited near Delhi was under more normal conditions, though this village too was a very poor one. There was no irrigation; the people were entirely dependent on the monsoon for their crops and when that failed, the people suffered. An Indian lady, who took a great interest in the welfare of these villagers had started handicraft and needlework for the women to help them eke out a scanty living and give them another interest. They did some beautiful work and she sold it for them. I went there to help with the Girl Guide movement which had been started by a friend and therefore made contact with some of the children in the village, especially the girls. I shall always remember how much they enjoyed our visits to them. When our cars drew up under a tree, out they all came to welcome us, looking fresh and clean with their dark hair carefully oiled and plaited. We discovered that their greatest pleasure was derived from games, for they had never played our games before and the delight with which they entered into them was a joy to behold. All else was forgotten, the drabness of their dusty brown village, their poverty, their ills and for an hour or so they just became the children they were at heart. They found learning to hop a most amusing occupation. We also discovered that they loved competitions and we used to set them to create something entirely original by themselves with the material they had at hand and quite amazing was the ingenuity they displayed as they proudly brought to us the results of their efforts. They also cultivated a little garden for which we gave them seeds. This was an accomplishment in itself, for they had to carry pitchers of water from the well several times a day in order to keep it watered. They tended it with loving care and displayed each blossom as if it were as precious as a jewel. Some of the girls were Muslims and had just reached the age when they would be no longer free to play about with the others, but would be restricted within the four walls of the *purdah*. I was interested to learn that at the same age the Hindu girls were not thus restricted. They were allowed the freedom of the open air and contact with all their fellows and creatures, but every effort was made to make them appear as unattractive as possible.

When the time came for us to leave these Guides, they invited us to lunch in a large shed where there was a small table at which we sat on wooden chairs from the village schoolhouse. The girls had prepared and cooked the entire meal themselves, which they served to us on banana leaves. It was delicious vegetarian food. Silently and gracefully they moved amongst us, always wanting us to have more and watching eagerly to see if we really enjoyed it. It was one of the loveliest social occasions I attended. We had been well coached by an Indian friend as to how to eat with our fingers in the correct manner and learnt that it would be against all politeness to use anything but the right hand throughout. I remember too that against all convention, it was a Brahmin boy and a fine lad too, who insisted on bringing the water from the well for us to drink on this occasion.

After the meal, and after we had tried to convey with *salaams* and smiles our great appreciation for all the children had done for us, we saw the formerly smiling faces sadden, for we were now leaving them for good. We both felt the parting, I think, and in order to mollify it as much as possible, we now asked if in this last visit we could do anything for them. They thought for a moment and then looked at the two cars we had with us and immediately the request was, 'Please take us into Delhi and let us see your houses'. There were about twelve of them and after gaining permission from their mothers, we bundled them all into the cars (which was not really difficult because they were so slim). Very excitedly they all started out, but just beyond their village there was a settlement of houses, some mud and thatch, where at this time was the *ashram* of Mahatma Gandhi, who had his headquarters there. As we went by, the excited voices were stilled, every head was bowed, their hands were folded as if in prayer and the cry went out from them "*Gandhiji ki jai*" (Victory to Gandhi). It was one of the most moving of all such demonstrations that I saw in India. As we motored into the Civil Lines of Delhi with the shady green trees and many old bungalows covered with bougainvillaea, the girls pointed at everything and talked animatedly amongst themselves. Nothing escaped their notice. It must indeed have been a great contrast to their dusty village. When we reached my house, they stepped into it hushed and awed, as we might on our first visit to a castle or a great hall. To them it was full of articles they had never seen before, furniture, pictures, mugs, books, china, silver, vases of flowers, ornaments, beds covered with silk bedspreads, bathrooms with water flowing in through taps, light which just appeared when a button was touched. Everything was looked at and talked about, but to my astonishment, the biggest wonder of all came when they entered a bedroom where there was a full size mirror and for the first time evidently, they really beheld their likeness. For a moment there was utter silence and then they began to laugh and gesticulate at each other's appearance. Some finally tried arranging their clothes and their hair and smiled and frowned at the result. Some remained looking serious as if they had just realized what kind of façade they presented to the world. It was now beginning to get dark. They had at last reluctantly to leave the mirror and we started the drive back to their village. The sun was setting, the laughter and talk had quietened down. As we passed the *ashram*, once more the dark heads were bowed and the cry, "*Gandhi ji ki jai*" rang out in the silent air. Before we finally parted, they ran into the village and came back with garlands they had woven of flowers from their own gardens which they insisted on placing around our necks. We could not help but feel a pang as we watched them with hands clasped, *salaam*ing and bidding us farewell. We drove thoughtfully back into Delhi, realising that these village children, with their charming natural characteristics, their sensibility to all life around them, their interest and wonder in all that is new, will bring, when the time comes, wondrous gifts of lasting value, not least those of the spirit, to the country of their birth.

An Indian Street

When I was a small child living in the West Indies, I used to listen attentively to all I could hear about a country called India. Perhaps the similarity in name struck me. I heard of people called Brahmins—the twice born, who wore the sacred thread and of others referred to as outcastes, who often had to hide themselves lest their shadow should pollute these Brahmin overlords. At a very early age I took part in a pageant featuring a Hindu wedding ceremony. It seemed to come out of a fairy tale; a bridegroom attired in gold and silver, a bride in the glittering folds of a sari, both walking round a sacred fire seven times; fabulously wealthy rajahs, their turbans flashing with jewels and riding gaily caparisoned elephants, dwelt in their marble palaces there; snake charmers abounded, and men who walked on fire and were not burnt and who lay on spikes and were not pierced. It was evidently a land of great pilgrimages, of holy rivers and shrines. It had been the home of great Mughal emperors whose legacy was written in stone in perhaps some of the world's loveliest buildings. I heard the mystic name of Taj Mahal. It was all so full of mystery and wonder to a child's mind. Years later when I went to live in this country of my childhood's memories, I was quite unprepared for the shock of an Indian street. It was such an utter contrast to the dull regimentation of the west. It pulsated with life and colour and noise. There the people were spontaneous and uninhibited in their behaviour. It was more of a stage on which the everyday comedies and tragedies of life were enacted and all India seemed to be contained in it.

The street itself was set amidst a medley of strange buildings of all sizes and shapes. A fine, well proportioned mosque with light airy arches and perfect dome, from which the call to prayer rang out at dawn and sunset, looked down on the humble open booths of the street vendors on either side. There were other sections of haphazard, highly decorative buildings usually two storied and surrounded by carved wooden balconies on which could always be seen grown ups and children in all stages of domesticity, amidst a clutter of cooking utensils, string beds and washing hung across the verandah. A fine modern bank compered a Hindu temple, whose bells and drums were sounded at regular intervals. On every side were various alleys and courtyards. In the narrow alleys could be found heavy doors built into the wall. Inside were some of the old city houses secluded from the bustle of the street and shaded by spreading *neem* trees. They were said to contain many treasures and were cool in the heat and warm in the cold weather.

Everywhere there were shops. They ranged from quite modern buildings with glass windows, from behind which costly and rare merchandise were displayed to where the street vendor sat cross legged behind his open stall. Many and varied too were the wares offered for sale. Generally each section of the street was confined to some particular ware or trade. On one corner, where newly made sweets were being made in full view of all, many were the customers attracted to it. These sweets differed greatly from the small boiled ones sold in the west. They were much larger and were composed of such delicacies as milk, butter, nuts, sugar and various delightful flavourings. An especially attractive one was green in colour and covered with finely beaten silver, while another, much loved on account of its succulent sweetness, delighted in the poetic name of *rasgulla*. To eat this one in public without becoming a sticky mess required some deft practice. Though loved and patronised by all and sundry, this shop was especially dear to the hearts of the children who, clasping their precious annas in their hot little hands, could be seen talking and laughing while they speculated on the best value for their money.

In another part and in the open, garlands, so loved by India, were being woven, and their fragrance filled the air, as many of the blossoms intertwined there were jasmine, roses, marigolds, as well as many other blooms. Also to be seen were those made of gold and silver tinsel. These garlands, one of the loveliest of Indian customs, are used for offerings to the gods, for weddings and funerals, and to welcome friend and stranger and again to speed them on their way. Long are the hours spent, great is the patience, and skilful are the hands that fashion into such a charming symbol, the welcome, hospitality and devotion of the people of India. Close by to the garland makers a brisk trade went on in the selling of bracelets, earrings and brooches, in fact in jewellery of all kinds. Their flashing colours and tinkling sound added a touch of magic to the scene, for great is the love of Indian women for these many and varied bracelets which so attractively adorn their delicate wrists and arms, worn in such numbers that their soft tinkling music can always be heard as the women pass by. In fact, an Indian woman, however poor, without such adornment is very rare.

There was also a special section reserved for the silversmiths, where delicate and highly skilled craftsmanship was carried on. Indian silver is beaten very fine and is noted for its softness, its light appearance and lovely intricate patterns. Where there was a Muslim quarter a great deal of carving was executed in wood and ivory. There wooden tables intricately inlaid with ivory were to be found along with trays depicting scenes and sayings from Mughal court life and light, exquisitely carved wooden screens. There were also miniature paintings showing the wonders of Mughal architecture in palace, mosque and tomb, or the faces of Emperors and Princes, along with ivory necklaces, brooches and earrings of gods and goddesses, animal inkstands, rickshaws, chessmen, and many other works of art.

Anther most attractive quarter was where the silks and saris were sold. Perhaps no where else can be found materials so lovely both in texture and in colour. The sari, one of the most graceful and yet most simple of garments is a joy to behold and a delight to wear, especially so perhaps in silk with its five or six yards of soft shimmering material, which drapes so becomingly around the human form, and supplies a headdress as well if required. Certainly in its variety of colours, plain and blended and with the finishing touch to a masterpiece of loveliness in the varied borders that adorn its edges, the sari commands admiration wherever it is worn. Silk saris are of course too expensive for the great majority of Indian women, but there were sold also at a very small price, cotton saris, cool and with lovely borders. These too assume the same quality of gracefulness and charm for their wearers. The men were also catered for with a variety of shirts and white baggy trousers caught in gracefully at the ankles in an embroidered band, as well as tight fitting ones and the *atchkan* or three quarter length coat buttoned to the neck, giving an impression of simplicity and dignity. A great deal of the men's clothing seemed to be white except where European dress had taken the place of Indian and had brought with it a certain drabness. Headgear was also very varied, and ranged from the simple Gandhi cap made of rough homespun cloth to the *astrakhan* Mughal hat, the red fez of Muslims and turbans of all colours and all fashions along with European trilbys and *toppes*.

Carpets and rugs were lavishly displayed; many of them were handwoven in rich colourings with red, gold, blue and indigo predominating. They were highly prized both for their finely woven and varied patterns of ancient beauty and for their durability. Some people decorated their walls with them, evidently prizing them too highly to be trodden on by passers by. Besides many other shops and stalls containing all manner of food, fruit, vegetables, grain, spices and the other necessities of everyday life, there was also to be seen the dispensaries of Indian doctors. These usually belonged to a hereditary group and were housed in what looked like little more than a large cupboard opening out into the street. Inside this cupboard apartment though, were kept many valuable medicines; many of them herbal which had stood the test of time. The patients who came to these dispensaries were usually very poor and could pay but little for medical attendance, and yet these doctors were noted for their compassion for and their understanding of the poverty and the dire need of those who came to them, and none ever seemed to be turned away. Perhaps they had the true feeling of a real healer; that it was their privilege to share in the task of helping their fellow creatures and no doubt their reward must have been a very satisfying one.

Around a large water fountain in the middle of the street, there was always to be seen large crowds; some fetching water, others quenching their thirst, some washing clothes or cooking utensils, others cleansing their teeth and washing out their throat with a rasping sound; others even managed to have a bath while washing and drying their clothes at the same time. This was not so difficult as it sounds for they have but to remove the long turban from their head, wash it and dry it, which only takes a few minutes in the hot sun, after which they substitute their turban for a waist covering and then wash and dry their shirts, loin cloths, or *dhoti*, which is a long length of material ties round the waist and often caught up between the legs. It is but a simple matter then to put on the *dhoti* and transfer the turban back to the head and the shirt on the back, and they are thus bathed and cleanly clad again before the public gaze with very little effort. Usually this was all done to the accompaniment of the pigeons' soft cooing and friendly acquisitiveness.

In another part of the street could be discerned the letter writer, sitting on the pavement with his clients and writing to their dictation, for in a country that is mainly illiterate they provide a most valuable service. Very interesting too was the phraseology of the letters thus written especially in English which takes on a form wholly oriental in style, yet having to be conveyed through an alien medium. A sample of such a letter thus written reads thus.

'Respected Sahib and Mem Sahib,

I gratefully acknowledge receipt of your kind letter dated 18th December... I am glad to inform you that I have collected usual present from Pedder Miss Sahib. Sir I am most grateful to you for kind remembrance and I wish you for Christmas and the New Year.

Sir, I pray to God that you may lead long and prosperous life. I would never forget those pleasant days which I have spent with you, and your generosity and affection which you have shown for me. Once again, I am very grateful to you for the kind present and remembrance. I am also most grateful to Mem Sahib for her kindness and treated me like her own children. I pray her long and prosperous life. God bless her.

> Live long Spear and Mem Sahib
> and God bless both of you.
> Wish you and Mem Sahib Happy New Year
> With affectionate and kindest regards,
> Obediently,'

A most patronised service was provided by the barber and hairdresser, both of whom quite unconcernedly carried on their activities before the milling crowds, while horoscope readers with their suave patter caught the attention and the money of many passers by.

The dust everywhere amidst all this motley and varied scene was indescribable; it covered everything and reached its height when the feckless gusts of wind so characteristic of the Indian plain whipped it into a blinding and most unpleasant fury, or worse still when a sudden dust storm descended from the leaden sky above and transformed the whole scene into a desert of sand. As the morning wore on, the glaring rays of the sun became more and more merciless until at last everything seemed to be held in a heat so scorching and relentless that by the afternoon all creatures, human and animal, sought some shelter in which to rest. Files appeared and were especially troublesome around the food shops where the vendors fought a losing battle against them as they endeavoured with inadequate fly whisks to stay this ever dodging army. The drains, usually open ones, ran down the side of the pavement and often gave forth most unpleasant odours. The pavements themselves were besmeared with what might have been mistaken for drops of blood, but was nothing more harmful than the result of chewing betel nut, a digestive, the red juice of which is finally spat out. No one could escape the dust, the heat and the smells, that were very mixed and highly varied, ranging from the unsavoury whiffs of sewage and dirty water, sweating humanity, spices and foods, to the lovely perfume of flowers and scent.

The noise of the street never ceased and was full of clangour and strident with shrill voices. This was due mainly to the highly diverse means of transport. Dangerously near the crowded pavement, noisy trams rattled by with bells changing continuously in their effort to clear the way before them of both pedestrians and animals. In keen competition came the tongas, small two wheeled traps, their lean horses jingling with bells. The passengers held on to a precarious seat in the rear, while the perspiring driver with flourishing whip and showing little or no sign of direction, whipped and cajoled his unwilling pony on. Rickshaw men also trotted wearily along wearing but a loin cloth, a form of attire which made more conspicuous their too slight forms and spindly legs. The passengers for the most part belonged to the privileged few with plenty to eat and inclined to corpulence and seemed quite unconscious of how humiliating to human dignity was their form of transport. At a slower and more dignified rate came the bullock wagons, those ancient and changeless chariots of the Indian scene for many centuries and still asserting their prior right as they crept slowly and monotonously along, quite indifferent to any hooting of cars or ringing of bells; as if to emphasise more clearly their detachment from all later forms of transport, the bullocks were often bedecked with garlands around their necks and their horns were painted in gay colours. Unique both in their appearance and in their perfect identity with the country, they still remained the primary means of communication between thousands of Indian villages. The camel cart too could sometimes be glimpsed bringing vegetables and other merchandise into the city. These carts were high off the ground and the camels' stride had a stateliness and contemptuousness not to be found in any other animal. Away from his desert home, where he is supreme master of all paths, he appeared now to look down in scorn on such an alien scene. At times a strange contraption appeared, carried by poles on human shoulders; inside this cage like box was seated a Muslim woman, cramped and almost hidden from view. In this stifling manner she was bumped and jerked along uninterested, it seemed, even in the scene around. A *dhobi*'s donkey too would stagger by always seemingly laden with bundles of washing too heavy for its legs to support adequately. Seeing these two, one could not help but remember the common Indian attitude to *Karma*, which expresses the hope that one may never again be born either a woman or a donkey.

In contrast came the more modern vehicles which fortunately did not depend on the suffering and abuse of the animal kingdom for their efficiency. Of these, bicycles were the most conspicuous, with their non-stop bells, as often as not on the wrong side of the road, and each carrying perhaps two or three passengers, one on the handle bars, one on the seat and the other on the back. The milkmen performed quite a feat on these bicycles as they came clanging along with great cans full of milk precariously swinging from the handle bars. Most of these milkmen had come from the villages around the some crossed the river on their route. It was said of these that the ferryman who brought them across was often given his fare in milk and this of course necessitated the filling up of the cans again, and what simpler and more economic way than to add the required amount from the "holy" river. Later comers to the street were the cars and buses, but their pride soon suffered a fall, for though the fastest and most recent they were by no means treated with deference. Despite all their fierce hooting their impatient drivers, geared to speed, had perforce to adjust themselves to the slower rhythm of traffic all around.

This description of the street would never be complete without a mention of the various stray animals that wandered about and are so taken for granted. One of the most familiar was the Brahmani bull who wandered aimlessly and quite harmlessly in his search for food. He was, luckily for him, considered sacred and so often helped himself from a stall or was fed by one of the stall holders. At other times he was to be seen chewing up paper, on which no doubt some faint imprint of food still remained. Cows too could be observed being milked from doorways or goats would leap nimbly across the road while cocks and hens narrowly escaped the wheels of passing cars. The pariah dogs, evidently no one's concern, often covered with sores and pestered by files, must arouse the compassion of all animal lovers as they raided any garbage or rubbish to try and allay their hunger. Still more heart-rending was the plight of the female with a little litter of puppies for whom she was the sole provider. But perhaps the greatest diversion in the street was stage by the monkeys, who appeared as if by magic. They had the best of both worlds as with great alacrity they descended on the roofs and quietly and stealthily made their way down, without any warning raiding a shop swiftly and cunningly while clutching their loot in their hands and just as nimbly swinging themselves out of reach before the shopkeeper's astonished eyes, only to look down again with amusement and surprise at the immobility of those beneath. I have seen monkeys snatch not only food, but towels, hand mirrors, combs and clothes on these expeditions. They are indeed the bold buccaneers of the highways and their antics aroused much mirth in those not involved in the loss of their goods.

The human occupants of the streets were a moving pageant of all types in appearance and outlook. The greater number were men and the majority amongst these were to be numbered among the poor in material wealth. They constituted the mass clad in shirt, loin cloth and *pugaree* or ruban. But amongst them could be seen the proud Brahmin distinguished by this caste mark displayed on his forehead, who passed by with the assurance of the inherent superiority of the caste who for so many years has dominated India's social and religious thought. In contrast to him came the Muslim with his smart three quarter length coat and tight fitting trousers. He represented in his outlook an entirely different code of religious beliefs and social patterns. Next the bearded Sikh, his long uncut hair rolled up under his fastidiously tied turban, at once indicated another side of Hinduism, whose men amongst other customs and traditions were not supposed to cut their hair or shave their faces. Most striking in his appearance and towering head and shoulders above the crowd around him, the Pathan or Frontiers man was one who could not be overlooked. With his gaily embroidered velvet waistcoat and wide white baggy trousers he was feared by all, not only for his fine independence in a land of servility, but because he was also a noted and ruthless moneylender and was certainly not to be easily reckoned with. An interesting comparison to him was the Jain, member of another religious sect, which included in its attitude to life certain Buddhist ideals. The Jains were easily distinguished by the small white cloth worn over the nostrils, a protection against the swallowing of the myriads of insects all around, for they had sworn never to take life. They were also often to be seen feeding no lesser of God's creatures than the ants. Occasionally an Indian lady in her beautiful coloured sari and jewels or a Punjabi woman in wide trousers, shirt and scarf and even a village woman in wide ballet like skirt in vivid green, yellow or blue often carrying her baby on her hips, passed along. All of them moved with the same perfect poise and balance, characteristic of these sandal' clad or bare footed women. In sad contrast came the Muslim woman shuffling along in a wide tent like all enveloping garment with just embroidered eyeslits through which to find their way, for to her was denied among many human freedoms, the freedom of the street. There were children everywhere, some gazing in shops, some wearing gay little frocks and still gayer little hats, the majority clad only in a brief shirt, but sharing with children all over the world, a common interest and wonder in all that was going on around them. Coolies too appeared to be holding out their large round baskets in the expectation of a shopping expedition. The sweepers, the most depressed class of all, with their small brooms of stick, mage futile efforts to clean up the ever increasing dust and rubbish around. Here too the beggar lay in rags on the pavement and along with him the crippled, the blind and perchance even a leper holding out his copper bowl and soliciting alms in the name of God. Next, India's "holy men", came passing by, their naked bodies covered with ash and their long hair dirty and matted; the *sadhu* in his saffron robe, ever seeking truth, would sit down on the pavement, oblivious of the world around, seemingly lost in a trance. In utter contrast to all these came the Europeans complete with *topees* and sun glasses always walking a little faster that anyone else and looking somewhat bewildered amidst such a panorama of contrasts. On Festival days were seen the pilgrims, hundreds of them, many coming in from the villages, clad in their gayest clothes and all hastening in the direction of the river to bathe in its sacred waters and have their caste marks duly inscribed on their foreheads by the pandits or priests who sat by the banks. Some beat their breasts and repeated the words "Ram", "Ram", (God, God) over and over again, some sang, laughed and talked, enjoying their outing in holiday spirit. Many carried offerings of food for the gods or pandits, and others held garlands. These festivals meant a great deal to the work-a-day Indian for it was their only way of obtaining a holiday from the monotonous toil of everyday life.

And then finally came a procession common to all streets the world over. Maybe a few Muslim men silent and dignified, carrying a coffin draped in white or green, depending on the sex of the one who lay within. They wended their way to the Muslim cemetery, where the body was reverently buried. When the body was that of a baby, it was carried with great tenderness in the arms of one of the family members. In contrast was the Hindu funeral procession where the body was borne on a simple stretcher and the occupant covered with a white or coloured cloth on which garlands were laid. The bearers made their way to the Burning Ghats often running and crying "Ram", "Ram", as they went. Other uttered the monotonous wail for the dead. Now and again they would stop and rest the body and it was noticeable that the feet of the dead were turned towards the direction in which he was moving for it was common Hindu belief that this would prevent the spirit finding its way back. To the Hindu with his belief in reincarnation this was an opportunity to be born into a higher stage of life.

Thus from early dawn to night the Indian street was teeming with life and activity in all forms and shapes, but at mid-night a hush fell, the shutters of the shops were closed at last, the crowd faded away into their homes, the lights were dimmed, and save for a beggar, whose bed was the pavement and the Brahmani bull who lay down close beside him, and the pariah dog, still rummaging among the garbage, all was silent, all was still under the watching stars of an Indian night.

A Stay in the Hills

A year after I arrived in India, we went to stay in a bungalow in the Hills for two months to escape the great heat of summer in the plains. I will always remember that journey, chiefly I think because we took our kitten with us. She was an attractive and intelligent little tabby. When we reached the station, we thought we had better book for her and so off we went to the ticket office to ask the cost of her transport. At that moment she was laying very quiet and still in the basket we had housed her in and no one would have known she was there. The booking clerk looked at us in some surprise and then consulted a list of those who travelled other than human. Evidently such varied creatures as dogs, birds and horses were accounted for—but cats were not included. After a good deal of talk and a very firm stand on our part that we could not possibly leave the kitten behind, he scratched his head with great determination and said that if that were really the case then the most likely category for the cat to be listed in, was that of a bird. Accordingly we paid a bird's railway fare and departed to our carriage. The kitten, I think, must have thought this an insult to her dignity for she started at once to mew and never stopped throughout all that long night's journey. We were indeed fortunate in that no one else entered our compartment. She refused food and drink and continued her mewing even after we had left the train and had been taken by car up a winding hill road to our destination. Once there, though, she settled down and thoroughly enjoyed life, following us all over the hillside—rushing up and down trees and getting into all kinds of scrapes.

Soon after we arrived, there was a terrific hill storm. We lay in our beds listening to clap after clap of thunder as it reverberated from hill to hill and shading our eyes from the vivid flashes of lighting that penetrated our room. We felt comparatively safe as we knew we had a good lightning conductor on the bungalow. Suddenly the rain came down in torrents and in a few moments the roof above us began to leak. Hastily we fetched tin baths and basins to try and stem the flood. A blinding flash of lighting followed by a terrific clap of thunder right overhead almost frightened us out of our wits and at the same moment we heard something heavy crash to the ground outside—a tree maybe we thought. Then into the room there rushed our little kitten, drenched through. She hurled herself in utter terror into my bed and disappeared under the clothing. We had put her to bed in a basket in an adjoining bathroom placing a heavy stone against the small opening where the bath water ran out so that she could not escape. What super force she had used to move that stone and get out we shall never know, but there she was snug in my bed now and she didn't stir from there till morning. When at last that all night storm had subsided and we looked out we discovered that the heavy crash we had heard early in the night was our lighting conductor lying on the ground.

A stay in the hills gave us an opportunity to roam the countryside thus bringing us into closer touch with hill scenes and the hill people. Once when we were strolling down a steep hill path, we saw eight men carrying what looked like a huge box on poles. But as we glanced closer, we saw that the box was more or less a platform surrounded by brightly coloured curtains and through a gap in them we caught a glimpse of the figure of a hill god with a brass head, gaudily attired and bedecked with jewellery. We immediately stepped aside feeling a hill god "on tour" certainly took precedence in his own territory, but the hillmen who were carrying him stopped, stepped courteously aside and *salaam*ed and withdrew their god to the inside of the narrow path. We could then only acknowledge such courtesy as best we could and pass on. Hill god are often carried round like this as they are taken to the Hill Fairs where the people bring them out and often dance with them. Once when we heard that such a Fair was taking place some three miles away we set out one fine morning to attend it. We scrambled down a thousand feet on a boulder strewn, scrub lined path, crossed a rushing stream and then ascended the other side. Here the slope was gentler and we soon entered a cone strewn wood of firs and deodars. At length the wood path emerged from the forest and descended into a valley which was comparatively broad, though there was little level ground. The land was terraced for cultivation with little channels leading off from the hill streams for irrigation. There were solitary little hill houses which dotted the landscape and here and there stood clusters of dwellings built in typical hill style—wooden houses with verandahs—gabled roof beams and slated roofs. In an open space the Fair was in progress and community dancing was in full swing. On one side were the women, dressed in heavy hill coats bound with gaily coloured sashes. They formed a crescent shaped line and with hands linked they moved slowly to and fro to a kind of solemn one step and at the same time chanted a plaintive air, slowly and continuously. The whole proceeding was punctuated with occasional bowings. Facing them were the men; they were not the young men but seemed to be the village elders—or perhaps one should say the state nobles—for his village was an important place in the tiny hill state of Kanethi. Some of them were gaunt and bent and some held covered swords which trembled in their unsteady hands. They seemed sad and rather tattered but they shuffled through their steps with great dignity.

There was also a band with drums and a collection of long and fantastic looking trumpets. The musicians did not seem to have had much practice judging from the weird and extraordinary sounds that emanated from the instruments they played. On another side of the space was, as it might be, the grandstand, where the spectators were assembled. In the midst of this group sat the local hill Rajah—his *hookah* by his side and his attendants standing round. He was a rather dark puffy looking man with the marks of indulgence on his face and with little sign of any animation. We exchanged polite greeting with him but most of the time he seemed more asleep than awake. Around us were the sedan chairs with the gods inside. They were apparently brought to preside over and enjoy this gala occasion. Now and again one or other of them would be taken out of his curtained seclusion and given a regular romp and dance by the excited hillmen.

As evening approached the fair began to dismantle in time for the performers and spectators to return to their villages before dark. This break up of the fair was the gayest part of the proceedings for it was only then that we realised how greatly it had been enjoyed by the participants. The solemn steps, the plaintive air, the feeling of restraint all vanished in a flash. Everywhere the departing faces were filled with animation and wreathed in smiles. The young men cheerfully and unceremoniously hoisted the gods on their shoulders, laughing and joking and even the Rajah unbent himself and gave his benediction to all.

On another occasion when we had climbed laboriously up to the crest of a hill over 10,000 ft. high in order to obtain a magnificent view of the snow capped ranges, we saw a number of people gathered near a small wooden hill temple. On the green slopes around grazed a flock of sheep with a shepherd in attendance. At first we took no particular notice of all this as we were absorbed in enjoying the grassy knoll we had ascended to and the breathtaking view of the snow ranges beyond. Suddenly we became aware that the shepherd was addressing us and we turned and tried hard to understand what he was saying—not too easy a feat, for we knew but little of the hill dialect he spoke. Ultimately, aided by much gesticulating, we gathered that the small hill temple was a Kali one, that is, it was dedicated to Kali, the Hindu goddess of destruction. They now wanted to build a larger and finer temple for their goddess and in order to inaugurate this undertaking, in a few moments they were going to sacrifice a sheep on a rock nearby. Even as he said this we glanced round and noticed that the other men gathered there were making their preparations for doing this—fire wood was being laid—huge knives were being sharpened with a rasping sound and a rope was being uncoiled with which the victim was to be bound. The shepherd himself was quite unconcerned about the coming sacrifice. He had no doubt witnessed many such. What he was interested in was the part we were to play in this drama and that quite evidently was expected in the form of a donation in money towards the construction of the new Kali temple. In the face of such simplicity and sincerity we deemed it only courteous to acquiesce. Unfortunately the first sum we offered was considered insufficient and was courteously but quite firmly refused. It was an insult to so great a goddess. We therefore proffered a more generous donation which was accepted with great dignity and a beautiful smile from our shepherd suppliant—and it was thus that we became humble participants in the building of a hill temple far away in the great Himalayas. As we turned slowly away from this scene the temple bells began to ring and we saw the shepherd seize one of his sheep and carry it towards the sacrificial stone before which the flames of the fire were now casting grotesque shadows.

Something we met the charcoal carriers. They were usually young women with long baskets full of charcoal slung on their backs so that they were invariably bent down under the weight. The married ones wore huge nose rings often six inches in diameter which hung down over their mouths and were, I should think, most uncomfortable. Often in addition to the basket of charcoal on their backs they carried their babies tied to them in front. The young women were of slender build with broad and smiling faces and would come along the hill paths laughing and talking together. One day one of these women appeared at our bungalow. I saw her just as she set down her load on the kitchen step. Seldom had I seen a more beautiful girl. In her hill attire, tight trousers, three quarter length coat, a scarlet scarf around her dark hair—with earrings dangling and bracelets gleaming—her lovely smiling face was such that only a genius of an artist would have done justice to her beauty. I asked her if in might take her photograph and she laughingly said that I could if I would take her husband's as well; so the next day she brought her husband along. As far as looks were concerned he stood out in contrast to his beautiful wife; but having, to her great delight, photographed them both together, she allowed me to take one of her alone, and hers is a photo I treasure to this day. On another occasion an older woman staggered up to the kitchen door, also with a load of charcoal. She had a terribly lined and scarred face, and white straggling hair. She looked very poor, her clothes were all ragged and shall never forget the sad and wistful face that looked up at me, when after depositing her load on the ground, she sank down wearily on the kitchen step to rest. When I offered her the money due to her for the charcoal, she shook her head sadly and said we were not to pay her, but that her husband would come for it. The next day he arrived, a strong well built man with an evil glint in his eyes and took that hard earned money. She was only the burden bearer.

Something along these winding hill paths we watched men carrying long wooden planks roped to their backs and extending for above their heads—some ten feet and more in length. These men too were bent low down under this heavy and unwieldy load and in order to rest their aching and cramped bodies, all they could do was to lean the huge plank against the side of the hill and just stand there with head bowed, the sweat pouring down their faces.

One lovely day when the air was crisp and the birds were singing for sheer joy, we set out in high spirits with two friends to walk to a dak bungalow some ten miles away. For the first part of the journey, we climbed upwards through a forest path strewn with pine needles and arrived at a village. Here we found the villagers in gala attire and there was a sound of merriment, music and dancing. A wedding was being celebrated and on the flat must roofs there women and a couple of men (evidently the professional dancers of the village) were treading a stately step to and fro to the accompaniment of a small band on the ground below them. We should like to have taken some photos but decided not to approach too near as we saw that most of the wedding guests were very excited and somewhat drunk and might resent our cameras. So we pursued our way through more forest scenery with rushing mountain streams rippling down the hill sides and disappearing into the valley below where we heard their musical rhythm as they gurgled and splashed along their rocky banks. By the edge of one of these streams we sat down to have lunch and were immediately joined by a very interesting Italian Professor, coming from the opposite direction. He said that he was studying the practice of Yoga (a system which concentrates a great deal on the power of mind over matter). To us some of the feats accomplished appeared to be almost fantastic and we listened with amazement when the Italian told us a rope had been tied round his neck and pulled both ways as hard as possible by two men and yet not even the mark of the rope was left on his neck. He had been told by his teacher that to obtain the best mental and physical results in a climate like India, he should stand on his head every morning. He was now very proud to say that he was able to do this and he gave us a demonstration there and then. He was a man of fifty-three or so and inclined to stoutness, and so had also been advised in order to reduce his weight to gradually swallow a length of tape and then pull it out again. He had not however progressed very far with this. He certainly was a most amusing and interesting lunch companion and we were sorry to see him go.

The pathway we continued on after this straggled down hill for some four miles and then quite unexpectedly ad a bend in the road, we saw our dak bungalow tucked away in a clearing in the forest. It was exquisite in its setting and perfect in form and colour—a site that was quite breathtaking. There was a bright green sward, very reminiscent of those in Switzerland, that undulated up and down and was surrounded on all sides by the deeper green of cedars and deodars forming ridge after ridge of outlined hills silhouetted against the blue sky, rising tier after tier and becoming more and more elusive as they faded away into the horizon. In the midst of this lush green grass, where sheep, cows and horses were grazing, there appeared a dark, mysterious looking lake surrounded with irises and tall grasses, and on whose waters sat a small crown like island of reeds and rushes, which at various times of the day, like a boat rowed by invisible oarsmen, moved silently across the lake. Legend said that when this tiny island sank and no longer took its mysterious journey to and fro, the British raj would cease to be. On the slopes around was a tiny village and a bazaar, and a quite large Hindu temple. We learnt later that the chief god at this temple was a king of snake god who was supposed to live at the bottom of the lake, and it was he they said who propelled the tiny island about when it pleased him.

When we arrived at the dak bungalows, we were told that they were both occupied. Quite undaunted though, for we did not mean if we could possibly help it, to walk the ten miles back in the dark, we marched into the dining room and called for the *khansamah* or cook. He was an old friend of ours and had looked after us well on a former occasion and still more important, we had reason to believe he rather liked us. He informed us that the new bungalow was entirely occupied by state guests (people who had permission from the Rajah to stay there) and that the two ladies of the party had taken ill on arrival and were still in bed. In the other bungalow a young Indian couple were on their honeymoon and had booked for fifteen days. In the only other bungalow were two sisters—one a doctor and the other a missionary. With al these people entrenched here the situation certainly did not look very hopeful for us—but our kind *khansamah* said that he would fit the dining room up for us to sleep in and covert the pantry into a bedroom for our friends. We thus retired into our bed-dining room (all the other occupants were fortunately having their meals in their own rooms) and here we were served and excellent seven course dinner—anything less we knew lowered the prestige of our *khansamah* friend. Tired out by the long day in the fresh air we were soon in bed, but alas for sleep, for the Indian couple next door had a gramophone which it pleased them to play all night. In the morning when our friends appeared for breakfast, we found they had fared no better in the pantry—as their night had been disturbed by a number of rats who, mistaking their beds for the pantry table, had danced tattoo over the bedclothes for most of the time. On the whole we decided, we had come off best.

After breakfast we sat on the verandah and watched the departure of the state guests. A Gurkha cook prepared their breakfast on a little stove in the verandah. They were taking no risks with our *khansamah*. A number of other servants were busily packing up their bedding and other requirements which seemed to amount to a great deal. When everything was ready, nine coolies were summoned and all the bundles and boxes were hoisted onto their shoulders. Two dandies were also brought for the ladies who now emerged for the first time and they were borne aloft on the shoulders of four coolies each. The cavalcade started with the dandies leading, then the one gentleman, and behind him all the personal servants headed by the Gurkha cook and finally the row of coolies with the luggage. At the same time on the sloping grass in front of us the cattle were being driven down by hillwomen and children. A contented and fine looking herd they were, for the pastures were indeed green and inviting, to which they were being driven. Two small village boys were playing golf with great gusto using a fir cone for a ball and a stick ingeniously fashioned like a golf club. Packs of mules who had arrived and unloaded were now having a well earned rest and feed in the grass below. A hill woman came bounding down the hill, complete with stick and cigarette. She was dressed in dark trousers and a gay skirt, and wore a marvellous mortar board effect in headgear. She was decorated with earrings, bracelets, necklaces, anklets and an immense nose ring, all of which jingled merrily as she walked by. After very energetically rounding up the cattle, she sat on a hillock close to us and shared her cigarette with a friend, as in between their talk one had a puff at it and then the other. She was delighted when we offered her another one, in fact two, one for the friend as well.

We next watched the coming of new arrivals to the bungalow. The first to appear were six tiny dogs with a servant in a dandy. They soon jumped out and scampered hither and thither in great excitement. They were followed by five mules carrying luggage, and perched on one mule was a live chicken, no doubt destined for the evening meal. A rather sly looking *khansamah* with a beard dyed red and a brightly gleaming *hookah*, headed the band of servants and finally an Indian official and his wife appeared, preceded once again by a servant carrying a large cage in which were a number of small birds. Both the official and his wife rode on horseback, and we learnt that they were on route for a stay in the neighbouring state capital. We wondered if the little dogs and birds were presents for the Rajah!

The next day we ourselves decided to visit the state capital, which was only some ten miles away. It had been raining during the night and when we set out in the early morning all nature was gleaming and sparkling with crystal drops and the leaves were tinted red and yellow amongst those trees for whom the year was waning. Many coloured plumaged birds darted from tree to tree filling the air with music. Quite unexpectedly the sun emerged from behind the clouds like a magician and cast gleaming rays of light in the valley beneath us. Each crystal drop shone like a precious diamond; each yellow and red leaf glowed gold and ruby. The birds' feathers reflected a hundred different shades hitherto unthought of and every flower quickened to a deeper and richer shade. We were walking in silence absorbing this lovely scene, when we became aware of fellow travellers approaching. They were two priests, the younger with a round jolly face, a long beard and a white cassock tucked into his stockings. The other was a gentle little man with white hair and a serene countenance. They stopped and greeted us, the latter one telling us with the delight and eagerness of a child that he had worked in the plains for thirty years and that this was his first trip to the hills. One could see with what delight he was enjoying every moment of it.

As we approached Chamba there was a six mile steep descent of some 5,000 feet; and it became hotter and more oppressive. By about 11 o'clock it was very not indeed. Rice fields soaked in water heralded our approach to this ancient capital which dated back to before the Norman conquest, when some Rajput prince from the plains came and conquered it. the wide river Ravi rushed over its rocky bed below the town. We crossed a fine suspension bridge and then found we had to climb a steep hill into the town which was built on a small plateau. Going up here disaster befell me, for I foolishly tried to walk up as quickly as possible. It was too much. I began to feel dizzy and the world began to swim around me. I just saved myself from fainting by sitting on a verandah and holding my head down. The townsfolk, wearily climbing up this steep incline with waterpots on their heads, regarded me with interest but apathy. I learnt later that my fate was a common one for visitors coming here and half way up the hill was the fatal spot. My companions managed to procure some iced lemonade and even a dandy in which I finished the rest of the climb. By the evening I was quite alright and we went out to explore the town. It was built on a slope and between the two main streets was a long wide lawn (a former polo ground), but now used for cricket and tennis. The houses were wooden and flat roofed. There were some very ancient Hindu temples. They consisted of curved buildings shaped somewhat like huge doorways, but embellished with highly decorative and skilled carvings and they were all situated together in a large compound. Within each building was a shrine on which was elevated the particular deity to whom the temple was dedicated, the effigies of Radha, Krishna and Shiva (with a carved bull at every entrance) were amongst the most common. These figures were all richly garbed, ornamented with jewels, and garlands of flowers and various offerings in small dishes were placed before them. In a special shed was kept a huge carved white bull, no doubt used for processions. At the other end of the town amidst a background of trees and flowering shrubs was a Scotch Presbyterian Mission Church and Hospital. The Church was simple, but it had been built by the Rajah himself in appreciation of the work done there by these good missionaries. There was also a small museum which had some quite fine paintings of Rajput life done by the court painters. The only piece of modern mechanisation in this remote part was the Rajah's car—bought for use on a five mile road.

The next day on our way back to Khajjia, we were caught in a heavy hill storm and got wet through. Our mules with the luggage were behind us, so having arrived at our bungalow with nothing dry to change into we again had to rely on the goodwill of the *khansamah*, who seeing our bedraggled plight, handed out to us a strange variety of dak bungalow curtains, in which we arrayed ourselves and ended up by looking like a fancy dress party when we sat down to lunch.

That evening was a most perfect one. We watched the full moon rise beyond the lake like a wondrous golden dome, and the stars light up the heavens in glittering array. All nature seemed to be lulled into a mystic silence by the magic of those silver rays, casting its shadows into the dark mysterious forests around, the distant snow mountains and the tiny elusive lake before us. Night held her gentle and mysterious sway, and save for the faint tinkle of the cattle bells, the cry of a lone night bird, and the sharp barking of the foxes, the world was hushed in beauty and serenity. I was standing on the grass, watching the rising moon, but was called by the rest of the party to come onto the verandah in order to get a better view. Unfortunately I had forgotten that at one end the verandah had no railings and being somewhat moonstruck anyway by this time, I hurried along, my eyes still on the glory of the heavens above me, only to run right over the edge and fall suddenly to a depth of five feet or so below. As far as I was concerned, I knew no more until I awoke and found myself in bed. My head hurt dreadfully, but otherwise there was no real damage, only a few bruises and in the morning, when we were due to return home, I felt much better. I was not allowed to walk, however, and a horse was procured for me. He was a quaint looking creature and I felt rather doubtful about him, but I was assured that he was most docile and sure footed. So I painfully climbed on his very angular back. Sure footed he was, though he always walked on the extreme edge of the hill path looking down into the precipice below, but what I was not prepared for was that the smell or sight of water acted as a powerful stimulant on him and wherever there was any sigh of it, he was off like a shot and didn't stop until he had located his prize and indulged in a good drink. As there was much water about, these sudden sallies of his were alarmingly frequent and it was only by sheer will power that I managed to keep company with him. He, however, took not the slightest notice of me. I might easily have not been there. Before I reached home, and owing to all these compulsory halts, the rest of the party coming on foot caught up with me and great was their mirth at my horse's behaviour, a sentiment I did not wholly share with them, I fear. As we approached our bungalow it was already getting dark and we saw men with lanterns coming towards us. It was our faithful *khansamah* Sibbu who, concerned about our safety and the danger of wild animals at night, had brought out lights to lighten us home. He had also heard, so quickly does news travel along these hill roads, of my misadventure on the verandah. We felt very grateful to him for his kindly concern for us and also for the roaring fire that awaited us, the good hot baths and the excellent dinner he had cooked.

Alas, these halcyon days spent in such idyllic surroundings had to come to an end and the descent to the hot dusty plains had to be made. It seemed hardly believable that two such worlds of such utter dissimilarity could be so near together and yet so utterly apart. But while our bodies struggled to adjust themselves once more to the discomfort of dust, heat and thirst, our minds and spirits were still on the mountain heights reliving again and again the experiences we had absorbed there of body, mind and spirit.

The Hindustan Tibet Road

Ever since I arrived in India, one of the great experiences I had been looking forward to was a trek in the Himalayas, and when the day arrived at last for the first stage of this journey, we set out in our car to drive from Delhi to Simla. To escape the heat of the day we drove by night; the evening was warm but not hot, with the exquisite perfume of the scented flowers still lingering in the air. Save for the usual convoy of bullock wagons ambling sleepily along in the middle of the road, we had the countryside to ourselves and it was fascinating to watch the dark shapes before us gradually emerge as trees and the strange looking blobs in the distance unfolded into the mud and thatched huts of Indian villages, where on string beds many of their inhabitants lay asleep under the glittering stars. Suddenly the silence would be broken by the sharp hoot of an owl, or a late hare would dart across the road. As the first light of the dawn appeared, our eyes turned to the rising sun, a ball of golden red coming straight up from the horizon and climbing majestically into a cloudless sky. In the loveliness of this dawn, the mountains stood up boldly before us, as they rose sheer from the plains, their outlines veiled in a mist so light and ethereal that they gave the impression of a fleeting vision, a kind of fairy world that might disappear at any moment. There was nothing so arresting, so unforgettable than this first glimpse of these illusive mountains catching the rays of the rising sun.

Life now began to stir around us. The village women in their lightly coloured skirts were seen coming towards the well, balancing with a perfect poise their shining brass pitchers on their heads: the men in their coarse white garments were getting the ox plough ready for another day's work in the hot fields and smoke began to rise from the village fires where the morning meal was being cooked. The children appeared on the road carrying sticks in their hands as they drove the cattle across to graze in the nearby foothills. Some of the late risers could still be seen getting up sleepily from their beds, others washing themselves in the village pond and cleaning their teeth with great vigour. Strange shapes crossed the road in front of us, their heads and shoulders so enveloped in blankets and shawls (for the morning air was chilly) as to be quite oblivious of the hooting o our car.

Having crossed an unbridged river bed with the charming name of the Ghuggar, about a quarter of a mile wide, we began a fifty mile ascent up a winding hill road, with innumerable bends and twists and ups and downs. As we pursued this somewhat hazardous but strangely exhilarating climb, we watched the valleys unfold beneath us, the tiny hill houses nestling in the olds of the hillside and the small steep terraced fields. As we went higher this was replaced by tier after tier of pine clad forests and barren rocky crags which culminated finally in the splendour of the first glimpse of the far away snow covered peaks of the great Himalayan range, glistening and white in a world untouched by man.

When we reached Simla, we began at once to make preparations to continue our journey along the "Hindustan Tibet Road". This we were going to do on foot with mules carrying our baggage. Before setting out, the route had to be marked out carefully, certain rest houses applied for and provisions stored. Finally all the arrangements were made and the great day for setting out arrived. Our cook, Sibbu, who was in charge of the expedition, appeared with mules, muleteers and baggage. Sibbu was tall and handsome and was dressed in a complete new khaki outfit with a most stylishly tied turban, canvas shoes and walking stick. He loved the hills and nothing gave him greater pleasure than to be on them. It was his most efficient handling of the whole journey which added so much to our comfort and enjoyment. His care of us was quite touching. At one rest house far away in a most lonely spot, he would not allow us to keep any windows open for fear of wild animals. On another occasion when we wanted to cross a river very early in the morning he decided we must wait awhile, because panthers and bears would be drinking there and they might be dangerous. But now on this morning amidst much talk and laughter the mules were loaded, unloaded and reloaded until weight was properly distributed. When all was finally ready, the party set forth with Sibbu walking at the head, accompanied by a hill boy who had taken upon himself the ambiguous tasks of a *chokra* or general helper; he had a merry smile on his face though, and carried a small wooden flute whose notes we were often to hear; behind and rather reluctantly ambled the mules, the bells around their neck clanging in the air, a warning to all others of their approach, and the muleteers, a rather fierce looking couple who carried *hookahs*. We in our turn fell in behind this cavalcade, but soon outstripped their pace and went ahead. A milestone just outside Simla with the inscription "Tibet two hundred miles", added to our feeling of exhilaration as we set out on this unknown path.

Most of our journey lay through the valley of the Sutlej, one of the great rivers of India which, having its source in Tibet, forces its way through the mountain ranges to the plains below. At times we would find ourselves in actual contact with it and walked by its banks where it flowed calmly and gently, and we bathed our hot feet in its cool water; on other occasions on climbing up to passes of 10 to 12,000 feet we would see its slaty coloured water in a deep chasm below us, looking like a gigantic snake winding in and out of the precipitous hill sides and finally dashing through deep gorges with sheer rock rising up on all sides. Here in the thunder and grandeur of that cascade sweeping all before it, was displayed the power and strength hidden in nature and we would stand watching it and listening to its tremendous roar. The sight and the sound of this river became a part of our daily life. This river was also used to transport logs of wood and we would watch them as they were carried along, tossed wildly about, or floating gently down. It also played a great part in irrigating the small hill villages nestling in some sheltered corner and surrounded by terraced fields, which in the autumn mapped out intricate patterns in red and gold on the green hillsides. The hill houses were usually built of wood or stone and were often two storeyed, the upper part being surrounded by a carved, closed in verandah, this design giving them a somewhat top heavy look. The cattle were housed in the lower storey, because such animals as panthers or tigers made it unsafe to leave them out, and of course shelter was a necessity during the long, cold winter. Sometimes the roofs of these houses seemed to be painted a brilliant red, but on drawing near, it was seen that this attractive dash of colour came from the red peppers drying in the sun. Always in the midst of a village, however small, was a symbol of worship depicted perhaps by a small temple above which rose a tall pole with a flag attached. When the village was very poor a tree would suffice, topped by a white flag, while often on its branches were tied pieces of red and white cloth, denoting the prayers and requests of its worshippers.

Once when we were staying in a rest house on the banks of the Sutlej the temple was just opposite to us. At sunset we heard the temple bells ringing out with their clear resonant notes suddenly breaking the silence around. We were told that it was the priest putting the gods to bed. The following morning we wanted to make a very early start, but we did not have to worry about waking up in time; the priest did that for us, for just before the dawn the bells rang out again as he woke the gods, ourselves and the village. As we approached the Tibetan border these little hill temples became more like Chinese pagodas and the hill houses had very steep roof to enable the heavy snow to come off easily. The buildings were also decorated on either side with carved dragons.

On the upper slopes of the hills were the large, somber forests filled with a secret lore and mystery all their own. There were the aromatic pines, swaying in the breeze and singing their wild sweet melodies sent out their perfume into the air. Mingled among them were stunted grey Himalayan oaks and the light green chestnut trees spreading out their magnificent branches in the sunlight. In the springtime were added the glowing colours of the rhododendrons intermingling their vivid hues with the many shades of green around. Higher still were the dark fir trees interspersed with the statelier and brighter green, and crowning all were the most majestic of all the forest dwellers, the splendid cedars and deodars. Then as if to lighten this dark and mysterious world the ground beneath was carpeted with jewel like little flowers of varied colour and the filigree foliage of many patterned ferns. These all turned to the sunlight glinting through their tall guardians above. Chasing each other too around their woodland homes came the butterflies dancing in the sunlight, their gorgeous colours of orange, blue, red, gold and amethyst sparkling in its rays.

The animal denizens of these regions, bears, foxes, wolves, panthers and snakes were rarely to be seen, but always to be reckoned with. Our cook, Sibbu, who went early in the morning to fetch water from a stream, once found two bears already there, whereupon he left his waterpot and tactfully retired. Another time when we were walking casually along a hill path a huge snake darted out in front of us from the bank opposite and crossed our path. We make the quickest halt yet. Another evening when we had been delayed and the darkness was overtaking us, we saw a wolf looking down at us from a rock above. It was not a pleasant experience for us to have to pass from beneath the rock for when we were under it, he would be outside our view but still able to observe us. When we came into sight of him again, we were relieved to see that he was still sitting there as if deeply studying us and he had not moved. At night the foxes often barked outside our rest house and on moonlit nights it was fun to go to the window and watch the cubs playing and gamboling about exactly like kittens. There were huge hill dogs too, which looked like bears with their thick shaggy coats and spiked metal collars which they wore in case of attack by other animals. Once three of them were at a rest house we were staying in and they came to breakfast with us. Although so large, they were extremely gentle, but somewhat overpowering in their demands and I was glad of a lavish amount of stale cake left over to regale them with. Their table manners were above reproach and they took each piece in turn very gently, but when afterwards we tried to photograph them, they decided this was in the nature of a game and began to race each other up and down the lawn and sniff at the camera in passing. The animals most to be seen of course were the monkeys and in the higher hills they were usually the lovely *langurs* with their long silky silver coats and black faces. They were the aristocrats of the monkey world and would at any time descend in troops, swinging from tree to tree in a perfect rhythm and harmony of mind and limb, hardly ever touching the ground. The most familiar sound was the clanging of the mule bells. They were the carriers of merchandise here and would come along in droves with their muleteers shouting and gesticulating at them as they ambled along in disorderly array. When we met them they always had the better of it for they refused to budge an inch and when the pathway was very narrow, we thought it the better part of valour to take to the hillside in order to escape the danger of being crushed against the rocky escarpment. Occasionally a flock of long haired sheep were to be seen trotting quietly along with little bags of salt attached to their backs. They were carrying the salt from Tibet to India.

High above the terraced fields, the pine and fir forests rose to great spectacular ranges of the Himalayan mountains spreading out in all shapes and sizes for hundreds of miles. Here, on these heights, dwelt the eternal snows and according to Hindu saying, "the Home of the Gods". They lay where earth and sky blend and where the soft silent snow glistens in the sunlight. From this gleaming radiance of crystal light shone froth a splendour elsewhere unknown. Above them the clouds, the master designers of the heavens, were a joy to behold as they formed, dissolved and recreated their never ending patterns. When the sun began to set, a hush seemed to fall as its golden rays caressed the world around in a leave taking of unsurpassed beauty. The pine trees were tipped with gold, the grass on the hillside reflected the shining light, the birds' wings glistened and revealed hidden and beautiful colours as they flew homewards; the flower petals already closing, sent out one last brilliant gleam, the dazzling purity of the snow was tinged rose red as if a fire glowed within. All life was bathed in the radiance of the setting sun in its evening benediction.

Amidst the quietude and strength of these mighty hills could be heard the mountain streams tumbling down in cascades of foam which gave a soft and harmonious melody to the scene; there was also the harsh notes of the long tailed magpies or the plaintive cry of the barbet, a longish green bird who, soaring high above, was forever uttering his lonely long drawn out notes, as if to personify the solitary spirit of these hills like the sad cry o the sea gulls does around the coast of Britain. There was also the shrill drumming of the tree frogs, those tireless little creatures on their never ending and seemingly inexplicable climb up and down the hill slopes; mingling with it all the tinkling of the cattle bells, the soft cooing of the wood pigeons, the plaintive notes of the wooden flutes of the herdsmen and the lovely ancient songs of hill women as they toiled in the fields. Occasionally the abrupt avalanche of great rocks falling into the depths below would echo all around. Most awesome of all was a sudden hill storm when the vivid flashes of lightning followed by green rolling thunder claps reverberating through the hills, filled the air with an all pervasive solemnity and awe as if some great giant of the mountains had suddenly awakened from his sleep and was bestriding his Kingdom in power and might.

Along the road we met a few of the people who lived isolated in these far away hills and villages. Some of them were remarkably beautiful with their light copper skins, fine straight noses, over faces and long black hair, usually slender in build and walking their hill paths with ease and agility. Nearer Tibet the physique changed, the cheek bones were higher, the cheeks more rosy, the eyes almond shaped, and the people of a shorter, sturdier build. The men wore their hair cut in a long bob and the women had long plaits tied with gaily coloured cottons. Very courteous too were these hill people and the greetings they exchanged might well have put to shame so called civilized peoples. Sometimes the mode of address was a graceful upward salute, the hand rising from the ground to the forehead; at other times the hands were folded together over the heart and the head inclined, while the words said were, 'Peace be to your presence'. Their dress was of homespun wool, the men wearing tight fitting trousers and knee length woollen coats and woollen or felt hats of various shapes; the women too often wore the same kind of trousers, sometimes skirts, and coats and over their hair were tied gaily coloured handkerchiefs. Now and again a hill blanket, home woven with a brightly coloured border did duty for a skirt. Round the waist of both men and women were coloured sashes which served as most useful pockets for concealing food, combs, matches and many other articles which were needed. The women often wore huge nose rings and earrings and some of them medallion looking ornaments on their breasts. Most of these people lived lives somewhat similar to those of people who lived in the Middle Ages in Europe, in that each village was self supporting. They had water mills by the streams, where the big grindstone was turned. They endeavoured on the steep hill sides to grow enough food for their wants and keep cattle for ploughing and milk. They wove their own garments and blankets from sheep and goat's hair. Water was always a precious commodity in the hills ad often had to be fetched from a long distance. I remember on one beautiful morning, when the sky seemed a playground for the white fleecy clouds that sported at will across it, meeting a water carrier as she slowly and laboriously climbed up the stony path bearing on her head a large brass vessel full of water. Long had been her walk down to the stream below to fill this gleaming water pot and burdensome was the journey back. She was dressed in a short coarse tunic that had known many a wash and over her head and shoulders was thrown a faded blue cloth; her thin brown legs and feet were bare, but the slender arms were heavily braceleted as they stretched up to support her water pot. A somewhat intelligent but thin face with great dark eyes was singularly attractive in its quaint old fashioned expression but at the same time somewhat haunting in the premature lines of hardship already marked there, which even the gay earrings failed to dispel. She was nine years old she told us, this solemn little water carrier, and when we asked her if we could help her with her load, she very firmly but politely said she could manage quite well alone as long as she stopped every few minutes to get her breath. Perhaps she was shy or perhaps she would have broken some caste rule if she had accepted our offer. I took out a small piece or ribbon I had in my pocket and offered it to her to tie her hair with, and I shall always remember how her face lit up with pleasure as she carefully removed the water pot from her head, set it on the ground and then with a deep *salaam* took it. In a minute she had torn off the strands of cotton binding her plaits and in its place now gleamed the brightly coloured ribbon.

The Rest Houses where we stayed for the nights on our trek were usually uniform in their pattern. There were a number of rooms strung out in a row with a verandah in front. Normally we were given two rooms and a small bathroom. They were provided with the necessary furniture, beds, chairs and table, some cutlery and china and a lamp. The forest bungalows we stayed in were built in a more varied style and often had a small garden and some books. For some unknown reason, though, they never seemed to own a lamp. After a climb of some ten to twelve miles up and down hill paths the first glimpse of a Rest House was a most welcome sight. We were always met at the entrance by the *"chokidar"*, the man in charge of the bungalow. These *chokidars* were most interesting characters and in a way they were often the closest contact we made with the hill people. At one hill capital thee was a most kindly and honest old man, who welcomed us with great dignity. His Rest House was spotlessly clean and even in this high altitude there were flowers on the table. It was evident he took the greatest pride in his work as he sat down in the evening at the further end of the verandah and polished the lamp glass and shade, till no lamp could have shone brighter and no poet could have been more proud of his poem, than when he presented this masterpiece of shining light to us. He was delighted when we bought two of the hill hats worn in that region and with a very real interest complimented us on our mode of wearing them. Another *chokidar* of an entirely different type was the young, handsome and Tibetan looking one, who welcomed us near the border of Tibet. He was most courteous, efficient and intelligent, and we knew we were in most capable hands, but he was quite detached. Then there was the willing but rather woolly type—who was quite willing to do what was required of him, but had little or no idea how to set about it and whom Sibbu dismissed with a smile by saying, 'He can't help it, he is only a *jungly wallah*'. Once we encountered one who came to meet us, accompanied by all his relatives and then immediately returned to his house, saying he had fever and nothing could stir him again or his relatives until the next morning when he appeared all smiles and bows demanding his *baksheesh* or tip. Another time we met the *chokidar* whom we dubbed The Laughing Cavalier. This gentleman was somewhat elderly with a most distinguished beard, but to our surprise he welcomed us with chuckles of delight and seemed highly amused for no reason that we could fathom, and throughout our stay this hilarious attitude continued, though it is to be said for him that he looked after us very well.

On our journeyings, we were always being asked for medicines, usually for fevers and chest complaints, but once while staying in a hill village Sibbu brought to me a woman with a terrible sore on her arm which was going quite septic. She had burnt her arm while cooking and then tried various remedies, which had been of no avail. The wound was in an appalling sate and she was in great pain: it was also her right arm. For a moment I felt there was nothing I could do, for the few medicines we carried where of the simplest kind but her distress and pain were so great and her faith so pathetic, that I decided to try a tin of antiseptic healing ointment which I had with me. It said it was good for burns. So I cleansed the wound as well as possible, smeared the ointment thickly on, and bandaged it and told her on no account to undo the bandage till I returned, which would be in a few days' time. Then in great trepidation I left her, wondering what would be the outcome. On our return, though, she was the first person I saw coming along the road to meet us, dressed in her finest array and *salaaming* with a smiling face as she said the pain had gone and she felt better. And sure enough when I took the bandage off I could hardly believe the improvement that had taken place, for the wound was quite clean and beginning to heal.

We always had to await the arrival of Sibbu and the mules when we got to a Rest House, and to our joy the most comfortable deck like chairs were provided on the verandah where we just relaxed and absorbed the lovely scenery around. One day they were very late coming as one of the mules had taken fright round a corner and had hurled one of the boxes down the hillside which they had managed to retrieve, really quite a feat. After the noise and bustle of unloading we settled down, unpacking what we needed for the night. The kinds of books and magazines found in these far away outposts always aroused an interest and curiously enough Christian

Science Magazines along with old Pictorials, some dating back to 1898, predominated.

At seven in the evening hot water was brought in kerosene tins and poured into a tin bath. The various Rest Houses in dulged in different colour schemes for their baths, some where painted white inside and green out, others were blue and white but the Forest bungalows retained the plain unvarnished tin. Whatever the colour scheme, though, all baths were most refreshing after the rigours of hill climbing, despite the fact that many a huge hairy spider watched the proceedings with great interest and sometimes form somewhat too close a range for those who did not care for the sudden and alarmingly swift manoeuvres of these creatures. Other inmates were scorpions and a sharp look out had to be kept for them, a none too easy task when the only light available was provided by a candle. After the bath came dinner round a log fire and with an oil lamp on the middle of the table, and never were meals more appetizing and appreciated; after being in keen mountain air all day it was just delicious. Then before we went to bed, we always stepped out once more into the verandah where under the canopy of the shining starts above, we would look out across to the opposite hills and see scattered here and there little lights shining out of the hill houses of the few dwellers around. They merged entirely into the beauty and pervading stillness of the night—just a gentle reminder that we were not quite alone, even in these great solitudes.

We were up with the dawn when everything swung into action again. Mules reloaded, dues paid and finally the Rest Houses Visitors Book was brought in and signed. All travelers passing through signed this, and also often added comments of their own, thus making this book quite an interesting document. Then once again we were out into the coolness and never to be forgotten beauty of the dawn, with the sun just touching the tips of the snow ranges with tints of soft rose and gold, and before us lay another day's unknown trek.

Moving Waters

One day we went in search of the Ganges, that holy and much revered river which, rising from its pure mountain source and winding its way through vast fertile plains has imbibed into its waters the very heart and soul of the people. It is to this river that every Hindu strives to make a pilgrimage in his life time, and it is to Mother Ganges above all that he desires his ashes to be committed. Here the saffron robed "holy" men of India wend their way and live in simple booths along its banks, seeking in meditation and prayer the underlying mysteries of life: many of them live lives of strict discipline and austerity, studying the ancient teaching of yoga and psychic phenomena. Along with them travel the inevitable hangers on, many of whom are rogues and fakes and all of whom live on the charity meted out to them by the people. Here too burn the funeral pyres, their tongues of living flame leaping heavenwards, a sign to all who pass by that one more Hindu soul has passed onwards on its journey. On festival days the pilgrims arrive in their thousands, and religious fervour mounts high. Epidemics like cholera and typhoid often claim many, but they would rather die here than anywhere else. Lepers, often presenting just stumps for limbs, the crippled, the blind groping their way along, the deaf and dumb, the beggars, all seek a refuge here where it is considered a religious duty to earn merit by giving alms to these unfortunate ones.

So one hot Sunday afternoon, we went forth to visit one of the small ancient towns on its banks which was noted for its annual religious festival. The town itself stood on a mound, displaying many temples and shrines from which flags fluttered in the air. As we approached, we heard the ringing of temple bells and Shiva's drum sounding its ominous note. We crossed on a bridge of boats and found ourselves on a vast stretch of sand on which grew clumps of tall pampas grass; there was not a tree in sight, nothing to shade the weary pilgrims who came there from the glaring heat. Suddenly the river became visible, its clear water shone like a trail of silver between those vast sandy banks. We could see in the distance the bathers, some washing themselves and some standing with their hands folded in prayer. One man was standing upright in the water on one leg, the other hunched up beneath him. We were told later that he had taken a vow to remain in this position for five days without moving. Fascinated, we watched him: we found it difficult to understand what he gained by doing so, but it was quite evident that he was much revered for attempting such a feat. At some of the little shrines near the water's edge, people were bringing their gifts—some carrying garlands and some food. Near us a few *sadhus* were sitting crosslegged and deep in meditation; they seemed to be quite oblivious of the life around them. A poor leper woman came up to us imploring alms in the name of God; her hands and feet were almost eaten away and the dumb suffering in her eyes would have wrung the hardest heart, and alas! she was only one of many such.

We looked round at this vast sandy stretch, the shining river and cloudless blue sky, and made our way further along the bank where we were going to have tea. We were conscious of a slight feeling of disappointment in this holy place of pilgrimage. What was the attraction that grew so many here? Something strange, almost eerie seemed to overshadow this silhouette of burning sand and silvery water, but that was most likely only our imagination. Gradually as the shadows lengthened and the sun began to sink, the sheer simplicity of the scene around absorbed us. It was so still, so hushed, so restful, that it seemed almost as if an everlasting spell had enshrouded if forever. Surely it was the genius of the Master Artist that, in this simple outline of flat white sand, shining water, tall green grasses, domed by the cloudless blue sky, flocked now by the many coloured tints of the setting sun, there should be conveyed to the Indian seeker a perception of the eternal pattern of life and a glimpse of the serenity of spirit. Suddenly a flight of wild duck passed silently over the water and disappeared into the far horizon, and a kingfisher like a flashing blue jewel sat motionless on a twig. Only the light green parrots broke the silence as they flew chattering by. We lingered long until the last glimpse had been caught of the sun, as in a ball of fire it sank beneath the horizon; then a brief afterglow lit up the fading scene, and clearly outlines against the darkening sky was the silver trail of water, the white sand, the grass clumps, the ascetic still standing motionless on one leg and the *sadhus* sitting crosslegged, withdrawn in meditation and prayer. Night fell, the crescent moon appeared and the stars shone brilliantly down on us from the dark sky above where the floor of heaven was indeed ablaze with the glory of its Creator. We stood in awe and wonder and at last turned reluctantly away, feeling that Mother Ganges had given to us a memory that would always abide, that of beauty in simplicity and of a calm and serenity that underlies and unifies all life.

Another day we decided to visit a very ancient site called Suraj Kund or the Sun Lake. It was situated some often miles from Delhi and in order to reach it, we had to take a two mile walk across the countryside. So we left our car outside a small Hindu temple on the roadside in the charge of a small boy, who bore the impressive name "Lion of the Faith". The first part of our walk was through barren, rocky land with goats and cows wandering about in search of food, but in the distance we saw the green palm trees and knew water was near. Very soon we climbed down along a welcome running stream bordered with shady trees and shrubs. Crossing the water by stepping stones we climbed the hill beyond, and quite unexpectedly as we reached its crest there lay before us the marvel that was Suraj Kund. In a dip in the land was a huge basin shaped amphitheatre with tier after tier of stone steps all the way around, and leading down from every side to a glistening lake of water. At one end of this great amphitheatre which could seat perhaps at a rough guess some fifty thousand people, was a majestic flight of stone steps rising straight up from the water. There stood the ruins of a temple. In addition to the steps was a wide elephant track, also leading to the temple. This was Suraj Kund, or the Sun Lake, the oldest Hindu ruin known in Delhi and said to have been built by Anang Pal in about 1050. It was a solemn, mysterious place, and as we sat on the stone seats, lost in their immensity and gazing across at the elevated Sun Temple across the water, we wondered what dramas had been enacted here so many years ago, who the thousands of people were who must have come here in order to take part in some religious ritual and who the people were who had undertaken the colossal task of building this mighty structure. Whoever they were, they had left no visible clue behind—no writings on the wall, no inscriptions, no initials, no engravings marked their passage through time. Thoughtfully we stole quietly away, not wishing to disturb the unseen watchers of this mysterious and forsaken place.

On another occasion we went to the ruined city of Fatehpur Sikri, some twenty miles from Agra. This city was built by the Mughal Emperor Akbar, who reigned at the same time as Queen Elizabeth I of Britain. It is said that he built this city because a saint who lived there called Salim Shah Chisti promised him an heir and this promise came true. Hence Akbar left Agra and built Fatehpur which, however, for reasons not fully known, but ascribed to lack of water, was left seventeen years later and has remained deserted ever since.

The city is some six miles in circuit and is built on a hill surrounded on three sides by a wall, and the fourth by a large, dried up lake. It is built mainly in Hindu style. We entered through Akbar's gate, above which was a balcony where the court musicians played to announce the arrival of the Emperor. Some distance beyond this gateway was a large building said to be the Imperial mint. Rare coins from here are to be found in the British Museum. Further down was the Hall of Public Audience, built in a huge courtyard, with long arched verandahs on every side and the Emperor's throne at one end. Inside were the Palace buildings. In Akbar's private apartments could be seen panelled walls with recesses for books and documents and the remains of painted decoration in the forms of flowers and birds. On the right hand opposite corner was the "favourite" wife's special "apartments". In the other half of the quadrangle was a life size "*pachisi*" board cut out on the pavement, a game that resembles "ludo", much played in those days, but often with human pieces, in the form of young women. Opposite to this was a unique little building, square in form, which was the Hall of Private Audience. It consisted of one vaulted room held up in the centre by a magnificent pillar, which at its summit branched out into four passages which ran into a gallery and went all round the inner chamber. This column is supposed to represent the Hindu symbol of the Pillar of the Universe, and Akbar placed his throne on the top of this tree so that he looked down on the supplicants. In another courtyard, the women had their apartments, delicate buildings with roofs of brightly coloured tiles. There were many other smaller buildings, baths, stables, hospitals, etc., but the most magnificent of all was the great Mosque built at the summit of the hill. Over its great archway these words are found inscribed: 'Jesus, in whom we have our peace, said, "The world is a bridge, pass over it, but do not dwell therein".' Sometimes we drove along the Canal Banks. It was very pleasant here for the road was lined with many trees and shrubs and the green grass grew on its slopping banks. There, a great deal of Indian rural life could be observed, as many villages straggled along its course. We first noticed the green of the irrigated fields on either side where the canal waters had converted the desert into a greenery. Sometimes we saw the young green corn just springing from the earth in all its freshness; a little later it would be almost hidden in a sea of brilliant yellow as the mustard flower, the herald of the Indian spring, added its golden loveliness to the scene. Later again at harvest time when the ripened corn shook before the wind, we watched it garnered with infinite toil and sweat by the patient villagers who, with small hand sickles and under the rays of a blazing sun, reaped and harvested these great fields. At other times we saw the sugar cane being cut, loaded on bullock wagons to be carted away to the mills. At times we had to be careful to avoid the cattle which came to the water to drink and bathe. They were usually driven by the small village boys who carried sticks in their hands. The most eager seekers of these cool waters were the large black water buffaloes, often the mainstay of the village milk supply, for if well cared for they gave milk of a better fat value than cows and were hardier and supposed to be free of tuberculosis. Being native to water and not being able to perspire like other animals, it was essential for them to bathe every day. One could sense their utter relief and enjoyment as they slowly and heavily sunk their great bulk into the water until only their grotesque and solemn faces were to be seen. Often the boys sat on their backs and played some kind of game, which seemed to entail jumping from one to the other without touching the water—and all of them took advantage of the interlude to swim about laughing and talking all the time. Often these were followed by a long trail of cows, whose bells we heard tinkling faintly as they slowly wended their way along a dusty track. The were beautiful creatures, greyish white in colour, but often painfully thin and emaciated. India reverences the cow and will not kill her, but at the same time these arid plains cannot support such numbers. They walked languidly to the water's edge and were content to stand there and drink of its cooling draught. Next, flocks of goats came skipping nimbly along. They nibbled any blade of grass they could find and tore the leaves off the shrubs. Sometimes they would even stop to have a playful fight with each other and the little goats were always up to pranks. Amidst so much apathy, they were a revitalising and welcome sight. Now and again a troop of camels appeared on the scene. From their lofty height they would strip the branches of the trees out of reach of all lesser breeds. One day a young camel was stretched across the road in front of our car. We thought he was injured or dying, for he lay so still, even when we hooted loudly at him. Not being able to move him, we tried to slip around him unawares; immediately one eye opened and gave us a wicked look, almost a wink and then he kicked furiously out at our car with his long legs for all he was worth. He was like a child in a tantrum and it took us all our time and skill to outwit him and get by without injury.

We were also able to catch glimpses of Indian villages. They were approached by dusty unmade roads and consisted mainly of mud huts. Now and again a brick house rose superior to the rest usually belonging to a village landowner or headman. Here and there were small temple towers and the dome of a mosque. On the outskirts were the still more miserable huts of the depressed class with their separate well. A touch of green was added to the brownness of this scene by the neem or mango trees, and by the glimpses of the bright colours worn by the village women. Most of India's millions live in these villages. They are for the most part simple, patient, hard-working folk, who live at bare subsistence level. Marriage, birth, death and religious festival are the all prevailing factors in their lives.

Sometimes we sat down for a rest in some shady mango grove and immediately we found ourselves sharing our world with the monkeys. They swung from tree to tree and gathered in groups on the ground. They would look at us somewhat suspiciously for a while and might even hurl a few husks at us from the nuts they were eating, but they soon lost interest and returned to their numerous activities. Often two of them would sit very close together and chatter in low, lover-like tones, on a mother monkey would round her small ones up and the morning toilet would begin amidst much squealing and many protests from the young victims. At other times she would hush one to sleep in her arms, softly crooning all the time. The male took no part in all this domesticity, but sat in solemn aloofness, his bright eyes gazing round, very much on the alert. As soon as the small monkeys escaped from their mother, they would climb nimbly into the trees and spring from branch to branch in an ecstasy of excitement and joy. Once there was a shrill chattering and cries of alarm as an enemy troop was seen to approach, and then the entire family immediately joined together and with many wild cries, alarms and excursions, drove off the intruders. Once a monkey climbed down the tree I was sitting under, and forgetting he was a vegetarian, I offered him a bone. Never shall I forget his look of disgust as he hurled it back at me and very quickly did I seize a banana with which to placate him. One day we saw some monkeys swim across the canal, but judging by their woebegone appearance and their eagerness to get dry again, the experience had not been a pleasant one. Only could some sheer necessity have compelled them to do it.

We also watched the lovely green parrots chattering away in the trees above, and tasting various fruits, some of which they approved and ate with gurgling sounds of delight, others which they rejected with loud and disdainful comments and threw down in disgust. The blue jay with its big head capped with blue, its wings barred in light and dark blue and its rufous coloured breast, often flew unsteadily across the water, its kingly robes gleaming in the sunshine. Nearer to the water's edge and quite motionless was the black and white kingfisher. Suddenly it would rise over the water, remain poised over some selected spot, and as soon as an unwary fish swam within striking distance, down it would hurl itself and seize the victim. Once we heard shrill cries quite close to us and on looking round saw a number of peahens followed by two peacocks. We remained very still, hoping to see the peacocks dance, and we felt much rewarded when these proud creatures began to spread out their magnificent tails, and at first hesitating and then growing more confident, began to trip lightly backwards and forwards and from side to side in short mincing steps, all the time displaying their gorgeously coloured feathers to the greatest advantage, though I must say it seemed to have little or no effect on the peahens who appeared to be rather bored at this display of masculine pageantry and pomp.

When it became cooler we left the shade of our mango grove and walked across the fields, and often would come across a *jheel* (pond). They were most attractive places as they were populated by many interesting water birds. There was the sepia brown sandpiper with his long beak running on the soft mud, wagging his small tail up and down and uttering his soft plaintive cry. Nearby was the red wattled lapwing, with his haunting call of, 'Did you do it? Did you do it?' as he is usually termed in imitation of his curious cry. With his black face, breast and head, and curious projection above and in front of each eye, he is familiar but quite striking in appearance. In contrast to him was the paddy bird who stood miserable and hunched up, his head drawn well in. this was deceptive, though, in that his inert and miserable looking posture hid the fact that he was really very wide awake indeed and was watching intently for any frog or fish that might come his way. More exalted and very lovely were the little egrets, snow white lovely birds, with long black beaks and long legs, who waded about on the soft mud and the grasslands, seeking insects and small reptiles. Once we saw emerge from the water a long, slender, snakelike head turning this way and that. This belonged to the snake bird, a black cormorant looking bird with silver grey streaks on the back. It had a long and very slender "S" shaped neck, narrow head and long pointed bill, and often it submerged itself altogether when on a fishing expedition, where it chases the fish at a great speed. On the tall grasses around the *jheel* we could watch the weaver birds making their nests. They were small, brownish yellow birds, and were chiefly noted for their remarkable retort shaped hanging nests, that looked something like straw bottles hanging down, and which they made from the coarse grasses around. The nest with its long entrance tube was woven with strips of grass, and had a small quantity of mud stuck inside near the egg chamber. Sometimes a second nest was made with a kind of bar across, on which the male bird was said to sit and sing to the female. To watch these small birds with the long grasses hanging from their beaks, weaving this perfect little model of architecture with the greatest agility and ease was a sight that cannot easily be forgotten.

Once we unexpectedly cam upon a small lake covered with lotuses. We stood spellbound before their loveliness, their delicate white and pink petals rising like a star shaped chalice from their bed of broad green leaves, their golden centres pulsating like jewels in the sunlight. As we gazed upon them, we understood why this flower has for centuries inspired poets and artists and has become a symbol of spiritual aspiration and attainment. How often had we heard said in invocation or prayer, and seen inscribed in wood and stone, the words, *Om mani padme om* (Behold the jewel in the lotus).

One evening on our way home, we were caught in a magnificent storm. It was not directly above us but all around us. Now in the east, now in the west, the forked lightning streaked the sky with brilliant flashes of liquid fire, the clouds gathered in a dark menacing mass and the thunder reverberated from all corners of the heavens. It was a spectacle awesome and grand till the rain fell in torrents on us and we were forced to bring our car to a halt. Then the heavens became angrier, the flashes more vivid as if the sky itself was rent in pieces, and it all came nearer and nearer while great bangs and claps of thunder filled the whole world around us with fear. Then just as suddenly it all stopped; an owl nearby hooted, a bat flew overhead and all along the canal bank and over the water, the whole place was suddenly lit up by myriads of fireflies, as if the awesome spectacle of the heavens we had just, witnessed had magically turned to a fairyland of soft, quiet, twinkling lights all around us.

People and Festive Occasions

We were fortunate in our neighbour for we lived in the midst of a large Hindu family, many of the members of whom had always been in Government Service. They had served in the Mughal Court and still prided themselves on their knowledge of Persian, which was the Court language then. Now they were equally at home in English and served in the government under British rule. In this family could be clearly discerned the impact of western thought and education, and the conflicts set up as it challenged some of their own traditions and culture. They still remained a large joint family and their first loyalty was to the family as such, but some of the younger ones now demanded, when they married, homes of their own. Their girls were educated and took up careers. They all gathered together on festive occasions at the large joint family house, but there were smaller bungalows quite near where the modern couples resided. We ourselves lived in one of these. We were treated very much as one of the family and on festive occasions one or other of the family would appear with garlands or offerings of fruit and sweets and we were always invited to their family gatherings. It was in their kindly care that I first had the opportunity of attending an Indian wedding. The first one I remember was when one of the sons was being married and we were taken to see him dressed for the wedding procession to the bride's house. First we had dinner with four other men, I being the only woman present. Then the bridegroom was brought in and introduced to us. He was a handsome young man of about 22 and wore a golden garland around his neck. We then moved to a balcony overlooking an open courtyard where we could not help but be struck by the picturesqueness of the scene below. Above, dazzling in its splendour was the starlit sky. Below were a number of women draped in their many coloured saris and adorned with flashing earrings and bracelets. With the intermingling of all these lovely colours in red, gold, pink, violet and green they presented a living picture of colour and harmony. There they all sat in a circle on a rich patterned carpet while on a white cushion in their midst sat the bridegroom. His mother with those sensitive hands and deft fingers, s characteristic of the Indian women, and smiling happily, helped him into a brocaded gold *atchkan* (three quarter length coat buttoned to the neck) and on his head she placed a mauve turban. A garland of gold tinsel tied to a garland of flowers hung around his neck and was so arranged that it circled his forehead and covered his face and chest. By his side was fastened a sword. All this was done amidst much laughter and talking. When he was finally apparelled to their satisfaction, we were taken to another balcony to see him set out for the bridge's house. The procession was made up of twelve men in red carrying lanterns, and various entertainers and performers; they were followed by the bridegroom himself mounted on a white horse. He sat with a small boy, a kind of page, I presumed, clad in purple velvet, in front of him on the horse.

While the bridegroom's procession went through the streets with music and dancing, we were quietly whisked away to the bride's house where the garden was illuminated with coloured lights. On the front of the house was an illuminated picture of Arjuna the famous warrior of Hindu mythology, shooting at a fish which circled round and round in a blaze of light. The time was May, a very hot evening, but an auspicious month for weddings. Here the excitement was mounting high as they all awaited the arrival of the bridegroom. There was children everywhere, their nimble little forms flitting to and fro in their wedding finery, almost like fireflies lighting up the night. In another part of the garden the servants were preparing the wedding feast which was being cooked in huge round copper vessels, and carpets were being spread on the grass for the many guests to sit on. We went into the house and saw the wedding presents and noticed that among the more customary ones of saris, cooking utensils, etc. were to be seen a set.

In the distance came the sound of music and there was a rush towards the gate, lights appeared, the music grew louder and the procession came into view. At its had the jugglers and tumblers performed their antics to the accompaniment of pipes, then came a blare of trumpets, followed by the old Mughal band, descendants of the old Court players with instruments identical to those used in Mughal days. They were followed by sword dancers who to the accompaniment of wind instruments, performed a picturesque dance featuring the old custom of the bridegroom capturing his bride in battle. Finally, silhouetted on his gaily caparisoned horse rode the bridegroom in his full regalia. The entertainers then doubled their efforts and the band struck out a grand crescendo as he dismounted and was courteously welcomed by the bride's family. This was followed by a dinner for all the men, who sat on the carpet, where water was provided in earthenware jars to drink and the food which was vegetarian was served on leaves. The younger men and the boys helped to wait on their seniors. This finished, they all vanished, the lights were turned out and the first ceremony came to an end.

The following evening the first people to gather were all the women in their gay saris, bringing with them the magnetic qualities of light and colour as they sat down and enjoyed their wedding feast. At eleven o'clock the actual wedding ceremony began. First the bridegroom was welcomed into the house by the bride's mother. She should have been behind the *purdah* while doing so, but this one had been able to break with tradition and we were able to see her gentle kind face and silvery hair prepping out from behind her sari as she performed that act. The bridegroom stood before her, head bowed and hands folded while she offered him various symbolic gifts and then inscribed a red sign on his forehead and waved some lighted candles over him.

After this the bride herself appeared somewhat shrouded and hidden from view in a red and gold sari. She was not veiled though, as was usual in orthodox families and we could see her gentle dark eyes and finely cut features. Her arms glittered with many bracelets as she walked round the bridegroom with a paper whip with which she struck him. This caused a great deal of mirth and cries of "Hit him harder, this is your last chance". She did not smile, but remained utterly enigmatic and with eyes cast down. After this somewhat lighter side of the proceedings, we all went into a large marquee at one end of which sat the bridegroom, and on his right hand the bride's father and beneath him, facing each other two pandits or priests, one from each family. They sat surrounded by various small earthenware dishes containing different kinds of grains and food; there was a geometrical looking drawing marked out on sand on the ground and by it wood laid out ready for a fire.

Then the pandits began to recite the marriage ceremony in Sanskrit, a language evidently not understood by the wedding party. The first part of the service I was told implied the worshipping of seven auspicious stars to which the bridegroom made offerings. Each star had its own separate rites which accounted for the length of the proceedings. Sometimes the pandits would disagree as to the actual words to be used and would begin to argue. At other times one pandit would get left behind in his recital by the other one and become quite annoyed in consequence. These dissensions between "the learned ones" caused great amusement to the assembled company. This part of the ceremony ended, the bride then joined the bridegroom and sat beside him; there was more offerings and a long list of injunctions were given to them both regarding duties, obligations and responsibilities between husbands and wives. Then came the long awaited lively climax when the fire was lit, the sacred cord produced, binding the couple together as they encircled the now blazing fire seven times and a vermilion sign was placed on the girl's forehead just at the parting of her hair, to signify that she was now married and must in future always were that symbol.

A delightful Hindu festival was Diwali, which marked the end of the rains and gave thanks for the return of light. Our kind neighbour often invited us to share their Diwali dinner with them, but before that we went down the Chandni Chowk, Delhi's most famous street, situated in the heart of the old city and where the Mughal processions complete with elephants, took place in former days. The whole place had been transformed into a soft fairyland of light by the tiny earthenware saucers filled with oil and wick which lit up verandahs, roofs, pavements, shop windows, houses and trees. These tiny twinkling lights, hundreds and hundreds of them, flickering in the gentle evening breeze, were the most beautiful illumination I have ever seen. The people too were all in happy mood, rich and poor jostling together where they were buying all manner of sweetmeats and toys from the loaded stalls. The toys were often made of clay and were mostly of animals, birds, elephants, cows, parrots etc., as well as the gods and goddesses of Hindu mythology. Children everywhere were dressed in new clothes if they could afford it. Their sensitive little faces, usually so serious, were now radiant with light as they clutched their toys to their breast and crunched the delicious sweetmeats which they had chosen. Mingling among this excited crowd was indeed a pleasure for no drunken brawl marred its happy welcome to the light.

While walking around we saw many of the shopkeepers garlanding an effigy of Lakshmi, their favoured goddess of good fortune. On stopping at one stall the owner, sitting cross-egged on the floor, looked up at us with a merry grin, after garlanding and placing offerings of food before this goddess. 'Ah,' he laughed, 'well this is what we call the worship of the money bags; well why not, they are worshipped everywhere'. And he laughed again heartily.

When we returned from the city, we were met by our gardener who presented us with a statue of Ganesh, the elephant god of good living, which was for our dining room and was evidently a favourite of his for we were given a fresh one each Diwali. Our house and garden too were all lit up with the Diwali lights, for indeed one dark house amidst the array of light all around from our Indian neighbours' houses, would have been a sorry sight. Finally we joined our large Hindu joint family in a huge marquee for dinner. Light, colour, talk and laughter greeted us as we sat down with them and enjoyed the beautifully prepared vegetarian meal that followed.

Another interesting Hindu festival was Holi, which marked the coming of spring and was usually in March when the fields were golden with mustard flower. It was celebrated by all, but especially in the villages where it was observed by the ringing of temple bells, beating of drums and blowing of horns, together with singing during the night and the squirting of coloured water on all passers by. Sometimes the villagers would paint themselves all over and then proceed to the town in rather too high carnival spirits.

Christmas too was beginning to find a place in Indians' hearts and we were always greeted by our orthodox Hindu gardener on Christmas morning with a specially culled buttonhole and the words, 'Blessed be the great day.' In the afternoon we arranged a Christmas tree and party for the servants and children in our compounds. This was not quite so easy as might be thought, as the servants included orthodox Hindu, Christian and the depressed class. The orthodox Hindu, our dearly loved gardener, could eat with Christians, but to eat with the sweeper and his family would "break his caste". After a good deal of talk and because of his special regard for so great a Master as Jesus, this Buddha as he was called, compromised. He was to sit at one end of the room, the sweeper and his family at the other and he was to be handed all his food first. He was sure we would understand his position.

So on Christmas afternoon the feast was spread, consisting of a variety of Indian sweets, a marvellously decorated Christmas cake, which the cook had stayed up all night to finish and plenty of fruit and the party foregathered, including always a very dear and courtly Muslim gentleman, who always came from the city to join us on this occasion, when he liked to sit on a chair aside and just watch the proceedings. Particularly, I remember how his face lit up, when after tea, we lit the many coloured candles on the Christmas tree to the strains of soft Christmas music played on the gramophone and then distributed the varied presents tied up in coloured paper. Everyone had a present, but to the children we gave those mainly of a musical variety and dearly loved by them, little drums, accordions, trumpets, bagpipes as well as bracelets and ribbons. Then came the climax, the pulling of the crackers. These children loved the bangs and for the first time their faces would light with glee as they searched inside the many wrappings for the hidden caps and trinkets; the caps they called "*topis*", and very soon all the dark little heads were covered with caps and crowns in a lovely array of all sizes and angles. Our bearer's father, a very old man, solemnly took off his own cap and replaced it with a jaunty paper clown's. For a few days after we were serenaded by all the tiny musical instruments till alack! to the great grief of their young players, one by one their music ceased.

At times somewhat striking visitors came to Delhi. One evening on going to church, we arrived to find it packed out, and we sat on benches that were hastily brought in. This was because a choir of some fifty people called Lushais who came from the Lushai Hills in Assam were staying in Delhi and were singing here that night. They had rather a remarkable history in that some forty years before they were noted as a very warlike people village rising against village and chief against chief and they cut off the heads of their prisoners and exhibited them on long poles outside the villages. It was said of them that the greater the number of heads, the better the hope of entering Paradise when they died. About 45 years ago, though, some Christians from Wales went to Lushai and their work met with much success despite persecution and opposition. The membership of the Lushai church was now fifty thousand and a great feature of their Christian worship was their singing, perhaps because of their Welsh teachers bringing the music of Wales with them. Now they had the special choir, conducted by a Welsh woman, and for the first time were touring India and giving recitals of their own folk tunes and the Messiah. They were a delight to look at and a joy to listen to. The young women wore a kind of white sari trimmed with red; their heads were quite bare, their black hair being parted in the middle and done up in a knob at the back. They sang beautifully, with all the rich tone so characteristic of the Welsh, their voices strong and musical and full of expression. They sang the Messiah extracts unaccompanied and one man with a lovely tenor voice sang. 'He shall feed his flock'. The Hallelujah Chorus brought the entire congregation to their feet, where they remained standing before the grandeur and majesty of its rendering.

Another time a Christian *sadhu* who was a healer came to Delhi. The accounts of his preaching (never less than one and a half hours), his miraculous healing power bestowed on all alike, Hindu, Muslim, Christian, had preceded him and aroused much interest. We went one Sunday evening to hear him preach. It was packed with Indian Christians. We noticed at once certain things that were not usual in India; the men and women sat together on benches not on the floor and the men wore no headgear. Strains of music filled the church as the organ began to play, and all eyes were turned on the Christian *sadhu* in his saffron robe as he came in accompanied by the Indian minister. He was tall, well built with black hair and beard, a kind open face and striking black eyes. He was altogether vital, magnetic and with a radiant countenance. His address, given in Hindi and translated into English, was extraordinarily vivid and original; he held his audience spellbound for two hours and it was interesting to watch the reaction of the audience. Sometimes they were all smiles, even laughter, other times serious and restful as he spoke in a kind and gentle tone. There were many testimonies to his healing power and the sick were brought to him. One case we heard of, which was quite authentic as we knew the family, was of a Hindu boy in the city who was blind. His father was a shopkeeper and one day the *sadhu* entered his shop to buy a blanket as it was getting colder. His fame as a healer had preceded him and when the shopkeeper saw him enter he besought him at once to heal his son. The boy was brought in and the *sadhu* remaining in silence and prayer touched the boy's eyes. The boy got his sight back immediately. The father was so overwhelmed with joy and gratitude that the *sadhu* was offered all he wished for in that shop, but he only took the blanket he had come for and insisted on paying for it.

Another time we went to hear Mahatma Gandhi speak at a public meeting. He was at this time touring India on a campaign for the depressed classes or outcastes. The meeting was held in a garden in the open. At one end a small raised platform was erected, covered with a canopy from which flew the Congress flag. Below this was another circular platform on which we sat with a number of others on the floor and all around us in an ever widening circle were thousands of people. We were the only English couple there, and except for a Belgian woman and a few Japanese from the Japanese Trade Delegation, the entire audience was Indian. When the Mahatma arrived, a small insignificant figure, clad in coarse homespun cloth, the crowd, consisting mainly of the depressed class, their faces alight with expectancy and reverence, bowed themselves to the ground and the cry of "*Gandhi ki jai*" (Victory to Gandhi) filled the air. He himself sat down crosslegged and seemed to take but little notice of the great crowd before him. Various speeches of welcome were read and garlands placed around his neck, and rose petals scattered over him. This was followed by the singing of national folk songs and a poetry recital. All these lengthy preliminaries seemed to irk the Mahatma and it was not until a bag of rupees was presented to him for his campaign that he smiled. Then he rose and spoke, telling them the long speeches were unnecessary and that the bag of rupees should have been very much larger. He said all this in such a whimsical manner that the crowd were delighted with him and cheered him again and again. There was always something a little puckish about the Mahatma. He then began to auction the speeches of welcome which were written and framed, and the garlands round his neck. Not content with the money thus obtained he cast his eyes on the expensive jewellery worn by the women on the platform with him and so compelling was his personality that ere long the piles of rupee notes rose higher and higher on the table in front of him and the jewels lay flashing at his feet. Towards the end the crowd, unable to contain themselves any longer, surged forward, breaking all barriers, as with on accord they prostrated themselves again and again to the ground with their cry of "Victory to Gandhi", "Victory to Gandhi". While this was happening the Mahatma slipped quietly away.

Another much loved visitor to Delhi was Sarojini Naidu, known as the Nightingale of India. I saw her first when at a women's meeting she was introducing the "Maharani of Travancore". A largish comfortable figure, she radiated warmth and kindliness wherever she went. Her sense of humour was inexhaustible and gave a wonderful balance to her whole life. She was also the greatest orator I had ever heard. Even at this gathering her speech was a masterpiece of eloquence, humour and seriousness perfectly blended. On another occasion at another meeting concerning Indian education I watched her deal with a very rubicund Anglo-Saxon Englishman in a manner so tactful, so witty, so tolerant, that before very long it was Sarojini who was expounding the ways and means of Indian education, while her opponent sat smiling and happily listening to her giving his assent to all she said. Perhaps that perfect blending of so great a heart with such a lucid mind sprang from her innermost mystic sense, which at times she had so clearly expressed in her poetry. I always like to associate one who was so universally loved and whose words were so wise with one of her own poems about the Buddha which seems to sum up all that can be said about one of India's great women.

Lord Buddha on the Lotus Throne
With praying eyes and hands elate
What mystic rapture dost thou own
Immutable and intimate?
What peace, unravished of our ken
Annihilate from the world of men?

The wind of change for ever blows
Across the tumult of our way,
Tomorrow's unborn griefs depose
The sorrows of our yesterday.
Dream yields to dream, strife follows strife,
And Death unweaves the web of life.

For us the travail and the heat
The broken secrets of our pride,
The strenuous lessons of defeat,
The flower deferred, the fruit denied,
But not the peace, supremely won,
Lord Buddha, of thy Lotus Throne.

The end, elusive and afar,
Still lure us with its beckoning flight;
And all our mortal moments are
A session of the Infinite,
How shall we reach the great unknown
Nirvana of thy Lotus Throne?

Endnotes

In Spear's essay there are references to individuals whom old-timers would recognise. I took the help of Rev. Daniel O'Connor, former Chaplain, St Stephen's College, in identifying some of them.

1. Ishtiaq Husain Qureshi (1903–81), did M.A. in History and Persian at St Stephen's College, and his Ph.D from Cambridge in 1940. He was a member of the staff from 1928–47, and was appointed Professor at Delhi University. He also served as the university's acting Vice-Chancellor. He suffered during the riots of 1947, and migrated to Pakistan. Qureshi was a member of Pakistan's Constituent Assembly, and was Professor at Lahore University. He was later appointed the Vice-Chancellor of Karachi University. Qureshi wrote extensively in Urdu and English, chiefly on administration under the Delhi Sultans and the Mughals. He passed away a year before Dr Spear (p. 21).
2. The Shakespeare Society (not to be confused with the older Shakespeare Reading Society) was started in 1924 by H.W. Padley, on the staff from 1924–33 (p. 21).
3. K.C. Nag joined St Stephen's in 1921 (p. 31).

4. Khub Ram, former student, on the staff of the college 1902–22, thereafter "Attached", and Reader in Physics and Dean of the Science Faculty, Delhi University; Rai Bahadur S.N. Mukarji (Mathematics), taught in St Stephen's College from 1912, and went on to become the sixth Principal from 1926–45 (p. 31).
5. Rai Bahadur Nishi Kanta Sen (M.A. Calcutta University) was on the staff of the College from 1906–45. He was Registrar of Delhi University and was later appointed Registrar of Visva Bharati (p. 31).
6. Rev. Alfred Coore designed many churches, chapels and schools in Delhi, including the Holy Trinity Church, Turkman Gate, Delhi, and in 1924 St John's in Mehrauli, which is striking for its incorporation of features of Indian architecture (p. 54).
7. Helen Jerwood was associated with the St Stephen's Community, Rajpur Road. She founded the Queen Mary's School in 1915, St Thomas' School in Simla in 1928, St Thomas' School in New Delhi in 1931, St Martin's School, Delhi Cantonment, and also schools at Kotgarh and Gurdaspur. Jerwood died in Delhi in April 1965 (pp. 56–57).

to notice. She continues without pausing: 'And Nico is complaining of a stomach ache. I'm worried. Do you think it's something he ate?'

'I doubt it,' Mr A replies evenly. 'He hardly eats anything.'

Mrs A frowns. 'Yes, I know, but that's besides the point. What if it's amoebiasis? You know, his friend Theo got it last year and was on antibiotics for seventeen days. Oh, drat this rain!'

I begin to drift off as tends to happen when Orang start talking about things I don't understand. How they go on and on. Caterers. Amoebiasis. Hmm. What a strange word. What is it? Is it tasty to eat, I wonder? It's my last thought before drifting off to the sound of driving rain on the roof.

❄

I wake with a leap that has me tumbling off the bed. But I can barely feel the pain, my ears are so full of the boom of thunder. What a storm! A crack of lightning outside the window lights up the rain slicing down onto the garden. The colours of the World have disappeared. Everything is white and grey and scary. Or, it would be scary to *most* cats. Few are as brave as I am.

Outside the bedroom I can make out the calls of unfamiliar Orang over the rain. I slide my paw around the door and pull it in, being careful to stick my nose out just enough to survey the scene. It seems that the caterers Mrs A had been so worried about have made it after all. The front doors are open and a number of Orang are trampling in and out, plastic bags over their shoes, carrying tables and chairs and serving dishes.

Mrs A is directing the traffic, dressed in a pink and gold saree. She looks just lovely. I saunter across to her, making sure to keep all the strange Orang squarely in sight, and rub myself across her legs. 'Soyabean!' she groans most un-maternally, and rushes over to a side table to grab a sticky roller brush with which she begins attacking her clothes.

Having had my love rebuffed over a few strands of hair, I make my way through the family dining room into the kitchen. Mrs A should try thinking of my fur in terms of aesthetic enhancement. Orang can be terribly limited in their outlook. I pass Mr A, who has had a shower and smells strongly of some perfume. It isn't particularly appealing. Someone should invent tuna perfume. Now that's a great idea that I doubt any Orang will think of. Another example of that limited outlook I just mentioned.

In the kitchen, Ibu Warsi is sitting on a low stool next to the ironing stand, sweat running down the sides of her face, fanning herself with a magazine. It would probably be less effort for her to just take off her jilbab, but she seems inordinately attached to it. The rendang and ayam bakar she'd prepared earlier are being ladled into serving plates and carried out to the drawing room. It's all rather noisy and disruptive.

My tummy rumbles. Just the thought of rendang does something to my mouth: it floods with saliva and

S
T

my throat vibrates uncontrollably. Ibu Warsi shoots me a warning look. I'm not sure how she always manages to guess when I have forbidden food on my mind. Slightly creepy.

My bowl is conspicuously rendang-free. I meow winningly at Ibu Warsi, even though I know in my heart that it's in vain. She looks pointedly back at the bowl and the stale kibble that lies in it.

'Hello, Soyabean.'

I startle as Tofu appears out of the shadows.

'*Meow*! You gave me a scare.'

'Sorry. I didn't mean to.'

'Where have you been? I haven't seen you all day. Hasn't it been annoying with the rain and all these people tramping about?'

Tofu doesn't respond immediately, staring at me in that unnerving, unblinking way of hers.

'Well?'

'I've been upstairs keeping an eye on Nico,' she finally replies. 'He's vomited and his stomach hurts. But he's resting now. I don't like how red his face has become. He looks too hot.'

I feel a flush of guilt. Tofu has that effect. She's so annoyingly noble and selfless. Thinking of others' well-being instead of food. Most uncat-like. 'Well, good to know the boy is resting. Is Ibu Mari with him?'

'Hmmm? Yes, she is,' Tofu replies distractedly.

'What's wrong?' I ask. 'Are you okay?'

Tofu sighs and sits back on her haunches. 'Soyabean, don't you feel we're getting old? There's this stiffness in my back legs when I try and leap up onto something high. It's even worse on rainy days for some reason.'

I think about it and realize that I don't actually leap up high very much. Understandably, given my impressive size. I'm not a tiny, Tofu-type cat after all. But there's no point in trying to make Tofu feel bad about her runtiness, and so I deftly change the topic.

'Age, my dear Tofu, is a just a number. And anyway, it's the old ginger that's the spiciest.' I'm quite pleased with myself for that last chengyu. One of Nai Nai's, of course.

A deafening roll of thunder has us both flattening our ears. Tofu's eyes widen into large saucers. Her eyes can look larger than her face sometimes

'I don't like this storm,' she says softly. 'It feels wrong in my bones.'

I don't know about her bones, but I agree that the storm's no good. Enough to take the edge off one's appetite, really.

'Imagine all the creatures out there tonight,' Tofu continues. 'The stray cats, the bats. Everyone cold and wet and miserable, trying to find some shelter. Trying to ignore the pain in their stomachs and their hearts. Trying just to survive.'

She looks straight at me and I can feel in *my* bones what she's going to say next. And sure enough:

'Imagine the poor rats out in the flooded sewers.'

I'm saved from once again having to steer this conversation away from its rodent-infested course by a group of Orang, who walk into the kitchen accompanied by Mr A. There's no sign of his earlier sulkiness. In fact, he's all smiles, chatting away with his friends.

Tofu is gone as suddenly as she'd appeared. Ibu Warsi gets to her feet and offers to take the bottles that some of the Orang are holding as presents for the As.

One lady with a humongous nose bends down and pets me on the head. 'What an absolutely glorious cat,' she croons. Now that I look closely, perhaps her nose isn't all that offensive. She does have good taste. 'Totally imperial,' the lady continues. 'What breed is she?'

'That's Soyabean,' Mr A beams proudly. 'It's a he, and he's no imperial breed; just an ordinary street cat from Beijing.'

'Ordinary' is hardly the best word to describe me. But scarcely do I have time to finish this thought before Mr A continues: 'Not that he's ordinary in any way.' That's more like it.

I begin to feel the warm glow of pride that the imminent telling of the story about my heroic exploits in China always brings on. Mr A is in top form, sparing few details, as he recalls how I had been tricked into modelling for a tainted pet food brand called Maomi Deluxe. But also how I'd gone on to bring the company's corrupt boss and his cronies to justice on live TV.

The friends are spellbound, and the big-nose lady can't keep her hands off me. 'Marvellous!' 'Clever cat!' 'Gorgeous fellow!' The compliments are coming in fast and thick, and I close my eyes to soak it all in, until a nasal sneer cuts through the admiring coos of my fans.

'Long haired, isn't he? Must be dirty having him shed all over the place. And where does he go to the toilet? Inside the house? Disgusting! It can't be hygienic.'

My eyes fly open and settle on the speaker, a sloping-shouldered, bushy-eyebrowed, mean-looking specimen of an Orang, whose appearance is as unpleasant as his opinions. 'Don't you have children of your own, Pak A?' he asks. 'How can you allow for them to be exposed to these unclean creatures?'

Mr A opens his mouth and then closes it. He clears his throat and tries again, 'Pak Bayu, our cats – we have two – are like our children. And they love our boys like their own family.'

Pak Bayu, whoever he is, does not look impressed. If anything, his expression curdles even more. 'Pak A, be careful what you say. I'm not sure the Lord meant for us to talk about these lower animals as though they were human.'

'Well, I'm not sure the Lord meant for you to be jet-setting around in expensive cars, attending diplomatic parties,' Mr A shoots back, his lips smiling, but his eyes angry.

There is a momentary hush, until Big Nose laughs nervously. 'Come on, everyone, let's go out and sink our teeth into some of that delicious food I can smell. Are those samosas?' The other Orang are quick to agree and leave the kitchen, with Pak Bayu trailing slightly behind them.

I follow them out too and find that the drawing room is whirling with strangers in glittering dresses and kebayas. The laughter and chatter rises over the rain. And there is much clinking of glasses and ice. My nose twitches, picking up on the crunchy scent of tortilla chips through the heavy smells of damp clothes and Orang perfume.

Following the scent, I arrive at a corner of the drawing room where Mrs A is sitting on a low-slung armchair, chatting with a couple of Orang whom I recognize as the mothers of some of Ishaan's school friends. I nudge the exposed leg of Mrs B, a blonde Australian, whom I know from past experience is partial to slipping me titbits. It's like pressing a button. Instantly, distractedly, she begins feeding me broken off bits of the chips.

I keep a wary eye on Mrs A, in case she tries to stop me. I believe she's read in some misinformed book that tortillas are bad for cat health. But why should some random Orang decide what we cats can and cannot eat? I'm sure whoever wrote that dratted book must chomp away on all manner of chips, probably at the very same time as writing the words denying them to cats.

Luckily, Mrs A seems too wrapped up in the conversation to pay me much attention. 'I worry about the children,' she says to Mrs B. 'They've been pestering me about their religion. I'm not sure they have enough of an identity, or a sense of belonging. Of place, you know? They were born in one country, live in another, speak the language of a third.'

She sighs and goes on. 'Their dad is from one place and their mom from somewhere else. They're a bit of this and a bit of that. But what if that means they end up as nothing?'

Mrs B breaks off another chip to pass to me. 'I wouldn't worry too much. It's increasingly common,' she says. 'Third culture kids, they're called. The world is their home. They don't need just one place, just one identity; they can choose as many as they like.'

'But that's not how the real world works,' Mrs A replies. 'You can't just go around picking your identity, like it's a carton of juice at the supermarket.'

'But that's what's so lovely about Indonesia,' Mrs C, another school mom, chimes in. 'If there is one place in the world where you can pick and choose and have all your multiple identities celebrated, its Indonesia. Bhinneka Tunggal Ika!'

Mrs A seems unconvinced. 'Yes, I know the mottos: unity in diversity; we are one, but we are many. They're lovely sounding, but I've been hearing things. Ugly things.

You know the elections are coming up and the stuff circulating on social media is unbelievably worrying.'

I'm beginning to lose attention as a sleepy, chippy, feeling spreads across my tummy.

Mrs B nods. 'I know! People are willing to believe anything. There's been a WhatsApp meme doing the rounds claiming that the President is allowing 10 million Chinese migrants to come in and take over local jobs.'

My head is drooping, but I snap awake hearing the word 'Chinese'. What did Mrs B mean? Are there millions of Chinese coming to Indonesia? It sounds good to me. I begin to think of the salty, preserved eggs and great steaming dishes of fatty pork that were served up in the restaurants along our street in Beijing. Despite my swollen belly, I feel like eating some more. It's impressive how I can do that. Be stuffed and hungry at the same time.

Mrs A massages her forehead with her knuckles. 'I'm just dreading some kind of a pogrom based on all this fake news. It can go up in flames like a tinderbox.'

She leans back into her chair. 'It's never taken much to turn things nasty against the Chinese. It's happened again and again. A whisper, a rumour, a WhatsApp message. The Chinese are poisoning our wells. The Chinese are atheists. The Chinese are driving up prices. Easiest thing in the world to scapegoat "outsiders" for everything that goes wrong, isn't it? Happens everywhere.'

Mrs B interrupts: 'But the President...'

'Yes. That's what I've been telling myself too. The President is a good man. He won't stand for any violence. He'll stick up for minorities. But have you seen the rumours flying around about him? Apparently he doesn't pray enough. Or he's the wrong religion. Or he's to blame for the millions of coming Chinese. It's...'

There's an enormous crash. I don't know if it's thunder or the end of the world. Orang screams fill the room and I'm lashed by the bottoms of dresses swishing this way and that. I crouch down low and fold my ears in, but there's water everywhere. I sputter as it seeps up my nose. My feet are soaking.

I hear Mr A's raised voice telling everyone to stay calm, to move out into the driveway or the backyard. Pak Nono is in the house and the caterers are in as well, and everyone is moving furniture out into the verandah. Mr A's voice sounds out again: 'Unplug all the electrical appliances. Hurry!' Somewhere I can hear glass shattering. And then Ibu Warsi is swooping me up in her arms and taking me upstairs towards the children's room.

Chapter V

Mrs A

Pelting Rice Cakes

Mrs A looked out of the plane window into a molten sky, the clouds ablaze in red and pink. But she hardly noticed the colours. The memory of her living room roof caving in was resistant to the splendour of the sunset. It played in her head on loop. The gaping hole where there should have been, had always been, a ceiling. The rain tunnelling in, the screaming guests, the cold panic. Deep breaths, she reminded herself, willing her heart to stop cantering.

It could have been worse. The children had been safe in their bedrooms upstairs. The cats were unscathed. In fact, the only person any worse for wear was Mr A, who'd suffered a cut from a piece of falling debris. But it had been a superficial wound.

Friends had pitched in to help, carrying furniture and carpets away from the flooded areas. Ibu Warsi had shrugged off the mayhem and made pots of tea for the helpers. Nico had been so delighted with the late-night adventure that no more was heard of his stomach ache. Mrs B had offered to put them up for the night. It really could have been worse.

The next day, their landlord had been all smiles and apologies. He'd discovered that the storm-water drain was completely clogged with plastic. On the night of the party, the rain had caused an enormous build-up of water pressure directly over the living room roof, causing part of it to give way.

The pipes had since been unblocked, the roof re-cemented. The landlord had sent them a gigantic fruit basket. Over the weeks, life had returned to its normal tempo. But Mrs A remained unsettled. She found it harder to feel the magic of the country that had till recently charmed her. She was more irritable. Why was everybody so laid-back when plastic garbage was being dumped into the environment, clogging up people's drains? Why did everyone smile so excessively? A long list of grumpy questions skulked in her mind, unbidden.

This trip to eastern Indonesia's island of Lombok felt like a raft that Mrs A was clinging to in the hope that it would carry her away from the quagmire of burst-pipe despondency to the white-sand idyll of journalistic accomplishment. The visit had been months in the making, having originated in a travel magazine snippet she'd come across in her dentist's waiting room. The moment that she'd read it, something had bubbled in Mrs A's tummy: a frothy mix of professional excitement and romantic idealism. She'd known immediately that this was going to be amongst her best work.

It was a description of Puri Lingsar, a temple complex in Lombok that advised tourists to time their visit to the island with an annual five-day festival held in November. Called perang topat, literally the rice cake war, the festival involved locals from different religious communities pelting each other with rice cakes before putting their ecclesiastical differences aside to worship jointly at the temple.

In that idea, Mrs A thought she'd found the pulse of the Indonesia she loved; the country that showed the rest of the world that there was an alternative to bigotry. That everyone was the same before god, especially when covered in splatterings of rice cake.

She'd been embarrassingly gleeful, fantasizing about the chance to bite her thumb at Pak Hendra. 'You want the real Indonesia, Pak?' she'd imagined gloating, as the dentist had polished her teeth. 'Well, you can take this: perang topat *is* the real Indonesia.' Even a hardened cynic like Pak Hendra would tear up at the story she would write.

'Are you okay?' the dentist had asked, looking concerned. He wasn't used to patients chuckling with apparent enjoyment while getting their teeth cleaned. Mrs A had flashed him a thumbs up sign and had gone back to her Pak Hendra–taunting reverie.

Once safely in Lombok, Mrs A breathed in the macet-free air and felt the stress of the collapsed roof dissipate. On the way to the hotel, her taxi passed expanses of paddy fields. Every once in while, she caught a glimpse of the sea, inky blue in the twilight. Mrs A wanted to open her arms and let Indonesia lap over her like a warm, salty wave.

That night, she found it hard to fall asleep; butterflies of anticipation flitted in her tummy. All those weeks of research were about to pay off. She was ready to throw some rice cakes and to write a piece that would inspire the world to join in.

The next morning, she headed to Puri Lingsar directly after breakfast. The taxi dropped her off at the foot of the rough, stone-hewn staircase that led into the temple complex. The air was alive with fragrances from the assorted offerings of betel leaves, lime and flowers, laid out besides long, tapered bamboo poles.

Mrs A scribbled furiously in her notebook, determined not to miss a single detail. She noted the presence of a number of glass bottles filled to the top with an opaque liquid, along with the instruction to find out what this mystery drink was.

But it was the large billboard right next to the entrance that left her truly puzzled. It featured, in lurid colours, a hosepipe snaking around a crudely painted mountain. Water sprayed from the pipe's nozzle, just avoiding the heads of two unsmiling men in the foreground. The man on the left was dressed in military fatigues, his eyes hidden by gold-rimmed sunglasses. He was shaking the hand of a portly civilian, whose swollen belly was barely contained by a white sarong. Neither individual was a likely poster boy for communal harmony.

Mrs A took a picture of the billboard to decode later and carefully stepped through the gateway. She'd been prepared to be wowed by the moment, but found herself deafened instead. The clanging of the gongs and cymbals of a typical gamelan orchestra was discordant to her uneducated ear at the best of times. On this occasion, the din was worse than normal. Two separate orchestras, each with about a dozen players, seated on opposite ends of a grassy square, were trying to outplay each other.

'Mrs A?' A middle-aged man, graceful in a black-and-red sarong, approached her.

'Yes. Pak Ketut?' she replied, folding her hands into a namaste.

Ketut Sumantri, an English teacher at a high school in Lombok, was to be her guide and translator at Puri Lingsar. They'd been introduced by the local Indian consulate, and had been exchanging emails for weeks.

'Welcome to our island, Bu,' Pak Ketut smiled warmly, revealing a mouthful of worn-out teeth. He handed Mrs A a sarong and showed her how to wrap it around her waist. 'You will be needing to wear this to go inside the inner sanctum,' he explained.

'Thank you! I can't tell you how excited I am to finally be here,' Mrs A beamed. 'To have people from both communities coming together. It's glorious!' She felt around in her handbag for a barrette to get her hair off her face. 'Thanks again for helping me out today.'

'It's my great pleasure, Bu,' beamed Pak Ketut. 'And an honour for all of us that a famous journalist like you is travelling so far to meet us.'

Mrs A blushed. 'Not so famous, Pak, and the pleasure is all mine. The way the world is, it's getting harder and harder to believe that people with differences in belief can still get along. Puri Lingsar offers us so much hope. Don't you think?'

Pak Ketut looked at Mrs A quizzically, his friendly smile still in place. 'Yes, Bu. It's wonderful. But please be careful also, Bu. Hold on tight to your bag. There are many people here today. And, of course, everyone from our community is honest, but you can't always trust the others. Too many people are getting their wallets stolen during perang topat.'

Mrs A had not expected her first chat of the day to proceed quite along these lines. She cast about for something to change the topic. 'Hmmm. Yes, one must always be careful in crowds. But tell me Pak, this music? What is it?'

'Oh, yes! The music, it is being very important,' said Pak Ketut. 'It is clearing the temple of evil, negative forces. Purifying the atmosphere, so that the wishes are granted. The one in that corner is our community's gamelan. Much more better than the other one, isn't it?'

Mrs A felt slightly sick, her discomfort only worsening as the conversation progressed. Pak Ketut was of the opinion that the children of his community were better behaved; that the women of his community were less oppressed; that the animals in his community were treated more humanely.

'You see,' he expounded with a reasonable air, 'these other people, their society is being very backward, stuck in ancient times. They are not modernized like us. Of course, not everything modern is good but the problem is simple: education. They are not being well educated.'

Mrs A wanted to clonk Pak Ketut on the head with her notebook. But she smiled instead. 'Should we go to the sanctum, Pak?' she suggested. 'I want to see how it all works.'

Pak Ketut was immediately obliging. 'Yes, yes, of course, Bu. Let us be going now. It's just over there.' He led her to the far side of the square where another stone staircase led into the sacred centre of the temple complex.

A hand-painted sign outlined a set of Dos and Don'ts. People were advised to wear 'neat and polite dress' and 'not disturb people practising the ritual ceremoni'. Amongst the list of forbidden items were: 'pork, pig, bee, menstruation impure, and hemorrhage women.' Mrs A stopped for a few moments to jot it all down. It would provide a nice bit of colour for her article.

Then she spotted more of the liquid-filled bottles amongst the other offerings along the stairs. Pak Ketut explained the drink was a kind of palm wine. Both communities imagined it to be a much-appreciated gift to the almighty. Mrs A smiled. There was hope to be found in Puri Lingsar yet.

Devotees thronged the sanctum, but a hush hung over the space, strangely loud given the sudden absence of the gamelan's cacophony. At the centre was a rectangular pool of still, sacred water. Men and women sat before it, their folded hands raised above their heads, eyes closed in contemplation. Others adjusted their prayer mats to ensure that they were facing westwards.

It was difficult to tell people of one community from the other. Most of the women were dressed in kebayas, tight-fitting blouses tied with a broad sash over sarongs. But Mrs A noticed that while some wore flowers in their hair, others covered their heads with jilbabs.

Along the long side of the pool, a raised platform shrouded in a thick white sheet functioned as a shrine.

Members of one faith heaped the right-hand side with mounds of offerings and those of the other belief did the same on the left. There was no physical barrier separating the sides.

The muscles in Mrs A's neck eased. She hadn't realized how tightly they'd been coiled. Here, finally, were the kinds of scenes she had travelled hundreds of kilometres to witness. It hadn't been a waste. The relief left her weak-kneed and she sat down heavily, behind a group of worshippers.

Pak Ketut dutifully settled down next to her. 'Are you seeing the pool, Bu?' he whispered loudly. 'It is the reason why everyone is coming to Puri Lingsar. It is fed by a holy spring: the source of the power of this place.'

Mrs A nodded. She'd begun doubting herself, wondering if Pak Hendra was right to perceive her as an over excited ingénue. But this moment in this temple was all the proof she needed to know that the Indonesia she believed in was not a fantasy.

Pak Ketut appeared to have picked up on Mrs A's improved mood and chuckled along in sympathy. He began to explain the temple's history. 'This holy spring, it was created by our God a long time ago. Maybe two hundred years before. And anybody who came here for worshiping always had successful harvests,' he said.

'I see!' said Mrs A. 'So it's all about harvests. Ultimately, everyone needs to eat and feed their families. How interesting! All that's needed to bring people together is something elemental like water.'

Pak Ketut looked at her indulgently and continued: 'Our religion, Bu, is being like that: open, tolerant, welcoming. So, we didn't mind whoever came here to ask for blessings of the deity.'

A pained look momentarily crossed his face. 'But.'

Mrs A caught her breath. 'But?'

Pak Ketut gestured at the people prostrating on prayer mats. 'These people cannot accept that the power of this temple is coming from our deity. Talk to their pemangku and he will tell some nonsense story about one of their preachers striking the ground with his staff to create the springs five hundred years ago. Ha, ha, it's a joke!'

At that moment, nothing could have been less funny for Mrs A. Her spirits, which had been soaring just moments ago, were now spiralling. It was like a bad roller-coaster ride.

'What's a pemangku?' she asked in a bid to maintain healthy journalistic curiosity.

'Pemangku? That is the temple supervisor,' replied Pak Ketut. 'There are two – one for each community. Ours is a holy man. Very simple, hard-working person, who only cares about others.

'But theirs...' he continued, making a disapproving hrumphing sound. 'Theirs...'

'Theirs?' asked Mrs A faintly, although in the sinking pit of her stomach she knew the response would probably be full of defamatory details of dastardly villainy.

'Their pemangku should not be in a temple at all. He is not being a spiritual person. Did you see his portrait on that big sign at the main gate? He is always dressed up in military uniform. It's because he used to be in the army. And got up to no good there either, I am sure. He's been appointed pemangku by the bupati as a government spy. Everyone knows that.'

Mrs A knew that bupati was the title of the top government officer at the local, regency level. She took out her phone and found the photograph of the billboard that had so bemused her.

'Is that the pemangku shaking hands with the bupati?' she asked Pak Ketut showing him the image.

'Yes, Bu. Not a bad painting; although the bupati is being a lot fatter in real life,' Pak Ketut giggled.

'What's that hosepipe in the back all about?'

'Oh, it is a symbol of water. The spring here at Puri Lingsar is feeding the whole entire irrigation network for this area. It is the lifeblood, Bu.'

The billboard finally made some sense, but that didn't help Mrs A feel any better. Everything was so much more convoluted than she'd imagined. Pak Hendra's words echoed in her mind uncomfortably: 'Dig deeper if you are going to do any real journalism.'

She opened her notebook with grim determination. 'So, tell me, Pak Ketut. Why does the bupati need a spy in Puri Lingsar? What's the point?'

He replied patiently, as though to a child. 'To keep an eye on our people, that's why. Whatever they might say in their tourist magazines, the fact is, they are not liking us. They don't like our customs, they don't like our rituals, they are not liking our Gods.'

He shrugged and went on, 'They are not happy with our success, Bu. They are jealous, because even though we are minority, our children are more educated than theirs – the majority.

'Bu, can I tell you the truth? Don't be disappointed. I know you've come a long way to watch perang topat. But actually, the government is not liking their people to come to our temple.'

'What do you mean by *their people*? Isn't the government for all the people?' asked Mrs A. She pictured Pak Hendra laughing at her even as the words left her mouth. '*You already know the answer to that, Bu. Open your eyes*,' he'd say.

The real Pak Ketut was looking almost as bemused as her imagined Pak Hendra. 'Do you really think so? How many people from our community are bupatis in Lombok? How many are bupatis in Indonesia?'

Mrs A had no idea what the answer was, but it did not seem like the appropriate moment to start googling it.

'You don't need all the fingers of even one hand to count them,' Pak Ketut said. 'They are tolerating us, Bu. That's all. We are pretty pictures for their tourism magazines. Our clothes are colourful.

'Tourism,' he said flatly. 'That's what perang topat has become. An excuse to attract tourists. You see, Bu, their leaders don't really want them to come here to Lingsar and pray with us. Maybe it has been a Lombok tradition for a long time. At least two hundred years. But now suddenly, they are saying that whoever goes to the temple is apostate.'

He went on, 'The ones who like to come here, they are always scolded: "don't pray like this, don't make those offerings, no drinking palm wine, don't fold your hands above your head, cover your hair like this". Bu, we are not wanting any problems. We are very few and they are very many. The best we can hope is just to be left alone.'

The sky had darkened, threatening rain. Devotees began picking themselves off the floor and making their way out of the sanctum. Mrs A watched them for a few moments and found herself missing her children. She conjured up Nico's minty breath on her cheek at bedtime, Ishaan's incessant questions; their abundant joy.

A random memory from a week ago arose. Ishaan had entered her study, having just returned from school, his hands smeared with dirt from the playground. 'When was the Bronze Age?' he'd demanded to know in lieu of a greeting. Used to this manner of address, Mrs A hadn't batted an eyelid. 'Thousands of years ago,' she'd answered. 'I think it started about 3000 BC.'

'Let's Google it,' suggested Ishaan.

Mrs A had looked rueful. 'Why do we have to Google everything? Why can't you just trust me to know?'

Ishaan had laughed, showing off his newly grown adult incisors. 'Mama, you know how some people trust in God? Well, I trust in Google.'

Back at Puri Lingsar, Mrs A was beginning to think that Google might indeed be preferable to god, if Ketut were to be believed about the state of His flock.

She felt a fat drop of rain splash on her head and looked up. 'Let's go, Bu,' Pak Ketut urged. 'It's time for the official ceremony. Perang topat will begin soon.' He paused to scan the sky. 'The weather is looking too terrible.'

Back in the square outside, the gamelan orchestras were nowhere to be seen, but rows of chairs had been lined up under a tent. Mrs A took a seat towards the back and busied herself taking notes. Mounds of rice cakes wrapped in coconut leaves were arranged in baskets on a makeshift stage up front. A cultural troupe of some kind milled about to the side, the women wearing elaborate headgear. A toothless old man sat cross-legged, hugging a drum. The drizzle outside thickened.

It was late afternoon by the time the bupati and an assortment of other local dignitaries made an appearance. Ushering them onto the stage were the two temple supervisors. One was familiar to Mrs A from the billboard. Outfitted in military regalia and wearing dark glasses, despite the failing light, he strode ahead of another man, whom Ketut pointed out as his community's pemangku.

Once the bupati was seated, a series of cultural performances clanged on soggily for over an hour. And then it was time for a round of speeches. A deathly dull report by a division chief of the tourism department of West Lombok was almost drowned out by the chatter of the audience, who were growing understandably restive.

The MC, a fast-talking man with a face like a friendly frog, took the mic once it was over. 'Thank you for that information. We can all see from it that perang topat is a famous festival all around the world. In fact, today we are honoured to have a famous journalist coming to cover this important event all the way from India!'

Mrs A felt a slow burn rise as half the audience turned around, craning their necks to get a look. 'You can easily identify her from her big nose,' the MC continued helpfully. At this, the bupati himself turned around from his throne-like chair to seek out the unusually large proboscis. He nodded in acknowledgement once he'd spotted it and turned his attention back to the stage, where the MC was now urging him onto the stage to declare perang topat officially open.

A few minutes later, a roar filled the air, accompanied by gobs of sticky rice being flung about. It was mostly skinny young men doing the throwing, with the women and the elderly looking on from under umbrellas. Fifteen minutes on, a policeman's whistle signalled the end of the event and people immediately began to swarm towards the exits, carrying armfuls of rice cakes away with them. The bupati had already departed after having thrown a single symbolic rice cake towards no one in particular.

Chapter VI

Tofu

Tikus

'What's the matter, rat got your tongue?' Tikus asked, startling me.

I was looking up at the clouds. They were so dense, although every once in a while they parted and the blue sky shone through. I thought that perhaps sadness was like that too. If you were patient enough, a patch of light would eventually break through.

But then Tikus crept up on me, and I forgot about sadness and clouds. Who would have imagined that a rat could be so enthralling? It was a benefit of the rat's job, Tikus said, to know the best stories. 'We squeeze into gardens and skulk under furniture. We're inside cupboards and behind sinks. There is no one who knows more about the lives of Orang than we do,' he'd hissed dramatically. But it was true.

The hours melted away when Tikus talked about the scenes he'd witnessed on his foraging expeditions. He told me about one family in the lane behind ours who owned a TV set that was so huge, it filled an entire wall of their living room. They had a servant whose only job was to clean the TV screen all day. She started with a dust cloth in the morning and slowly worked her way across the gigantic surface, left to right. Then she would fetch a ladder and start rubbing from top to bottom. When she was done, she simply started again at the beginning. 'And, do you know?' snorted Tikus. 'I've never seen anyone actually watch that TV!'

In another area called Kemang, across the main road near our house, Tikus was a regular visitor to a mansion where there were always bits of the choicest morsels to be found on the floors. The family's only child never sat down to eat. Instead, he ran about all day, grazing from the outstretched spoons and forks held out by a battalion of nannies stationed across the house, bearing bowls of his favourite foods: watermelon slices, fried bananas, chicken satay and chocolate donuts.

'There's always an overflow onto the floor. If the nannies stoop down to pick up the dropped food, they risk a screaming fit from the brat because the piece of watermelon or whatever it is that he expects to be

available to him, at mouth-level, at all times, is not there. What a place. It's a pa*rat*adise,' Tikus had grinned naughtily, his sharp teeth glinting.

Littered with the homes of the rich, and their excess food, our neighbourhood was prime real estate for rats. Tikus explained that his family had to fight off rival gangs of rodents almost every day in order to maintain their territory. The stakes were high. Many of his cousins operated only a few kilometres away in a kampung. 'Kampung' meant village in Bahasa Indonesia, but it was also a way to describe a slum.

Kampung was where the servants and nannies, who cleaned TV screens and followed fat children around with plates of food, lived. Their one-room shacks were hot and overcrowded. Stinking, open sewers lined the narrow streets. Tikus said that the Ren who lived here washed their clothes and even their dishes over these drains. The water they drank often made their children ill. And they were constantly bitten by mosquitoes. Sometimes after being bitten, they got such high fevers that they died.

Most rats lived in areas like these because there were no beady-eyed security guards to chase them away. And there was easy access in and out of the drains. 'The Orang who live in kampung are like Orang Rats,' Tikus once told me. 'No one likes them. And they are seen as dirty, like us.'

I'd understood immediately. I had been born in a dented dustbin. My family were Dustbin Cats, and I had once lived with the Dustbin Ren who had come from the poorest villages in China to build sports stadiums in Beijing for the Olympic Games. Yunqi could be a heavy burden.

One or the other of Tikus' kampung cousins died every day, but so many were born that their numbers only grew. They lived their short lives on the verge of starvation. Tikus and his siblings took scraps of satay or bakso or anything tasty to them, whenever they could spare the time.

For not only could rats be enthralling storytellers, they were also kind. Becoming friends with Tikus had brought many surprises. Sometimes, I felt a pang of jealousy when he talked about his large family and how they looked out for each other. Every cut-off tail or injured foot was soothed. Every bite was licked. It made me miss my own brothers. There were five of us once, but we were scattered to the wind now, and I had drifted the furthest.

It wasn't always easy following Tikus' stories because all of his family were also called Tikus. There were hundreds and hundreds of them scampering along Jakarta's sewers. For my sake, he tried identifying them by adding their relationship to him in front of their names. 'Aunty Number Two – Tikus had a terrible day yesterday,' he might say.

He explained that to rats, each Tikus sounded unique because it involved a tiny difference in the pitch of the squeak. Once again, I understood him quickly. Tikus in rat language was like Chinese, except with limitless tones. Chinese, the way it was spoken by Ren in Beijing, had four tones. The same word in a different tone could mean a completely different thing. Tang, for example, could mean soup, sugar, or boiling hot, depending on whether it was said in a flat tone, a rising tone, or in a falling tone. It was like singing. Which made me realize that perhaps a squeaking rat could also sound quite musical. It depended on how you decided to listen.

Tikus was a bit grumpy today. He said he'd been next door all morning at the home with which our garden shared a boundary wall. I had never seen the Ren who lived there. The wall was too high for me to jump up onto. But Tikus was convinced that there was something peculiar about the place.

'They have six, SIX, fancy cars lined up in the driveway, and they can't be bothered to put out a dustbin for their sampah, their garbage? How do you explain that?' he asked, more to himself than me.

I agreed that it was strange. I'd caught Mr and Mrs A discussing it too. Before Mrs A went away on her trip, she'd asked Ibu Mari to talk to the helper next door about the trash problem. Instead of putting their rubbish in the tall steel cans placed in the driveway, like all the other houses, our neighbour dumped his trash in unfastened plastic bags onto the pavement outside his front door. The garbage man, Pak Jubaid, only came around to collect these three times a week. For the rest of the time, a mess of eggshells, milk cartons, chicken bones and other smelly things lay strewn outside, often spilling out in front of our garden wall as well.

Mrs A was convinced it was why Tikus liked to come into our garden. I guess, that was part of it. The trash was like the gateway, but beyond the garbage, the rat came because it was pretty here. He liked a break from the foul drains in which he slept. And now that we were friends, we both enjoyed our chats. The stories he told me about the World reminded me of my conversations with Da Ge in Beijing. There were so many exciting things to learn; all the better because I could learn them from the safety of home.

At first, I'd found Tikus' contempt for the neighbour's dirty habits unexpected. But he'd explained that although objectively throwing sampah about was good for rats, it also lowered the high-class reputation of this neighbourhood. Tikus and his family felt satisfaction in being the rats of our area. It brought them status. 'As my Older Brother Number Four–Tikus says: we might not be a pride of rats – because we're a pack – but we still have pride *as* rats,' Tikus declared, whiskers aquiver.

The strewn sampah wasn't Tikus' only gripe with the neighbour. The rat had an uncomfortable feeling about the whole place. He said that the house was often filled with people dressed in white, who spent a lot of time typing on computers. There were so many different Ren that Tikus wasn't even sure who the owner actually was. Sometimes, they gathered in a large room on the second floor and held meetings. 'They open a book and read out from it,'

Tikus said. 'And they complain a lot about foreigners in the neighbourhood.'

'What about them?' I asked, my heart suddenly skipping a beat.

'Oh, that they have loud parties and drink wine and dress the wrong way. Look different, smell different, eat different. Everything different! But, what's wrong with being different?' Tikus snorted. 'I'll tell you what. Nothing! Nothing at all.' I felt an utterly impossible rush of love for this rat. '*We're* different, Tofu; you and I,' he said and he didn't need to say more.

But Tikus wasn't done yet. 'That place is just so gloomy, Tofu. The shades are always down. I might as well stay in the sewer, what with the garbage and the dark,' he snorted. 'And all those Orang look so angry, thumping their books and frowning.'

The rat paused, suddenly uncertain. 'There's one other thing.'

'What?' I whispered, but my tail already knew that I would not like the answer. It drooped.

'It's about Pa'harto.'

Pa'harto? I was confused. Was Tikus talking about the As' driver?

'What?' I asked again.

'I'm not sure,' said Tikus, sitting back on his haunches. 'They were complaining about him. I was on a high shelf when I overheard, so the voices weren't clear.

Something about him having a bad character.' He looked uncomfortable. 'Something about teaching him a lesson.'

My skin crawled like a thousand fleas were running on it. Pa'harto was the kindest Ren in this house. I didn't spend much time with him because it was difficult for me to be around Ren in general. But I knew instinctively that he could be trusted. Soyabean took every chance he got to jump onto the driver's lap for a cuddle. And Pa'harto never refused, even though Soyabean must be rather heavy.

The children loved him too. Before helping Nico into the car, Pa'harto sometimes lifted the boy high into the air and flew him around like he was an airplane. Nico's laugh was the happiest sound in the World. It could part any clouds and the sky that showed through was the brightest blue. Pa'harto did not have all his teeth, but what he did have, without any doubt, was a good character.

I turned towards the driveway. It was partially hidden by the frangipani tree, but I could see the driver sitting on a stool next to the parked car. He'd slipped off his shoes and had one leg crossed over the other. His flowery shirt was unbuttoned almost to his large stomach, and he wiggled a foot in time to the dangdut that Pak Nono was blasting from the radio. The security guard was smoking under the covered garage at the end of the driveway.

Pa'harto looked up and caught me staring at him. He smiled kindly. 'Ke sini! Come to Pak, little cat!' he called. Oh, no! Tikus! If any of the Ren spotted the rat, he'd be in trouble. I whirled around, but thankfully, Tikus had disappeared. He was an expert at making himself scarce at the right moment.

Pa'harto was now slapping his thighs and making clucking noises, trying to attract my attention. Ren did that a lot. I've never figured out why they don't understand that if we happen to be ignoring them, it's on purpose. I looked away from the driver and stretched out on the grass, turning my head towards the sky. Pa'harto went back to his newspaper. Then, just as I was getting ready to go back into the house, the angry growl of an ojek shattered the calm.

I jumped up and hid behind a nearby bush. Whoever was driving that ojek was now hammering loudly on the gate. Pa'harto looked towards the noise and then back at Pak Nono who was standing with his arms by his side and his mouth slightly open, staring. 'Open up. Go on,' Pa'harto urged. His words seemed to unfreeze the security guard who began to jog forward, calling out, 'I'm coming, I'm coming!' But the hammering didn't stop.

Pak Nono unfastened the bolt and had only just started to push the doors open, when a bony, fierce-looking Ren, burst in. I recognized him at once. It was Pak Eman, Ibu Mari's kiai husband. His strangely pale eyes flashed in his dark face. He looked very angry, this Ren. I peeked out of the bush as far as I dared and took a good look at him. He was dressed, like I'd always seen him, in a long white shirt and loose trousers. His beard had grown longer than I recalled, but his lips were as fat as ever.

He pushed past Pak Nono roughly and marched up the driveway. 'Where's Mari?' he barked. 'She's with the children inside the house,' Pa'harto replied. 'Come, have a seat here while you wait.'

The driver heaved himself off the stool that he'd been sitting on and offered it to Pak Eman. But the kiai only curled his fleshy lips and took out a phone from his shirt pocket. I edged closer. This Ren needed an eye to be kept on him.

'I'm outside,' he said curtly into the phone, and then, 'How long?'

I couldn't hear the answer, but I assumed he was talking to Ibu Mari.

The conversation over, Pak Eman stuffed the phone back in his pocket, and began pacing up and down the driveway, glancing at his watch every few moments. Pak Nono and Pa'harto exchanged looks. The driver shrugged and opened up the newspaper he'd been reading again. But Pak Nono approached the kiai. 'Would you like some tea?' he asked.

'No!' snapped Pak Eman, without even looking at the security guard. 'I don't drink tea. Water is enough for the pure.'

'Well then, sorry for asking,' said Pak Nono. He walked across to where Pa'harto was sitting and lit up a clove cigarette. 'How about a smoke? Would you like a cigarette, kiai?' he called out.

I think he was teasing him, but Pak Eman did not look amused. 'It's a disgusting habit,' he said. 'Blackens the heart as much as the teeth.'

Pak Nono laughed, showing off his stained teeth. 'Well, white clothes don't automatically make for a white heart, kiai. Kindness does. And a little dancing.' The security guard began to prance about, wiggling and thrusting his hips to the beat of the song playing on the radio. 'Come on, kiai,' he called out, extending his hands towards Pak Eman. 'Come, dance with me. This song is one of my favourites.'

I flattened my ears. My body was preparing for something before I was even aware that there was going to be a something. Pak Eman walked over very slowly to where Pak Nono stood. He was shorter than the security guard, but his anger made him dangerous.

'You fool,' he roared, spit spraying from his mouth. 'You listen to this corrupt music instead of the Lord's prayers.'

Pak Nono shrank back, shocked at the poison in Pak Eman's tone.

'What do you *do* with your life?' the kiai asked. 'Life is a gift from God. And you spend it smoking and drinking tea. You will rot in hell, Nono, that much I am certain about.'

Pa'harto got up to his feet and tried to get between the two Ren. 'Now, now, kiai,' he said soothingly. 'Why are you so angry? To each their own. Let others live their lives in their own way, Pak. No one has all the answers. We are all trying to make our way through this world the best we can. Everyone makes mistakes.' He put his hand on Pak Eman's shoulder.

But the kiai flung it off. He turned to Pa'harto, bringing his face close to the driver's. 'Don't you touch me, you dirty, faithless old man,' he said, each word like a blow. 'Serving these foreign people. Drinking alcohol at their parties. The Lord knows I have told Mari to leave, but that sampah of a woman won't listen to me. What kind of a job does she do? Looking after filthy animals and half-breed children!'

Both Pa'harto and Pak Nono were now backed up against the wall, staring at Pak Eman as he raged, his voice rising higher and higher. 'But these days will soon be over, I can tell both of you that for sure. Indonesia is no longer going to tolerate this corruption of the soul. We will be cleansed. And that means getting rid of the likes of you.' Pak Eman pointed a shaking finger at Pa'harto.

'Stop it. Please, stop it now. The children can hear you!' It was Ibu Mari. She had come hurrying down the back stairs that led directly from the kitchen into the garage. She was close to tears as she pleaded. Pak Eman turned furiously to face Ibu Mari and there was so much anger in him that I felt he was going to hit her; and I knew with every standing hair on my body that I would gouge his eyes out if he did.

Chapter VII

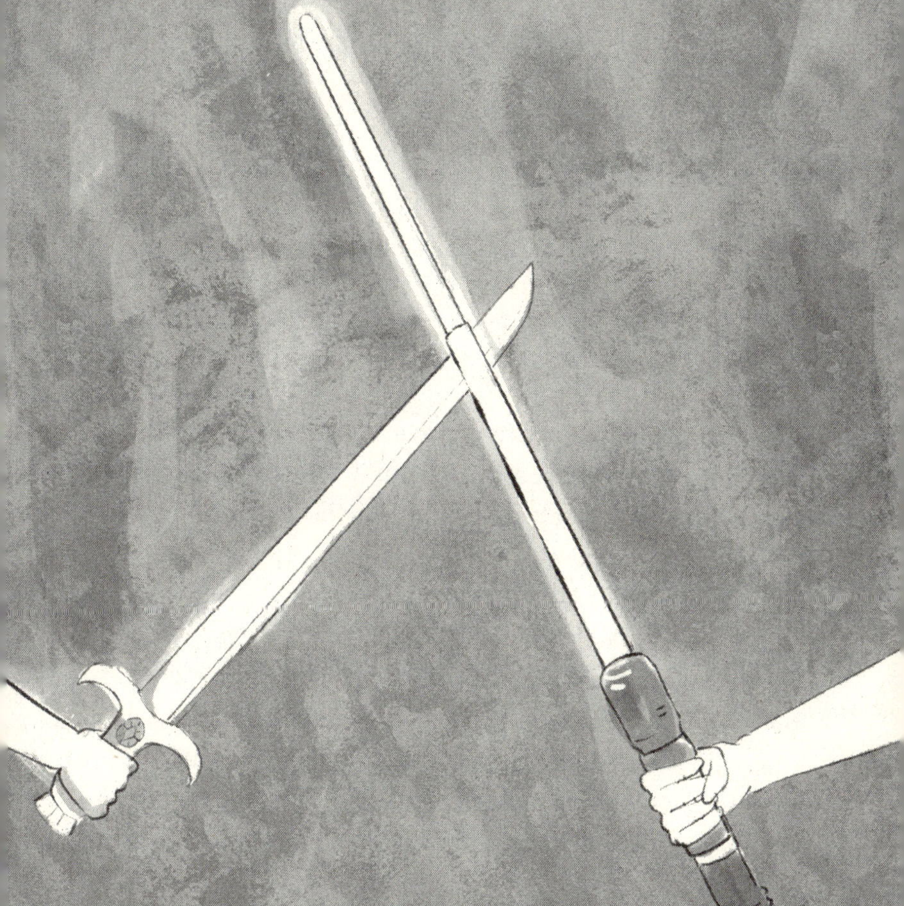

Soyabean

Darth Sidious vs God

It's the third time I'm trying to get up this dratted wall. Why does it have to be so high? Couldn't Orang architects be more considerate towards those who may no longer be as sprightly as they once were. But I suppose one may as well wish that Orang were quicker on the uptake in general. Well, a cat must make the best of what is.

My nails are almost filed off from all the sliding down the wall they've suffered on the last two attempts. But this time, I'm going to make it. Watch me soar, like an eagle, into the air. I crouch, gathering strength into my powerful hind legs, ready to spring. Hang on a second. There's an urgent itch behind my ear that I need to take care of.

Okay. That's better. I'm ready now. Deep breath, razor-sharp focus on the goal: the top of the wall. I uncoil and fly: up, up and... *Splat!* My ears clear the top, but my snout hits the concrete. Another slow, nail-scraping descent. The indignity is shocking. I'd give up, if curiosity didn't kill me so. Something is going on next door. I can hear heaving and scraping. Mrs A and Ibu Mari have gone outside to look, but I'm stuck behind this absurdly high barricade.

Perhaps, I should get a snack to recharge. A little egg yolk would hit the spot. But whom am I kidding? I'd have more luck getting Ibu Warsi to wander about on all fours, meowing for a tummy rub, than feed me an egg. The best I can hope for is a boring pour of kibble. Hmm. Maybe a scratch on the frangipani tree? Or not. My nails have had more than enough of a filing for one day.

I look around the garden. Everything is as it should be. The grass is still bright and damp from the rain this morning. And there's a muddy puddle in the corner that might be fun to roll about in later. The driveway is empty. I suppose Pa'harto has gone to pick up the children from school. Pak Nono is outside with the others, watching whatever is going on. It's a rare, rat-less moment too; although that's no thanks to Tofu. The crazy cat has begun to spend more time with random rodents than with me. She's encouraged them to no end. They frolic about without a care, as though they own the place.

Okay. I think a last, last try is in order. Taking a deep breath, I tense, ready and release. I stretch my paws out as far as I can. I'm in the air, and still in the air, and yes, my paws touch the wall! For a moment, I'm hanging. Yikes! I shouldn't have eaten so much breakfast. I can feel that can of tuna dragging me down. But my sinewy forearms kick into action and I pull myself up. I am king of the wall, conqueror of heights, Soyabean the Spectacular.

Scrape, scrape, *thud*. The curious goings on that I can finally see distract me from being impressed with myself. The noises are coming from a scruffy Orang, who seems to be building some kind of partition on the pavement in front of our row of homes. He's stacked up a low line of bricks so that it divides the path in front of the neighbour's house from ours. Strange. Why?

I spot Mrs A, Ibu Mari and Pak Nono huddled together outside our front gate. They're staring at the Orang too. Mrs A looks annoyed. I pad across the wall until I'm right above their heads and can listen in.

'Ibu Mari, but what happened exactly? Can you tell me again? In detail,' Mrs A is saying. Ibu Mari is wearing a jilbab. Something she's started to do even when she's inside the house. Also, the circles around her eyes are becoming very dark. Could she be sick?

'I go yesterday in the afternoon, like you say me, Ibu,' Ibu Mari replies. 'The pembantu answer, but only after Mari knocking on gate for long time.' 'Do you know who she is?' Mrs A interrupts. 'No. It was man, Ibu. He only open gate very little, so Mari cannot see inside.'

'I ask to talk to the Mister because I have message from you, but pembantu say he not home. I ask when he come back. Pembantu say he not know, but maybe very late. He say I should tell him the message and he would tell to his Mister.'

She then adds, 'So, I explain about rat coming in our garden, because of all sampah they throw outside gate. I say some also spill in front of our house wall. I ask why they not put in trashcan, like everyone else. I say my Mister and Misses want to talk to his Mister to discuss.'

'Could you see inside? What was it like?' Mrs A asks.

'Only little bit, Ibu. The pembantu block view. Mari can see many cars parked in the garage. And there is bad smell. Rotting sampah, maybe.'

'What on earth is wrong with these people,' fumes Mrs A. 'They have no standards of hygiene at all. The entire neighbourhood could fall ill. It's ridiculous! And, what? Now, they're making a partition?

'Yes, Ibu. Mari talk to pembantu again this morning. He say his Mister say the wall will make sampah stay in front of their house, not spilling our side.'

'Are you serious? They'd rather build a wall than just get a trashcan? Who is this man? Neither of you know anything about him at all?' Mrs A asks, throwing her hands up.

Ibu Mari shakes her head and Mrs A turns to Pak Nono. 'Pak, can you go over later and see if you have better luck getting us a meeting with him?'

Ibu Mari is staring at Mrs A's back strangely. She opens and closes her mouth, and fiddles with her jilbab. I don't think Mrs A's noticed, but my cat senses are particularly acute. Something is wrong with our nanny. I'd bet my whiskers on it.

Ever since her husband came around yelling at everyone, she's changed. I rarely see her smiling these days, and she's stopped her tea sessions with Pak Nono.

I was napping at the time of the husband incident, but Tofu told me everything. It was lucky that Mrs A had returned from her trip to Lombok at just the moment she had. Tofu said she was worried the husband might actually have *hit* Ibu Mari if Mrs A's taxi horn hadn't blown just then.

Pak Eman had left in a huff once Mrs A arrived, and we haven't seen him since. But Ibu Mari has gone all droopy. If she had a tail it would be tucked between her legs, she seems that sad.

'Bu, one thing there is,' Pak Nono is saying. 'Sometime Pak Nono wake up in night because next door gate is loudly close. Nono think many people coming and going there in night.'

'What? That guy has friends? He has parties?' Mrs A frowns. 'Pak Nono, we really need to get to the bottom of this. Does he have a family? Does he live in that huge house all alone? It's bizarre to know so little about your neighbours.'

Yes. It is odd. In Beijing we had neighbours coming out of our ears. There was Xiao Wang and his pet crickets, and Old Lady Fang, who ran the corner shop. No one came or went in the hutongs without everyone discussing it during gossip sessions outside the public toilet. But here, the walls are so high and the cars have tinted windows, and the toilets are very private. You can see the pembantus arriving for work sometimes, but the owners might as well be invisible.

Mrs A and Ibu Mari are going back in. I suppose I should too. Oh wait, here's Pa'harto driving up. The kids are back. I think they deserve a little treat after a long, hard day at school. Perhaps I'll allow them to pet me. Except, it isn't much easier jumping off this accursed wall than getting up it. *Ouch!* Hard landing. I think I'll just lie here for a minute to recover.

I haven't even got my breath back when the screams start. The car doors are open and an endless number of shouting children are tumbling out. By my whiskers, it's Keanu, Krisna and Kei: monsters masquerading as Ishaan's friends. I've been at their mercy before, during demonic rituals called playdates. Oh, the poking, prodding, the indignities!

Ripples of terror paralyze me even though I know I should run like the wind. But my girth and my beautiful, vivid colour betray me yet again. The children have spotted me in the garden. I meow pathetically. Pa'harto shoots me a sympathetic glance.

'Let's play with Soyabean,' one of them yells, and the pack bears down on me, as I watch, helpless. Time slows down. I can see their little faces screwed up in grotesque grimaces as they run across the garden.

'He's so fat,' says Keanu, as they crowd around me. This boy should speak for his own big fat self. He's a particularly nasty one, with his glasses and spotty face.

'Awww,' says Kei. 'Soyabean's cute.' Now, that's better. Yes, this Kei child is a tad more bearable than the rest.

I close my eyes in resignation and roll over onto my back. I've learnt from bitter experience that to give in is the best way to bore them into leaving me alone. But, for the moment, their breath is on me. It's clear none of them are sticklers for dental hygiene. In fact, cleanliness of any kind is not their strong suit. Sticky fingers attack from all sides. Should I give them a lick? Remnants of jam sandwiches might linger on them.

'What exactly does he *do* all day long?' It's that spotty Keanu again. I'm trying to keep my cool. My Nai Nai used to say that in bad times it's helpful to remember that day always follows night. Well, this is pretty black. I need a new day. Pronto.

Now I'm being lifted up. I think by Ishaan. 'Let's take him inside.' And then: 'Wow, he's heavy.' Well, no one asked you to carry me about, did they? After being half dragged into the house, we are all in the playroom. The boys plonk me on the sofa and gather about arguing about how best to torture me.

'Should we play Star Wars?' suggests Krisna, the shortest and skinniest of the bunch.

'Yes, let's! Soyabean can be Darth Maul,' chimes in Ishaan. Traitor! No cuddles for him tonight.

'Let's attack him with swords?' says Keanu eagerly.

'Or maybe he can be Princess Padme, and we can be jedis rescuing him from Darth Maul?' adds Kei.

Will the sun ever dawn on this long night?

Nico produces a collection of lightsabers and swords as I hunker down for the worst. The boys grab one each and begin hacking at each other with bloodcurdling battle cries. It's hellish, but has the fortunate effect of summoning Mrs A.

'Come on, boys! Put those away. You could hurt each other,' she says. 'Let's have a snack, shall we? You must be hungry after school.' She goes into the kitchen and comes back a few minutes later with plates of grapes and cookies. Ibu Mari follows with a carton of orange juice and some glasses. I could do with a snack too, but of course, no one concerns themselves with my needs.

The boys settle around the table and reach for the food, the lightsabers mercifully forgotten on the floor. Mrs A leaves them to it. She's always locked away in her study, typing on her computer these days. The room remains off limits to me. A pity that my potential as a muse is so underappreciated.

I position myself under the table, alert to stray crumbs. The boys are yapping.

'Is Albert Einstein real?' asks Kei.

'And what about Frank Einstein?' says Nico.

'Gosh, you are so dumb, Nico!' Ishaan snaps. 'It's Frankenstein, not Frank Einstein.'

The older boys snicker. Cookie crumbs hail down. It's just as Nai Nai said. The night is passing and the dawn is sweet.

The conversation drifts back to *Star Wars*. I cast a nervous eye at the lightsabers, but they still lie forgotten. 'Can Batman defeat Darth Sidious?' Nico asks.

'No, dummy!' smirks Ishaan.

'Can a megalodon defeat Darth Sidious?' Nico persists in a sing-song voice.

'Noooo,' groans Ishaan. The other boys chuckle.

'Can God defeat Darth Sidious?' asks Nico.

Ishaan opens his mouth and then stops short as though unsure of the answer.

'I'm not sure God is real,' he says eventually.

'That's true,' Nico agrees. 'I've never seen God on TV.'

Krisna and Kei burst out laughing. 'Ishaan, your brother *is* so dumb,' sputters Kei. Ishaan grins, but Nico's face has crumpled.

'I am *not* dumb,' he shouts and leans over to hit Ishaan on the head.

'Ow! Stop that,' yells Ishaan, and the two are about to go for each other, when Keanu abruptly gets up and puts his hands over his ears. 'You shouldn't talk like that,' he says loudly.

So far I've been taking in the chatter with only one ear. But there's something in that porky Keanu's tone that makes me pay attention. He's gone purple in the face. The boys have fallen silent and are staring at him. 'You shouldn't talk like that,' he repeats. 'Like what?' asks Ishaan. 'I don't know what you mean.'

'About God, like that,' Keanu shouts. 'It's wrong. My parents wouldn't like it. I don't like it. You are not good people.'

Everyone just sits there. I consider meowing, if only to break the silence, but perhaps it's better if I remain unnoticed. This Keanu kid seems a bit crazy. 'I want to go home,' he says, tears in his voice. 'Now! Can your driver take me?'

'What? Are you serious,' asks Krisna, finally finding his voice. 'Come on, Keanu. We were just joking. What's your problem?'

Keanu has gone even more puffy faced and is refusing to look at anyone. 'We shouldn't joke about God. It means you are a bad person, and you will suffer after you die,' he says, eyes screwed shut. 'I don't like it here. I should have listened to my parents. This is not a good house. It's because you do not have a religion.'

Ishaan flushes red. 'What do you mean, Keanu?' he asks. 'I do have a religion.'

'Really?' Keanu looks at Ishaan. 'Well then, what is it?'

Now everyone is looking at Ishaan. 'Actually, what is your religion, Ishaan?' asks Krisna. 'You aren't in any religious study class at school. You do that moral studies thing instead. Why? Doesn't you family believe?'

Ishaan looks as distraught as Keanu looks triumphant. A growl is working its way up my throat. I don't like his spotty face. A scratch or two, or three, amidst those spots might be in order. But before I can make up my mind, I notice Tofu. It's spooky how she just emerges from the shadows. She walks up to Ishaan's feet and puts her nose on his legs. I love this cat, rat-friend or no rat-friend.

Ishaan is struggling to hold his tears back. 'We *are* good people. This *is* a good house. You guys are my friends. Why are you being so mean?' Both Tofu and I rub our cheeks against his legs. But it is Nico who has picked up a lightsaber and is pointing it at Keanu.

'Leave my brother alone,' he says, holding the toy steady, even though his voice is shaking. 'Of course we believe. We believe in the Jedi. And in Superman too.'

Chapter VIII

Mrs A

Dark Times Call for Poetry

Mrs A sat out on the verandah by the garden, staring moodily at her laptop. The story was due in a few days, but progress was elusive. The air was distractingly still, and she felt a bead of sweat trailing down her cheek. Wiping it off, she moved her neck in small circles, trying to ease the pressure building up around her shoulders.

Her trip to Lombok had proved disheartening. The story was not going to have Pak Hendra eating humble pie like she had once naively, if gloriously, imagined. Worse, it was turning out to be complex. And there was nothing that seemed to give magazine editors ulcers like complexity. The last email she'd received from her boss had smarted: 'It isn't clear what point you are making.' The cold fact was that she agreed, because she was no longer sure herself what the point was.

What was the real Indonesia? Were the things that had attracted her – the pluralism, the mixing and mingling – real? Or was it all rose-tinted glasses disguising hate and prejudice? The answer felt existentially important, but no matter how much she edited and shifted paragraphs around, it remained just out of her grasp.

Tofu's whiskers tickled her shin. The cat was rubbing her cheek against Mrs A's leg. She felt a rush of love for this dearest of cats with the roundest of eyes. Bending down, she scooped her up onto her lap. 'Gorgeous thing,' she whispered as Tofu wetly nosed Mrs A's neck. They looked at each other.

'What are you thinking?' mused Mrs A. 'What do *you* make of this world?' Tofu met her eyes steadily. 'Do you like it here, baby cat? It's so hot, isn't it? I bet you wish you could take off all that fur.'

Mrs A sighed and thought, not for the first time, how much nicer it was to be a cat than a human. 'It doesn't matter if it's a black cat or a white cat as long as it catches rats,' she murmured, and bent her head down to snuggle against Tofu when she felt the cat stiffen under her. 'What? What's the matter?' she asked following Tofu's gaze towards the corner of the garden.

A moment later, she was on her feet screaming, having dropped Tofu unceremoniously. 'Pak Nooonooo, that rat is here again. Come! Come quickly.' Mrs A hopped around, disgust rippling up and down her body. She squeezed her eyes shut to erase the image of the rat's creeping scaly tail, but her skin broke out into goosebumps as the dark, furry body forced itself into her mind.

'Ibu? Is everything okay?' Pak Nono finally appeared, panting.

He shouldn't smoke so much, Mrs A thought, even as she pointed towards the rat. But the rodent was gone. 'Oh! Thank goodness,' she gasped. 'It's run off. But we can't have this happening so much. Rats in the garden. It's disgusting, Pak. Yuck!

'And have you figured out anything about the neighbour? That little partition of his hasn't helped much, has it?'

The security guard scratched his balding head. 'Ibu, Pak Nono go many time, but always only pembantu open gate, say the Mister not home. Even Pak Jubaid very angry. He must to lift all rubbish they throw with hands only. Very dirty.'

'Pak Jubaid's the garbage collector? Why doesn't he complain?' Mrs A asked.

'He try, Ibu, but pembantu say him go away. And he cannot make too big noise. Pak Jubaid only little man. What he do if lose job?'

Mrs A felt a stab of guilt. People could be so callous. Was she callous too? What gave her the right to be the 'Misses' of this huge house, attended to by a gaggle of helpers. She was especially worried about Ibu Mari. It was like something had switched off inside the nanny. She no longer flounced around the house trying to get Ibu Warsi's goat. The song was gone from her, quite literally. Mrs A hadn't seen her singing along to Pak Nono's dangdut music for ages. Not since she'd returned from Lombok.

No one had been forthcoming about what had gone down with Ibu Mari's husband, but Mrs A knew something was awry. The way that Pak Eman had glared at her, his face ugly with accusation, as she'd gotten out of the taxi, had been unsettling. The kiai had taken off on his ojek almost immediately after, without so much as exchanging a greeting. Pa'harto and Pak Nono had busied themselves helping with her luggage with a mechanical politeness, but had refused to make eye contact. And Ibu Mari had disappeared into the bathroom for a long time.

There was a time she'd been considering asking Ibu Mari to help organize a reporting trip to the pesantren where Pak Eman taught. Mrs A thought a spotlight on these religious boarding schools might help dispel some of the stereotypes about them as breeding grounds of a radical, even violent, theology. She had met a few graduates of these schools in Indonesia, who had described the experience to her in completely different terms: as places of camaraderie and character-building.

Pesantren still interested her, but now did not seem like a good time to approach Ibu Mari about her husband. There was obviously bad feeling there. It was difficult to know how much to intervene, unsolicited, in another person's private relationships. But Mari was her employee and she had a responsibility to her. Mrs A felt overcome by a sense of helplessness that was becoming depressingly familiar of late; of layers unpeeling to reveal a world off-balance.

A loud rap sounded on the front gate. Mrs A started. 'Pak Nono,' she called out to the security guard, who had already begun to move towards the gates. 'That will be my friend, Pak Hendra. Could you let him in, please?' A few seconds later Pak Nono unlatched the doors to reveal the bespectacled Indonesian journalist, standing next to a pretty young woman dressed smartly in trousers and a batik top. Mrs A waved them in. 'Selamat siang! Come in, come on in.'

Pak Hendra nudged his companion forward and the two walked up the driveway briskly. 'Sorry, Bu,' he smiled. 'We got late.'

'Macet?' Mrs A asked.

'Of course,' replied the journalist. 'This is Jakarta after all. But it is worse than ever, if you can imagine that, by everything being dug up along Jalan Antasari. It's the MRT, Bu. The President claims it might actually start working while, God willing, we are still on this earth!'

Mrs A laughed. The MRT was a mass rapid transit system that the Indonesian government had been touting as the solution to Jakarta's epic traffic jams for well over two decades. Successive leaders had held groundbreaking ceremonies to launch the project, but dug up roads were where the progress always seemed to halt. The current President had promised rapid implementation and digging was taking place with renewed vigour, but bitter experience had left most Jakartans cynical of the outcome.

'Should we go inside to chat?' suggested Mrs A. 'This garden looks lovely, but it's not to be trusted. There are rats around.' She was ready to launch into a diatribe about the neighbour's habits, but Pak Hendra seemed distracted. His thoughts were still with the MRT as he followed her into the house.

'Don't get me wrong, Bu,' he said, accepting a glass of water from the tray that Ibu Warsi carried out to the table in the family room. 'This city needs the MRT as much as a starving man needs rice. If this government can pull it off, I will forgive them many of their other sins.'

'Are there that many sins to forgive, Pak?' asked Mrs A, standing up to help Ibu Warsi put bowls of nuts and fruit down. 'Is there much water in the ocean, Bu?' Pak Hendra retorted, eyes creased in amusement. 'But I am forgetting my manners. Let me introduce you to my friend, Debbie.'

The slender woman accompanying Pak Hendra had so far been silent. Now she placed her right palm over her heart and bowed slightly in greeting. 'I'm sorry to come to your house like this, without any invitation. But Pak Hendra said you wouldn't mind.'

'I don't. Of course not,' Mrs A said quickly. 'You're very welcome, Ibu.'

'Debbie is an atheist,' said Pak Hendra casually, before helping himself to a slice of watermelon as a prelude to a long monologue on the putative benefits of the MRT. Mrs A felt it was an odd way to introduce someone, but couldn't think of how to pursue more information about Pak Hendra's unexpected guest without seeming rude.

Debbie sat back in her chair with the indulgent smile of someone used to listening to Pak Hendra's voluminous views on the state of mankind's affairs. 'You see,' he held forth, 'the MRT won't just ease congestion, it could be the greatest boost to our city's health. You know, Bu, how we spend hours sitting around in traffic every day? The obesity, the stress. It's terrible!'

He broke off mid-flow to bend down. 'Oh, selamat siang! Who are you, little kucing?' Tofu looked up unblinkingly at Pak Hendra. The cat had disappeared and then appeared again as was her custom.

'That's Tofu,' Mrs A said. 'I've rarely seen her be so friendly towards a stranger before, Pak. She's usually really jumpy around people.'

'Perhaps we have met in another life, this cat and I,' said Pak Hendra, 'and so we are not strangers after all.'

It was difficult for Mrs A to tell if he was joking. Tofu certainly seemed to recognize him as she settled at the journalist's feet, looking uncharacteristically relaxed.

Pak Hendra turned his attention back to the snacks on offer. 'So, Bu,' he said starting on a second slice of watermelon. 'How are you feeling about Indonesia these days? You had said you were going to Lombok for perang topat. What did you think?'

Mrs A felt a flush rising. 'It was interesting, Pak,' she said finally. 'The tradition is really unique.'

'And?' persisted Pak Hendra.

'And, obviously, it's complicated,' said Mrs A, hating her use of the word.

But Pak Hendra only chuckled. 'Indeed, Bu. It is that. It is always that, don't you think? In a country like ours, there are many truths. And why shouldn't there be? There are, after all, many people and many customs. What was that famous quote by Oscar Wilde?'

'The truth is rarely pure and never simple,' muttered Mrs A.

'Yes, exactly,' beamed Pak Hendra. 'But we mustn't let that lead us to believe that we cannot judge right from wrong. Now that would be dangerous indeed.'

The journalist leaned back into his chair and took off his glasses. He reached for the handkerchief that peeped out from his shirt pocket and carefully began to clean the lenses, blowing on the glass before each wipe. 'Ibu,' he said casually, 'I wonder if you have heard about my recent troubles?'

Mrs A shook her head. 'No. No, I haven't. What's wrong? What kind of trouble?' Her hands twisted nervously in her lap.

Pak Hendra fluttered his fingers in the air dismissively. 'Nothing terrible, Bu. Nothing to worry about too much. Not yet.'

'But, what?' Mrs A persisted.

He exhaled slowly. 'There have been protests outside my house every day for the last week. They are calling for my arrest.'

'What?' It was as though all other words had been knocked out of Mrs A's throat.

'Apparently, I am an apostate, a blasphemist, the devil himself.' Pak Hendra smiled. 'They say I belong in jail, that I will destroy the fabric of this country.' He laughed out loud. 'I had no idea I was so powerful.'

'But, why?' Mrs A asked. Threads of dread clung to her like sticky cobwebs.

Pak Hendra shook his head. 'Ah! Now, that's where things get interesting, Bu. A month ago, I published a short blog criticizing what had been done to a young man from Sumatra. From Medan. Have you been there, Bu? No? You should go. There's a Little India there. Something for you to write about. But I was telling you about Agus, the young man, who is now rotting in jail. He wrote a Facebook post last year. A Facebook post, Bu! And now he's in jail. Bravo Indonesia!'

'What was the post about?' asked Mrs A.

'Does it matter? What can you possibly say on Facebook that should send you to jail?' The journalist pushed his plate to one side, dribbling watermelon juice onto the table. 'What he said was that he was an atheist. That there was so much suffering in the world that he could not find it in his heart to believe in God. That God was not rational. Something along those lines. How many young people around the world have felt the same, Bu? Millions maybe. But this one is in jail because this one happened to live in this country.'

'He's a good man, Ibu. A teacher,' Debbie spoke up forcefully, even though tears snaked down her face. She made no attempt to wipe them. 'I've known him since university. He's my best friend.'

'Debbie and Agus run a group: Indonesian Atheists,' said Pak Hendra.

'There's a group for atheists in Indonesia?' Mrs A asked, her head spinning.

'Oh yes, Bu,' replied Debbie. 'We need it. A space where we can allow ourselves to think, to breathe. Many of our own parents don't accept our beliefs. Mine tried to get me treated by a doctor. They said I had a mental disease.'

Debbie smiled wanly through her tears. 'Agus was the first person who understood me. Before I met him, I was all alone and so scared. I was afraid of my own thoughts. Wear these clothes, eat this, don't eat that, heaven, hell – none of it made sense to me. I just wanted to work hard and have friends and live well, regardless of clothes or food or the afterlife. I didn't even believe in the afterlife. I didn't believe in god.'

Debbie's voice dropped. 'It's absurd. Even now, even here, I am afraid to say it. I don't believe in god.'

The sound of Pak Hendra chomping on almonds was loud in the pause that followed.

'You have nothing to be afraid of here,' Mrs A said easily. 'I'm not sure why people are threatened by anyone else's beliefs. But I am not. Some believe in ten-headed gods and others in a heaven full of fairies. A belief is only as good as it's believer.'

Debbie nodded. 'It is absurd, isn't it? But whenever I tried talking about my opinions, my mother would start crying and my father would shout, his face so red that I thought he might collapse. I had no friends. In school people realized I thought differently, and it was like I had a disease that no one wanted to catch. They kept away.'

She paused, out of breath, but Mrs A looked at her encouragingly and she continued. 'Then I met Agus, on the very first day of college. He was like a drop of honey in a bowl of vinegar. A group of students had surrounded me in the corridor outside one of the lecture rooms. We were all studying public health, but my hair was uncovered and they couldn't stand that. "Do you have no shame?", "Do you think you're better than us?" They were snarling at me, saying all the standard things that people say when they see my hair. These are people who are unmoved if they see a beggar child wasting away with hunger on the street, Ibu, but the sight of a woman's hair has them agitated. What a joke!'

There was a muffled snort and Debbie started. It was only the cat. 'Tofu tends to sneeze sometimes,' Mrs A said absently as Pak Hendra pulled the cat onto his lap. 'I'll make an appointment with the vet soon, but please, Ibu Debbie, do go on. How did you deal with all the bullying?'

'I found Agus,' Debbie replied simply. 'That's how.' She leaned forward in her chair. 'That day in the college corridor, he happened to walk by and when he noticed what was going on, he intervened. He told everyone to leave me alone. "She wears a jilbab on her heart, where it's important," he said, and no one seemed to know how to respond to that.' Debbie's eyes danced at the memory, clear of the tears that had flooded them earlier.

'I knew in that moment that I finally had a friend. It was all I needed. Oh, Ibu, I don't know if you can understand what it feels like to have just one person with whom you can share a joke. Agus gave me that. Three years later, during our last year at university, we organized our atheist society together.'

The sound of Pak Hendra munching on nuts changed back to that of Pak Hendra slurping on watermelon chunks. Mrs A shot him a shushing look. It was difficult to hear the young woman clearly above the noise.

'We've never caused any trouble,' Debbie said. 'Agus became a high school science teacher in Medan. I moved to Jambi, to the forest in East Sumatra. Do you know it? People are very poor there; it's such a remote place. There are almost no doctors, no hospitals. I've been trying to set up mobile health clinics.'

'But what happened to Agus? How could he be jailed for a Facebook post? I don't understand,' interrupted Mrs A.

'It was some of the teachers at the school he taught in,' said Debbie. 'Agus was popular with his students, but the teachers didn't like him. Maybe he was too much at peace with himself. Agus is a very joyful person. *Was* a joyful person. I doubt there is much happiness in prison.' She took a quick sip of water.

'These teachers, they started a whisper campaign, sending each other WhatsApp messages accusing Agus of being a communist, a non-believer, a criminal. Apparently, these are all the same thing.'

Pak Hendra chuckled, but Mrs A felt her stomach turn.

Debbie continued: 'One evening, last year, maybe a week after he posted that message on Facebook, Agus was stopped by two police officers right outside his house. They asked him to accompany them for his own safety. He called me that evening from the police station. He'd sounded more annoyed than frightened. The cops had told him that WhatsApp rumours were circulating about his communist activities. They said they were worried he might be attacked by some kind of mob.'

'And were there any communist activities?' asked Mrs A.

Debbie snorted. 'Our Indonesian Atheist group had maybe twenty members, at most, in Medan. We met every few weeks in coffee shops or cafés, on the sly, as if we were criminals. We chatted and swapped books. But no, we are not, and never have been communists. We don't believe in Stalin or Mao or Marx any more than we believe in god. We believe in people, Ibu, in human beings.'

Mrs A leaned forward, 'What happened to Agus?' The young woman squeezed her eyes shut. 'The next day, he was formally charged with blasphemy and a month later sentenced to two years in prison. Pak Hendra has been helping us to fight for his release, but...'

'But it hasn't helped,' Pak Hendra finished the sentence.

The journalist picked up Tofu from Pak Hendra's lap and began scratching her under the chin. 'Mrs A, I am a believer. My wife and I, we share a deep faith. Our faith is in a God who is merciful, not vengeful. In a God that no one should be forced to believe in, for forced belief is not what He wants. There are some cultural customs we follow. My wife wears a jilbab. I fast during the holy month. But it is not these things that make God happy. What makes God happy is knowing that His people are kind. And I know, as clearly as I know that God knows, that Ibu Debbie is a good person.

'She might not believe it herself, and maybe she does not care,' Pak Hendra continued, 'but she does, in fact, please God. Not by what she says or what she wears, but by what she does.'

Debbie slid off her chair to kneel by Pak Hendra's. She held on to his armrest. 'Oh, Pak!' she said.

'Debbie is helping to get Orang Rimba, people who live in the deep forest, basic medical attention. Many children there are not vaccinated against even the most common illnesses. They get coughs and die. They get upset stomachs and die. None of the so-called righteous, who are so worked up about Agus' Facebook post, care to visit these places. But Debbie's clinics provide some medicines, some relief. They've even got a volunteer dentist from Medan. If this is not God's work, what is, Bu?'

Mrs A looked from Pak Hendra to Debbie trying to find the right words to respond. She felt outraged, but, at the same time, somehow ashamed at her discomfort. It only brought her cluelessness into relief.

'I'll tell you what is not God's work,' Pak Hendra said. 'The work of internet trolls, the work of spreading fake news, of making lies in the name of the truth. It sickens me. Who are these monsters who whisper their wicked perversions into the winds of the internet?'

Despite herself, Mrs A smiled. 'That's quite poetic, Pak.'

'Dark times call for poetry, Ibu,' smiled Pak Hendra.

Debbie interjected: 'Pak Hendra might joke about this, but he could be in real trouble. If they could lock up Agus for a Facebook post, they can certainly lock up Pak Hendra for publishing a blog in his support. Already there are many tweets going around about how he is a Communist Party member. How he is anti-god. The protestors outside his house do not look like nice men, Ibu. I'm worried.'

'Wah! What is that?' Pak Hendra stood up suddenly, his head cocked towards the windows. 'Can you hear it?'

Mrs A rose to her feet as well. There was definitely some kind of disturbance out on the road – muffled shouting and crashing. And then a loud scream of pain.

'Ibu, hurry!' Pak Nono was at the door, gasping for breath as he frantically signalled to them. 'Come quickly. It's Pa'harto. They killing him.'

Chapter IX

Tofu

Making Lies in the Name of Truth

At first, all I could see was a blur of Ren bodies. They were baring their teeth like beasts at a kill. And then I saw him. Pa'harto bent low in the centre of the circle, hands over his head trying to fight off the blows and kicks. His trousers were torn, stained dark. I could smell blood in the shouts, on the clothes.

'Stop!' Mrs A screamed, as she ran into the blur, the other Ren, Pak Hendra and Debbie, right behind her. They grabbed and tugged at the attackers, but were pushed out of the circle that was closing in tighter and tighter on Pa'harto.

But a cat is smaller. A cat is quicker. And a cat has claws. I spied a narrow gap and, in a flash, I was through it, scratching and biting. I went for eyes, ears, any patch of skin I could see. Hands yanked me off and threw me about, but at least some of the nasty shouting changed to screams of pain.

And then I felt my head explode. A hard slap sent me sprawling onto the road. My skin split. This was what the World was really like: not gentle like the silk cushions on the As' sofas, but rough enough to tear through flesh. I felt a knee in my ribs and a stab of pain somewhere else. My tail? My mouth? It was hard to tell when everything hurt.

I struggled to get up. As I turned my neck, I found myself staring directly into Pa'harto's swollen eyes. He was difficult to recognize without his glasses, with blood running down his face. But he saw me. His mouth formed the word 'kucing', as he moved his hands away from cradling his own head towards me. To cover *me*, to save *me*.

A kick landed on his ribs and he rolled away, until he lay very still. I tried to drag myself over to him, but Pa'harto was swallowed up by all the Ren and their rage and their shouts of 'infidel'. I remained on my side, panting, willing myself back on my feet.

'Is this what your God tells you to do?' Ibu Warsi's voice cut through the din of the mob like a sharpened claw. 'Tell me, good men, in what religion is it acceptable to attack a helpless old man like this? What holy book teaches you to be so cruel?'

'Tell me. What is this authority?' Her words were cold and strong, unwavering. Under their weight, the rabid circle that had formed around Pa'harto went slack. The Ren whose eyes had sparked with hate only a moment ago dulled, like they were suddenly coming back into their own bodies from another place. Some looked at their bruised hands wonderingly.

Ibu Warsi had on the gleaming white mukena she wore to pray. She was tiny, but, at that moment, she seemed taller than all the other Ren. 'In the name of our merciful God,' she roared in Bahasa Indonesia, 'get out of here and leave this good man alone. Go home! Wash your faces and wake up. Wake up to your actions. Try and wake up your hearts.'

Some of the Ren had already begun to slink away. But one of them stood his ground, staring at Ibu Warsi blackly. I recognized him. It was Pak Eman, Ibu Mari's husband.

Mrs A and Pak Hendra were now crouching next to Pa'harto, who remained motionless on the road. 'Pak Nono,' Mrs A turned to the security guard, worry lines slashed across her forehead, 'can you call an ambulance? We need to get Pa'harto to a hospital immediately.'

'It might take a while, Bu,' Pak Hendra interrupted. 'The macet was really bad today. We should carry Pak Suharto inside while we're waiting.'

Ibu Warsi and Pak Nono gathered around to help lift the driver up. I looked at him, and thought of how much he loved eating his favourite pisang goreng, but a second later, all thoughts of bananas were driven out of my mind. Pak Eman had noticed me.

The kiai's beard was wet. I couldn't tell if it was with spit or blood or something else. The way he was looking at me was terrifying – a strange smile flitting across his face that stopped short of his eyes. I felt the breath leave me. I knew I had to get away from him. But, as I stood up, my front paw buckled and I fell again. A moment later, Pak Eman's arm clamped around my neck and hauled me up. He shook me as though I was one of Nico's cloth bunnies and stuffed me inside his robes.

I bucked and squirmed with every ounce of strength I could find, but he held me down. 'Stay still if you know what's good for you' he hissed, squeezing my snout with his huge hand. I was choking. He chuckled, 'Oh, this will teach these ungodly foreigners and their cursed household a lesson alright. They love their filthy animals more than God. Well, they can enjoy looking for their darling kucing all they like, but it's not coming back.'

I could feel the kiai walking, although I had no idea where he was going. He was holding me too tightly for me to be able to peer out from under his clothes. I felt his thighs slap against my body and shuddered. Desperate, I unsheathed my claws and blindly dug them in wherever I could. He yowled once, and then punched me. I fell into darkness.

❄

Everything was red, and unsteady. It took a few moments for me to realize that the strange colour was actually pain. I wanted to vomit. Most of all, I wanted Mrs A. To be curled up in her arms, as she crooned, 'My little owl.'

Slowly, the red haze lifted to reveal a deep blackness. Where was I? I jumped up, but collapsed even as the memories came rushing in. Pa'harto! Was he alright? The crazed mob. And Pak Eman. I fought against the pain and stood up again. Where had he brought me?

I took a slow step forward, almost immediately bumping into something. Forcing my eyes open as wide as they could, I strained to make out the shapes that crouched in the gloom. Wherever this was, it was crowded with things: piles of boxes and stacks of paper. It wasn't a large space. My tail brushed against something smooth and solid: doors. It clicked into place. This was a cupboard that I was inside.

My heart began thudding loudly as I imagined Eman bursting into the closet to shut me up again. Would he kick me? Or squeeze my neck tighter and tighter until there was only silence. I shook my head. This was no good. I had to calm myself. I remembered Mama telling my brothers and me as we sheltered from Beijing's dust storms: 'Dustbin Cats don't have the luxury of fear. Panic is only good for *jifei goutiao*, flying chickens and jumping dogs.'

My breathing slowed as my ears rotated out, alert. I crouched, head extended, and moved forward quietly, the tip of my tail curling up, feeling the air. I pushed against the doors with my nose until they opened a crack. The light washed over me like the cold spray of rain. I blinked. I had never seen anything like it before. What was this? Where was this?

It was a large, bright room. Tangles of electronic chargers lay everywhere. Computers, mobile phones and keyboards were piled high on the tables that lined the room. The clackety clack of typing filled the space. There were many, maybe ten, Ren staring into screens, headphones over their ears. Some slurped on bowls of Indomie. I recognized the instant noodles immediately. Ibu Warsi ate them for lunch every day. Discarded plastic packets of the noodles and other snacks lay on the floor.

I didn't know what to think. What a strange place. Why had Pak Eman brought me here? What should I do? I weighed my chances of sneaking out and escaping. I had to try, even if it was risky. But just as I edged a paw out and around the door, a booming voice filled the room and I shrank back in.

Through the crack, I watched a tall, bulky man saunter in. His beard quivered like the legs of a dying cockroach as he spoke. 'How are my warriors doing?' he asked. 'Do you need more snacks? More Indomie? You need fuel for the fires you are fighting, my boys. You are the armies of God. We cannot have you weak.'

The Ren in the room began to stand up, although some seemed reluctant to take their eyes off the screen. They looked so young – like Ishaan, maybe a few years older. What were these almost-children doing in this bad place?

One of them clasped a hand to his heart and bent forward in a bow. A few strands of hair dangled from his chin, but his cheeks were smooth. 'By the grace of God and your goodwill, we are well, Pak Halim,' he said. The cockroach-beard man laughed out loud and ruffled the boy's hair.

'The Lord be praised! You children are the light of my eyes. Your rewards will be rich, I can promise. In this life, and in the hereafter as well. But, tell me. What is the news today, Sigit? What progress?'

'It's been a good day,' the boy, Sigit, replied. 'Pak Eman sent us two new recruits from the pesantren yesterday.' He gestured to the table next to him, where a couple of young Ren stood straight as sticks, wide-eyed and nervous.

'Welcome, sons,' boomed Pak Halim. 'This is your home now. You can ask me for whatever you need. More noodles. More tea. Work hard and you will thrive. There is plenty of money.'

The two boys nodded silently, but Sigit had more to say. 'We've set up fifty new accounts on social media this morning, Pak. And everyone is on target. A hundred posts every day on Twitter, and ten on Facebook from each account. We have about a dozen accounts each. Instagram is also going well. We are working hard, Pak. We can feel God's will in our work.'

'By the grace of God, that is excellent! Such good work. But, Sigit, there is one thing, my child. Remember that it's not enough for us to post. We must also be believed. And for that, we need to mix up the messages.'

'Pak, I...' Sigit began, but was interrupted by Pak Halim's upheld palm.

'You cannot become one-dimensional in your work. I know that good boys like you are filled with righteous anger. But you can be more effective if people believe you are "real". Humanize your posts, my warriors. Mix them up.' Sweat glistened on Pak Halim's face. His eyes shone.

'Can you instruct us further?' Sigit asked. 'I'm not sure I understand. What should we do, Pak?'

'It is not difficult, young Sigit. Only distasteful. You are paid to spread lies about the enemies of God, yes? This is war, and our weapons are tweets and posts. We spread stories about our enemies, infecting information networks like a virus. Eventually, our viruses will sicken those who stand against us, so that the virtuous can rule.'

The young men drank in the words, their eyes wide and faces shining.

'But it is not easy, as you already know,' Halim continued. 'Our fellow countrymen have long become debased in these godless times. They are swayed by images of fancy restaurants and filthy pets more than by the true word of God. To win them over, we must get into the gutter with them.'

'I know you will find this difficult, my children, but you must mix up your posts with "clickbait". Do you understand? For every few posts about the heinous ways of our opponents, stick one in there of a cute puppy or some new fairness cream. Make people like you. Gain their trust. Speak their language.'

I felt a snort tickle my nose. But I knew I couldn't make the slightest noise and fought it back. Halim was still talking.

'It's not good enough to tweet 100,000 times if you just have five followers. Your goal, *our* goal, is for some of your 100,000 tweets to get retweeted by the kind of buzzers who have 100,000 followers. You have to get noticed by *them*.'

'Yes, Pak. We will do this,' Sigit bowed his head obediently. 'I will guide everyone accordingly. Were there any particular pictures that you had in mind?'

'Cat pictures are always popular, aren't they? And I brought you boys one just today. Personally, I think it's as ugly as a toad, but these bule-types seem to like it.' It was Pak Eman's voice.

The kiai sauntered into sight, fat lips folded upwards into a dreadful smile. 'So, where is the cat, Bapak? You haven't eaten her by any chance, have you?' Eman guffawed, looking pleased with himself, but Pak Halim seemed less amused.

'Eman, I still don't understand why you had to bring that unclean creature into this house,' he frowned. 'We don't want to draw any more attention from next door than we already get, what with their infernal complaints about the sampah. Hmph! Where are all these Indomie packets supposed to go?'

The kiai flopped down on a chair next to Sigit. 'There's nothing to worry about, Bapak. Taking their cat is a great idea. They will now be tied up in knots over their beloved kucing having gone missing. It will distract them. And help us. That Indian woman and her bule husband are up to no good. You know, they are thick as thieves with Hendra. He was there with his atheist friend this morning when we conducted the operation against the infidel driver.'

Pak Halim's face tightened even more. 'Hendra must be brought down. Forget about the likes of drivers like Suharto. They are just worms. We need to zero in on the big fish. Hendra's been causing us trouble for too long. It's time for that blasphemous dog to be sent to jail, once and for all.'

'Sabar, patience, Bapak. It will happen. Soon. We are spending most of our energy on him. Stories about his communist activities are already rife. When the moment is ripe, we'll launch a mass protest. A filthy doubter like him doesn't stand a chance; his days are numbered.'

Sigit, whose face had begun to glow, cut in. 'Yes, Pak. We will bring him to his knees. We are willing to work around the clock for this noble cause. You can depend on us.'

He hesitated. 'There is one request, kiai. Is there any chance of a few more hands? I feel with another half-dozen fighters, we can win this battle quickly.'

Pak Eman turned to the young Ren. 'I can't conjure men out of air, Sigit. I already sent you two new recruits just yesterday. There are no more suitable boys at the moment.'

'Then what about girls?' asked Sigit. 'There is a pesantren for girls near your school, isn't there, kiai?'

Pak Halim looked aghast. 'No. No.' He paused, and then repeated himself, 'No!

'Females are unreliable. The less they are exposed to the internet, the better. The Lord knows it is dangerous to give them too much access. They cannot control themselves like men can. It is easy for them to stray. No, I will not allow girls here.'

The kiai nodded vigorously. 'Absolutely, Bapak. You are wise. My own wife is impossible. Working with those dirty bule next door, wiping their nasty children's bottoms. I've been telling her to leave that job, but she dares to defy me.' Pak Eman's face had become mottled with rage. I forced myself to keep listening, even though I wanted to turn away.

'You need to bring her under control, kiai,' boomed Pak Halim. 'Get her out of that godforsaken house before it is too late for her to be saved.' His words swirled in the air like nightmarish yangui. I no longer cared if I was seen or not. I needed to get back home. I had to warn Ibu Mari. I had to protect the children. I knew at that moment that I had been born a cat so as to use my teeth on the Ren in this room. I was alone and I was small, but I could cause a lot of damage.

I arched my spine and raised my tail stiff. I was going to step out of this cupboard, come what may. I closed my eyes to steady myself and took a deep breath, the fetid instant noodle–air filling my nose. 'Tofu,' a scratchy voice whispered. I sprang to attention, blood pumping in my ears and looked straight into a pair of beady eyes. It was Tikus.

Chapter X

Soyabean

A Cat in Pain

I'm pacing up and down the back verandah, feeling as though the walls are collapsing in on me. The sun is up high, but I'm cold to the bone. I shiver in the heat. It makes no sense; not much does. A crow flies overhead, cawing like a cat in pain. Its dark wings are reflected in the swimming pool water. It feels ominous. Everything does.

My stomach growls. I can't remember when I last ate. I am a substantially sized feline who needs steady nourishment. But every time I wander over to my bowl, a wave of nausea washes my appetite away. Drat that do-gooding Tofu. Why did she have to go running out onto the street like that? What chance did a little cat like her

stand against a mob of crazed Orang? Where was I when she needed me? Napping! Why am I always napping?

Oh, I can't stand the guilt. She's put me through this once before, in China. But I'm not sure I can take it again, at my age. And I had the help of her older brother last time. Who's going to help me in Jakarta? Much though I love Mr and Mrs A, they are Orang, with all the limitations of their species. Their talents lie in cuddling cats, not rescuing them. And no one even knows where to rescue her, whom to rescue her from.

The crow continues to caw somewhere in the background as I pad back and forth, a series of desperate images rising in my head. I can see myself heroically vaulting over the garden wall, wandering the humid streets of this alien city, the days stretching into weeks. No food, no water except for the foul seepage of the sewers. Yet, never giving up, ever searching. My eyes swim with tears, moved by my selfless actions, by my pitiful state, by my stout heart.

Overcome with emotion, I stop pacing for a moment, when, all of a sudden, I am rigid with shock. Someone is screaming and screaming. There is so much terror in that sound that I feel I will never be able to breathe again. I am paralyzed, my spine stiff, but I will myself to creep towards the cries, ears flat in the knowledge that something is terribly wrong.

The scream is coming from the family dining room. Every hair on my body is taut. I know I will find something in there that I never want to see; that no one should ever have to see. And yet, I must. I drag myself forward, steeling my heart for what is to come, willing myself not to vomit. I am a brave cat, I tell myself. I am a brave cat.

And then I see her. It's the nanny: Ibu Mari. She is standing on the blue carpet in the middle of the dining room, blood flowing down her face like red rain. Her mouth is open, twisted. But it is what she carries in her arms that I stare at. It's Tofu, a bloom of crimson at her neck. She's not moving at all, her tongue lolling out of her mouth. And I know in that moment that she is dead. All feeling drains from me as my head hits the floor.

❄

'Soyabean, Soyabean, it's okay. It's okay.' Mrs A is planting soft kisses on my forehead, leaning over me, massaging my belly. I am woozy, sick to my stomach. I lie there for a while, allowing her caresses to chase away the dread. The relief is overwhelming. It was a dream. A dream! It's most uncat-like to be so happy, but I could leap with joy, high enough to pluck a dragonfly out of the sky. Let me just think it aloud: I love Tofu. I love that annoying, sanctimonious bundle of dark fur. And she's not dead.

Wait a second. Not dead? The sinking feeling in my tummy returns. If 'not dead' is the best you can say of a cat, the scenario is bleak. She may not be dead, but she is still gone. And we don't know where. And we don't even know for sure if she's not dead.

It appears I will have to wander the streets in search of her after all. I snuggle deeper into Mrs A's soft body, aware that soon I must leave such comforts behind. I will have to forage in trashcans. Will my delicate stomach be able to handle the rotting scraps, the putrid leftovers of rats? I suppose there might be an Orang or two imbecilic enough to wonder why I won't just eat the rats. If only these innocents actually saw one of the monstrous beasts that inhabit Indonesia's gutters, they would know better than to entertain such ridiculous ideas.

These are no succulent rodent roulades, but indigestible and frankly, abnormally huge, rancid rodent rascals. I would rather eat plastic. Oh, drat that Tofu for the millionth time. Who am I kidding? I would rather eat egg yolks and strawberry yoghurt.

And now, even as Mrs A cuddles me, I can't get rats off my mind. That stinky brute that Tofu was always waxing eloquent about, Tikle-something-or-the-other, has been skulking around, trying to catch my eye whenever I go out into the garden. To my credit, I've managed to ignore him. Now is not the time to attract attention to a rat infestation in the garden. Mr and Mrs A have enough in their bowls already.

They've hardly been home since Tofu's disappearance. They're either at the hospital visiting Pa'harto or patrolling the neighbourhood looking for Tofu and putting up 'lost cat' posters offering a reward to anyone who has information about her. There's been no response.

Everyone in the house is puffy eyed, even Ibu Warsi. The children are the worst. They've stopped fighting. Their lightsabers lie untouched in their toy boxes. There's no arguing or complaining. It's what I've always fantasized about: peace and quiet. But this silence is suffocating.

❉

There's a knock on the door, and Mrs A puts me down to go and see to it. She returns with Pak Hendra. The Indonesian journalist has been in and out of the house for the last couple of days. He's been helping the As put up their lost cat posters. But I doubt he's going to have much luck. I'm pretty sure someone stole Tofu. She wouldn't have just wandered off by herself and gotten lost. For all her mooning at the clouds, she isn't dopy enough to do that. The question is, who would steal her? And why?

'Bu, Debbie and I have covered all the neighbourhoods we can think of,' says Pak Hendra, taking the cold glass of water Ibu Warsi has brought in. He collapses into the worn-out sofa (it is a particularly comfortable piece of furniture), and sighs.

'How about you, Bu? Any leads?'

Mrs A's face is pinched. She shakes her head tiredly. 'Nothing, Pak. It's like she's disappeared into thin air.' Then, pursing her lips, she adds, 'Although I doubt air, thin or thick, has anything to do with it. More likely, it's one of the goons that attacked Pa'harto.'

'How is he, Bu? I've been meaning to go and visit him, but there's just so much going on, I hardly have time to breathe. And with the macet, it would take me an hour each way from home to the hospital,' Pak Hendra says.

'Don't worry, Pak,' Mrs A replies. 'Pa'harto is fine. A few bruises and cuts. They've kept him in hospital this long because he's old, and with his diabetes, there could be complications. And he still doesn't remember much of the actual incident. But apparently short-term memory loss isn't unusual.'

She begins drumming her fingers on the dining table surface. 'The worst of it is psychological. The poor man is traumatized. He can't understand why anyone would attack him so viciously. *I* can't understand it. None of us can. He's such a good man.'

'But, it's the good men that are often the most vulnerable. They're the ones that stand out, so it's easier to shoot them down,' Pak Hendra says, placing his glass of water on the small table next to the sofa.

He leans forward, the lines on his forehead deepening. 'Bu, about your cat. I don't want to sound too harsh but you should not hold onto false hope. This is a city where people disappear all the time. Few have the time to care about lost animals.'

Mrs A draws a long breath, and is about to say something when the car horn sounds in the driveway. The children are home. Mr A has taken the last few days off from work and has been ferrying the boys to school and back. I'd heard him talking to Mrs A about finding a replacement for Pa'harto. They'd agreed that it was not something they could face now.

I get to my feet and trot out, towards the car. Mr A and Nico have already gone into the house through the door at the back of the garage, but Ishaan is sitting on top of the steps that lead up from the driveway to the garden. I sit down next to him. He glances at me and puts an arm around my neck. 'Good cat,' he whispers so sadly that my ears droop. Little boys and pets: we're a 'thing'. Tofu's disappearance is probably the hardest on the children.

I am overcome with generosity, so I offer my body to Ishaan to stroke and manhandle however he likes. He buries his face in my neck which makes his words muffled, but I can make them out nonetheless. 'Soyabean, I don't like it without Tofu,' he breathes into my fur. 'I'm so confused. Papa says I should be brave and focus on school. But if I really was brave, I'd have left school to go looking for Tofu everywhere until I found her.'

I put a paw over his thigh. This child is as brainless as Orang-young tend to be. Him running off to look for Tofu would only compound everyone's problems. We'd have to look for Tofu *and* Ishaan. But I understand that he means well. Strangely, I feel a purr arising. This body is so weak. It responds to stroking, no matter the circumstances. I suppose we must enjoy that which we cannot control. I'm just about to close my eyes and give in to the Purr,

when I notice an unattractive grey shape lurking under the frangipani tree.

It's him, that horrendous Tiktok what's-his-name. I am afire with indignation. The gall of this creature, intruding upon our house at a time like this! These rats truly have no shame.

In a second, my lips are curled back. I leap towards him, a magnificent golden missile, flying. Unfortunately, as I've mentioned before, my colour and size make me rather conspicuous, and what with lacking practice in recent days, or years, the rodent manages to escape. Drat, drat, drat!

'Come back here, Soyabean!' Ishaan calls out to me. I lift myself off the grass and walk back with as much dignity as I can muster. To show humiliation is even worse than being humiliated. I'm sure there is a Chinese proverb about this. Better a smiling mouse than a scowling rat? My Nai Nai would know. She knows most things worth knowing.

Back in the family room, Mr A is talking to Pak Hendra and Mrs A. 'Go up and get changed,' Mrs A says to Ishaan, only half turning towards the boy. 'Nico's upstairs already, with Ibu Mari.' The child complies reluctantly, dragging his feet. Mrs A returns her full attention to the conversation.

'No, Pak Hendra, you need to be more careful.' Mr A is sounding unusually stern. 'It's not a game, Pak. If these thugs can attack Pa'harto so brazenly, outside our home in broad daylight, they can get you too. Besides, the elections are coming closer. There are people willing to try desperate things to win. It won't take much to tip the black campaigns against you online into physical violence.'

Pak Hendra grins. 'What will I get for being careful, Mr A? At least, by being myself, I can try to change things. Being careful will change nothing.'

Mr A does not smile back. 'But it's not just about you, Pak, is it? You endanger your friends too.' He looks directly at Mrs A.

'I don't care,' she interrupts, flushing. 'I know there are risks, but like Pak Hendra said, there is no change without some risk. We can't just sit around with blindfolds on and let good people like Pa'harto get hurt.'

'Yes, of course, I understand about *change*,' Mr A snaps. 'And you are an adult. You make your own choices. But what about the children? We've had the driver attacked just outside our home. Our cat is gone. What if the kids are next in the line of fire? I can't bear even the thought.'

Mrs A reaches out and clasps his arm. I nuzzle closer into his legs. 'Darling, it'll be okay. We can't let the bullies cow us down. Can you imagine if they are given free rein?' She tosses her head. 'The worst is not knowing who *they* are. Do we know anything for sure?' Mrs A looks from Mr A to Pak Hendra.

Mr A shakes his head. 'Not much. I went to the police again this morning. They're next to useless. I told them again, about the shouts of "infidel" from the attackers, and do you know what they asked? They asked if he was in fact an infidel! Whether Pa'harto was properly pious or not. I could have throttled them.'

'It's all part of the same cancer, Mr A,' Pak Hendra joins in. 'It's an everyday occurrence these days. Some vigilante gang or the other beating up people, attacking rock concert audiences, beauty pageant contestants, traditional theatre performers. Who knows when it will stop? Where they will draw the line?'

'They'll certainly not draw it at you, Pak,' says Mr A, his eyes twinkling for the first time. 'If they get hold of you, you're a goner.'

'What's a *goner*?' Pak Hendra asks.

'Nothing good,' replies Mr A. 'Nothing good at all.' He turns to Mrs A and adds, 'Nono insists he saw the kiai, Eman, in the mob. Is Mari still denying it? Have you spoken to her about it again?'

'I have, yes,' Mrs A pauses.

'And?'

'There is something there,' Mrs A says slowly. 'But I don't want to push her too much. Whatever's going on with Eman, it's not her fault. The worst would be if he turns on her. He's already constantly on her case because she works for us. We must handle this very carefully.'

Pak Hendra stands up all of a sudden. 'Bu, I don't feel comfortable. Perhaps it is best for all of you if you have less to do with me from now on. Mr A is right. Everyone is in danger because of me.'

'Please sit down, Pak Hendra,' Mrs A says. 'Let's not be hasty. We don't know if the attack on Pa'harto had anything to do with you at all. And you know better than anyone, Pak, cowardice only begets cowardice. If anyone is in danger, it's not because of you, but despite all you do.

'I don't want the children "safe" in a cocoon, while the world around them turns nastier every day. It's *for* the children that we must not back down. They're the mongrels that these "righteous" types despise. The thugs will come after us regardless of you, Pak Hendra. Our family will never be pure enough for them.'

The words begin to wash over me in a tide of boredom. Orang talk and talk. And talk. But what about Tofu? What's the plan to help her? This Pak Hendra is pompous enough, but not much more competent than the rest. Gosh, it's hard to be a cat sometimes! It's tough being so much cleverer, swifter, more powerful than those that surround you. But I must cope. What choice is there?

I stretch and jump lithely off the sofa, where I've been squeezed between Pak Hendra and Mr A. It's stifling in here with all this gloomy talk. Not to mention the even gloomier facts. I wander back into the garden, where the late afternoon sun is hidden by gathering clouds. It'll probably rain later. I don't need to spend hours staring up into the sky like Tofu does to deduce that. Oh, why do I miss that dratted cat so much?

I make my way to the frangipani tree and hoist my front paws onto the tree trunk, tingling in anticipation of a good scratch.

'Soyabean! Soyabean!'

My name has never sounded slimier. I topple over. What fresh horror is this? What sinister being is calling to me so hideously? I scramble back up to my feet. Luckily, no one important is around to witness the failure of my usual composure.

I crouch in readiness for battle and scan the scene. Oh! It's only the rat. Again. It appears the rodent simply cannot take a hint. I must be upfront with him. Looking at him with as much contempt as I can muster, I tell it like it is. 'Rat, you are not welcome here. Please leave before I tear you apart from your scaly tail to your offensive nose. Scat!'

But the rat stares back at me. 'Soyabean, please hear me out. I have information. I know where *she* is.'

My heart starts hammering so loudly I can hardly hear myself ask him who he's talking about. Could it really be?

Chapter XI

Mrs A

WhatsApp

The rumah sakit, hospital, wasn't far from her home, five kilometres at most. But this was Jakarta, where distance was a traffic jam–addled creature that had lost its objectivity. That's quite good, thought Mrs A of the sentence that had wandered its way into her mind as she waited, and waited, in the MRT-engendered gridlock of Jalan Antasari. She'd left the hospital almost an hour ago. It would have been faster to walk, if there had been any pavements to walk along.

She sighed and considered switching on her meditation app, but dismissed the notion almost immediately. It would be impossible to focus on her breathing. The mob closing in on Pa'harto, the hate in their voices, the rancid smell of their bodies: these memories slapped away any quiet she reached for.

Mrs A pushed her phone roughly into her handbag, as though burying it might help quell her uneasiness. She was irritated by her anxieties. This wasn't the time to be overwhelmed. She needed to pull herself together and face up to adulthood. No one was going to be able to kiss the hurt away and make everything better for her. She was the one who needed to do the fixing, the making better.

Pa'harto needed care. Pak Hendra needed support. Mr A needed to retire from his temporary driver position and return to work. And the children were so sad about Tofu. Her baby cat! Such a fierce, sweet bundle of fur she was, with her wise owl face.

Mrs A thought back to the first night Tofu had spent in their courtyard home in Beijing, all those years ago. It hadn't been easy to separate her from her littermates. Poor kitten. She'd been terrified and for the first couple of days, she hadn't let the As near her, baring her tiny teeth if they approached. Eventually, she'd begun exploring the house, her belly always close to the floor for security. Whenever a human got too close, she'd scoot behind the large chest of drawers in the living room.

It was Soyabean who'd managed to finally persuade her to trust them. Over time, she'd begun to copy the bigger cat in his interactions with the As. But there was always a corner in her heart that remained untamed, and a little sad. Mrs A knew this and her own heart ached for her baby cat. She straightened her back and tucked a loose strand of hair behind her ear. She needed to come through for everyone. She was going to find Tofu.

The only concrete lead they had was Pak Eman. Nono had sworn he'd seen Ibu Mari's husband in the mob, and this morning Pa'harto had confirmed it. The driver was slowly regaining memories of the attack. He remembered seeing Tofu and reaching out to grab her. 'Sorry, Bu,' he'd said, red-faced with shame. 'Pa'harto trying to help kucing, but someone kick me. So much pain, Bu. Pa'harto not remembering after that.'

But he did recall seeing Eman. 'Even with too much pain, Pa'harto sure it was kiai, Bu. Very bad man. He was laughing.'

The driver's face had crumpled like a discarded piece of paper. 'Why they do this to me? What bad thing Pa'harto do?' These were questions he asked every time Mrs A visited and as usual, she had no answer except to lay her hand on his arm. It wasn't good enough. She owed him more.

She was going to have to speak with Ibu Mari again. The nanny was scared, that much was apparent. And no wonder. Her husband sounded dangerous. Mrs A briefly toyed with the idea of trying to track the kiai down directly at his pesantren. But what if he became enraged? What if he attacked Ibu Mari?

Her phone buzzed from inside the bowels of her bag. She dug it out. It was a message from her editor. Apparently, she was still not making enough of an argument in her perang topat piece. 'I can't make out if you think the two communities love each other or hate each other. Is the festival a sham or something beautiful? You need to work through it,' the message read. 'It seems you're confused.'

Mrs A laughed out loud. It was a gaspy sound devoid of any real mirth. She checked the time on her phone. It had been seventy-five minutes since she'd flagged down this taxi outside the rumah sakit. But the worst was over. There was only one traffic light left to clear before they could finally turn off the main avenue, into the neighbourhood lanes that led to the house.

❄

Pak Nono opened the gates as the taxi drew up. 'How is Pa'harto, Bu?' he asked, holding the car door open for Mrs A, although she was still hunting around in her wallet for change. 'He's better,' she replied, handing over the exact fare to the driver. She heaved herself out of the taxi and looked at the security guard.

'The doctor says he can go home within a day or two. And he's beginning to remember everything more clearly. Why don't you go and visit him for a few hours tomorrow morning? He was asking about you.'

Pak Nono grinned, his cigarette-blackened teeth on display. 'Thank you, Bu. Pa'harto is like father for Nono.

Always telling Nono: stop smoking, stop wasting so much time listening dangdut.'

Mrs A smiled. 'I know, I know. You go see him tomorrow. He'll be thrilled. By the way, Pak, is Mari upstairs?'

'Yes, Bu. Children still in school. Ibu Mari waiting. Maybe in kitchen?'

Mrs A walked up the short flight of stairs to the front door, her heart skipping with nervousness. She could no longer put off a proper conversation with the nanny about her husband. 'Ibu Mari,' she called out as she took her shoes off and changed into house slippers. 'Ibu Mari, are you there?'

'Coming, Bu,' Ibu Mari answered. Mrs A walked into the family living room and flopped down on the worn-out sofa. It would be better to have this talk sitting down.

Mari entered, her hair slightly askew. She wasn't wearing the jilbab she'd been wrapping around her hair recently. 'You want Mari pick up children, Bu?' she asked.

'No, don't worry,' replied Mrs A. 'Mister has gone to get them in the car. But, please, come and sit down with me for a little bit.'

The nanny looked startled, but made her way to the sofa without comment. She sat on the very edge of the seat cushion, holding her body straight, as if in readiness for flight. Mrs A took a deep breath. 'Ibu Mari,' she began. 'I spoke to Pa'harto in the rumah sakit this morning.'

'How is he?' Mari asked quickly.

'He's well enough,' replied Mrs A.

'By the grace of God!' Mari whispered.

'Yes, well. The thing is Pa'harto is beginning to remember more details from the attack and, Ibu Mari, I might as well tell you directly. He says that he's sure he saw your husband in the mob. And you already know that Nono thought he saw him too. Do you know anything at all about this?'

Mari sat still, the weight of her silence bearing down on Mrs A as she searched the nanny's face for a clue to what she was thinking. A loud meow broke the spell. It was Soyabean, nosing at Mrs A's feet.

'Cat hungry. Mari go feed.' The nanny got to her feet.

'No! Please stay here and answer me,' said Mrs A, putting a restraining hand out. 'Do you know anything at all that could help us find out more about what happened with Pa'harto? And anything about Tofu?' Mrs A almost choked over the words. 'Please, Ibu, can you help me?'

Mari sat back down with a plop. She looked Mrs A in the eye for the first time in days. 'My husband not coming home already three day, Bu. Mari no see him after Pa'harto hurt.'

The nanny folded her hands into her lap and sighed. 'Maybe because Mari no good wife, but Eman being bad man. Always shout at Mari, never happy. Telling me leave job with dirty bule, who no believe God. He say: children are dirty, no have country, no have religion. He tell me:

stay in home, no go work. But, Bu, he give no money for family. Only pray, pray all the time. Many time he not come home in night. Not tell Mari where he go.'

Wild-eyed, the nanny continued, 'What Mari can do? She like job. She like bule family and children. She need money. Oh, Ibu, please forgive Mari. Everything my fault.' Ibu Mari broke into a storm of sobs.

'Ibu Mari, nothing is your fault. Why do you say that? There's absolutely no need to cry.' Mrs A reached out to hug the nanny, who collapsed into her arms like a grateful toddler.

'Oh, Bu, but it is me. It is me!'

'Who is you? What is you, Mari? What are you talking about?'

The nanny disentangled herself from Mrs A's embrace, wiping away her tears. 'It is me telling him about Pa'harto. When Eman say dangdut bad, this bad, that bad, I am telling him Pa'harto say nothing bad if you have good heart. When Eman say I must to leave job because God not like me work for bule, I tell Pa'harto say bule or no, not matter. I talk back to husband. It is me who make Eman angry with Pa'harto.'

'You mustn't believe that, Mari,' Mrs A said urgently. 'People like Eman don't need an excuse to hate. He's come here so often to pick you up. He's talked to Pa'harto directly. It's got nothing to do with you. Eman might be your husband, but you haven't made him do anything. You've stood up to him. You've continued to work here even though he disapproves of it. Mari, you are a brave woman. I'm proud of you, Ibu.'

The nanny let out a little yelp as Soyabean landed on her lap, purring against her belly. 'This kucing is too much fat,' she gasped. 'Mari getting big shock.'

Mrs A couldn't help feeling that Soyabean understood every word, the way in which he immediately recoiled on hearing her. He lowered his ears and sloped off looking so insulted that she had to smile despite all her worries.

'I know. He is dreadfully overweight, but what to do? He loves eating so much. I've been talking to Mister about putting him on a diet, but we've tried it before and it makes Soyabean terribly depressed. He loses his purr.'

Mari looked quizzical. 'You know, he loses his spirit, his personality. He goes all droopy,' Mrs A explained, putting on her best sad cat face.

The nanny still looked dubious, but Mrs A didn't notice. She was thinking about Tofu again. 'Do you think anyone is feeding Tofu? She hardly eats at the best of times. Oh, Ibu Mari, I'm going crazy imagining she's lost, or worse, being harmed in some way. Can you try and find out something, anything, about her from Eman? I know you haven't seen him, but do you know where he might be? Can you find him? Talk to him?'

'Maybe Eman in pesantren, Bu. Mari not know, only guess. But what he do with Tofu? He not liking animal. If he see dog or cat on road, he kick it. Even baby animal.'

The nanny's voice dropped. 'My husband bad man, Bu. He like to hurt.'

'He not hurting Mari, or Ibu Warsi beat him up.' The cook had entered the room without anyone noticing and was shaking the broom in her hand menacingly. She walked up to Ibu Mari. 'Bu, if you need, Warsi come stay in your house. Mari not worry. Warsi take care of any bad man.'

Ibu Mari looked at the tiny, fierce Ibu Warsi and burst out laughing. It was a full-throated laugh, a clear sound that filled the house with an energy that had been missing since the attack on Pa'harto. Mrs A reached out and the three women clasped hands for a moment – the big nosed Indian journalist, the cardamom-scented cook and the still red-eyed nanny. 'The two of you have meant...' Mrs A began, but her mobile buzzed loudly in her pocket, jolting her attention away.

❄

'Just a second,' she said and took out her phone. She had a new WhatsApp message. 'It's from Pak Hendra,' she muttered and began reading. When she looked up a few minutes later, she was pale.

'What happen, Ibu?' Mari asked. 'Everything alright?'

Mrs A held out the phone wordlessly.

The nanny and the cook stared. It was a picture of a cat, but not just any cat. It was Tofu. And she was wearing a jilbab.

Chapter XII

Tofu

Clickbait

There was always so much food at the As' house that I'd forgotten how the stomach bloats with air and hunger when it's empty. Perhaps that's why I had been thinking so much about my Mama. It was almost like I could smell her hard belly, as my siblings and I pressed up against it, waiting for the dust storms to pass. I could taste the hunger as her teats ran dry. Or perhaps I was chancing upon these almost forgotten moments from my kittenhood because time hung so heavy in this cupboard. Sifting through memories helped pass the hours I spent shrouded in the darkness, even though the glare of the computer screens and phones outside never dimmed.

The number of boys hammering away on the keyboards changed every once in a while, but the room was never empty. Pak Halim strode about with his cockroach-beard, handing out packets of Indomie. Plastic wrappings lay scattered on the floor. No one seemed to notice them. The boys' eyes were glazed as they stared into their screens, into another world.

At first, I was mostly ignored, although Pak Halim occasionally flung open the cupboard door and stared at me as if trying to make up his mind about something. I didn't know what, but I knew that it must be bad. Once, he picked me up and held me so close that I could smell his rotten-egg breath. But for much of the time, I was left to myself and my memories.

I'd been in the cupboard for a while, maybe two days or three, it was difficult to know, when the doors creaked open slowly; too cautiously for it to be Pak Halim. I dropped close to the floor, ready to spring, steeling myself for the worst. But it was only that boy, Sigit.

He just stood there, looking. Was he confused? Curious? Gradually my muscles loosened. This did not feel like a cruel Ren, only a very young and unsure one. Eventually he reached out a hand towards me, but snatched it away just as it was about to touch my head. He tried again and snatched his hand away once more. A strange realization dawned on me. This young Ren, Sigit, was afraid of a cat, me.

The next time he began to hold out his hand, I stepped forward and before he could withdraw it, I rubbed my face against his palm. His hand jerked but stayed put. I rested my chin in it and looked up. His eyes softened, but he was still on edge, and so I tickled him with my whiskers until he smiled. Then he turned and left, closing the doors behind him.

A few minutes later, he was back, holding a saucer of milk. He held it out and eyed me nervously. When I took a lick, his face burst into sunshine. 'Oh, kucing!' he laughed out aloud. 'Oh, kucing!'

I licked the saucer clean in seconds, and sat back on my haunches, my tummy singing. When Sigit reached to pick me up, I didn't complain. The boy smelt safe. He carried me a few steps to his desk, which was covered in a mess of cables and paper. He pushed it all to one side, making a clearing and placed me next to his computer.

I looked around the room, my heartbeat quickening. I wasn't sure what was going on and, after all that time in the cupboard, I felt exposed, uncertain. But the young men who filled the room didn't take their eyes off their screens. No one remarked on my appearance at all.

Gently, Sigit pushed down on my back, until I was sitting on my haunches. He moved me a little to the right, looked dissatisfied and then tugged me back to my original position. Then he took out his phone and began taking pictures of me. By my whiskers, I couldn't understand why in this World he'd want to photograph me. It seemed very odd.

But he did me no harm. Only made me sit this way and that: on the chair, lying on my back, even stretched out across his keyboard. After a while, he sat down on the chair by his desk and thrummed his lips with a finger, looking thoughtful.

'Kucing, stay here for a moment, okay?' He hurriedly left the room while I shrank into myself, wondering what would happen to me if he didn't return. But he was back only a few minutes later, clutching a long black scarf in which he began wrapping my head. I found my voice and began to meow loudly.

'Shhh. Don't worry. It's okay,' the Ren murmured, as he continued to drape the cloth around me. He stood back and smiled. 'This is perfect, you adorable kucing.' And then once again he began taking pictures, until I heard a voice that turned my blood to ice.

'We need to raise a cyclone, not just a storm, Pak. Our work is still going too slowly. The elections are very, very soon.' Every word out of Eman's mouth felt like a kick to my ribs. I began to shake.

'We just need to get that Hendra. Everything else will fall into place.' Pak Halim's booming voice was also unmistakable. 'Don't you worry, kiai. You have sent us good boys. They work hard and our support is growing every day. God willing, Hendra and his friends will get what they deserve. No one can be blamed if he gets hurt.

After all, he has wounded the feelings of the pious again and again.'

'Kucing, what's the matter?' asked Sigit. The boy put down his phone and picked me up, placing me on his lap. 'Why are you shaking? There's no need to be scared. Sigit is here.'

I looked towards where Eman and Pak Halim's voices were drifting in from and Sigit followed my gaze. 'Oh!' he breathed softly. 'I see.' And with that he carried me back to the cupboard and, after stroking me on the head a final time, closed the doors. The darkness swallowed me.

Later that night, there was a familiar scrabbling that sent my tail soaring. It was my friend, Tikus. The rat's visits had become my window to the World, and the only reason I was just waiting in this closet and not trying to escape. Tikus said, and in the end I agreed, that trying to make a break for it would end badly. The room was never empty and I'd only be caught and hurt. Maybe worse.

Tikus had been trying to figure out a way to get me help, but it was hard for a rat. Mrs A and Pak Nono would only scream and run away if they spotted him. Ibu Warsi would attack him with a broom. And Soyabean, that melon of a cat, had been ignoring his attempts to talk.

I always asked him for news of Mr and Mrs A, of the children and of Pa'harto. But he didn't know much. He said the boys were quieter than usual and that Pa'harto no longer came to work. Everything felt hushed at the As' home. Even Pak Nono had stopped playing dangdut on the radio. I was heartsick thinking of all of them. They were so close and yet seemed far, far away. Why did I always lose the ones I loved? Mama, my siblings, and now the As.

On his last visit, Tikus had also been sad. He'd explained that his Niece Number Fifty-three – Tikus, one of the kampung tikus, had met with a bad accident. She'd spotted a squashed piece of bakso lying on the road and had run out after it, even though it was daylight and she ran the risk of being beaten to death by Ren. In the event, it was a Bajai that ran her over. She was still alive, but her hind legs were crushed and her tail gone.

Tikus' Auntie Twenty-three – Tikus, Niece Number-Fifth-three–Tikus' mother, was looking after her. 'But we think she might be going to the Boss Tikus in the Sky,' my friend said. His eyes had been even more ringed in red than usual. I asked who the Boss Tikus in the Sky was. The rat managed a weak grin. 'It's where cats finally get their just desserts.'

I must have looked alarmed because he'd hastened to reassure me. 'I'm just joking, Tofu. Some tikus believe in the Boss Tikus up there; but to be honest, I'm an atheist. It's not the most popular opinion among the tikus, but then I've always been a cashew amongst candlenuts. I mean, my best friend is a cat!'

A slow warmth had crept over me, which I later realized was happiness. I was his best friend!

On this particular visit, Tikus was triumphant. Not because his niece was any better, but because he had finally managed to talk to Soyabean. 'It's not been easy, believe me, Tofu,' he sighed. 'Your Soyabean has a long, fat stick up his big backside.' Was it wicked of me to smile? I tried not to. The good news is that they were now trying to figure out a rescue plan.

Tikus went on, 'The problem is that the orange cat is not very bright. All his ideas seem to involve him leaping across the boundary wall. Given his belly, that is about as likely as a tikus sprouting wings. And, even if by some miracle he does manage to jump, what will he do then? Won't Eman or one of the other Orang here just capture him too?

'But don't worry!' Tikus must have seen my face fall because he forced his lips into a grin. I wished he hadn't. As much as I loved him, a grinning rat did not look all that reassuring. 'We are working on something. You stay put, and just try to stay out of trouble. We'll get you out before long.'

But how long? I did not know how much time we had. I did know from the conversation between Eman and Pak Halim that Pak Hendra could soon be in trouble too. I'd already failed Pa'harto. I could not bear to fail again. I remembered snuggling against the journalist's feet when he had come to visit Mrs A. He had felt so familiar. When he joked that we knew each other from another life, I had wondered if it was in fact a joke.

❄

'Kucing! Kucing!' Sigit was calling for me.

Tikus had left hours ago, and I was cramped and starving. The cupboard doors opened to reveal the boy holding out something in his hand. I moved forward, the scent diving into my tummy: ikan goreng, fried fish. I snatched at the offering gratefully. It was slightly rancid, but I hardly noticed.

'Come, Manis,' Sigit said, using the name he'd taken to calling me, once I was done eating. He lifted me up and quickly touched his nose with mine. 'The posts with you in it are getting more likes than anything I've got before.' I had no idea what this Ren was talking about, but it seemed to make him happy, so I was glad. He was very chatty and kept up a steady banter as he walked towards his desk. 'You are one of us now, little Manis, a warrior for our cause. With you as our mascot we can defeat the infidels and keep our country safe.' He scratched me on the head.

I was immediately uncomfortable for I didn't want to be a warrior and the only cause I had was to protect the creatures, both Ren and animals, that I cared about. I had only known Sigit a short while, and I knew he was working with bad Ren, like Eman, but the boy himself was not bad. He was kind. I did not know what to do. How to help Sigit? How to defeat Eman? How to protect Pak Hendra? I was only a cat trapped in a strange, confusing World.

'Sigit, my boy!' Pak Halim's voice reverberated across the room. 'Good work with the posts of this kucing.'

He came striding up to us, white robes swishing, fat belly jiggling. 'This is exactly the kind of clickbait I've been talking about. Bagus! The picture with the jilbab was pure gold.' He slapped Sigit on the back, a sharp thwacking sound.

Sigit glowed and crossed his hand over his chest in thanks. 'Pak, our work is going viral thanks to this kucing. Your guidance was absolutely correct.'

Pak Halim chuckled. 'It's your hard work, my boy. I am just here to make sure you are all well-fed. How about some pisang goreng after lunch today, as a treat for everyone to celebrate the good news?'

Sigit smiled. 'Thank you, Pak. You are always kind to us, but how about a treat for the real star instead? This kucing. I fear it is not getting enough food. Could we buy some snacks for it? And maybe a blanket for it to sleep on?'

In an instant, Halim's beaming face changed to a snarl. 'Dungu! Idiot! These are filthy, unclean animals. We might have to use them to achieve our goals, but do you think the Lord would approve that you are spending so much time thinking about dirty creatures like them? What is wrong with you, boy? This kucing has brought your brain out onto your knees. You must remember to keep yourself pure at all times to do God's work effectively.'

Sigit was cowering, hanging his head lower and lower.

Pak Halim went on, relentless. 'I think it best that we give this kucing back to the kiai to dispose of. It has already served its purpose.'

Sigit's head shot up. 'No!' he said loudly.

Pak Halim's face turned purple. 'You dare defy me? You insolent, wicked boy,' he roared. 'I will talk to Eman about disciplining you.' He raised his hand high and struck Sigit on the cheek with an open palm, so that the boy dropped to his knees.

In that instant, I sank my teeth into this evil Ren's wrist, clamping down so hard he couldn't throw me off even as he flung his arm about, screaming in pain. Finally, he prised me off with his other arm and walloped me on the head.

'Disgusting, cursed creature,' he spat. 'Look what it's done!' Drops of red flecked his wrist. 'If this becomes infected, even God will not be able to protect you.' Halim shook his hand at Sigit, before turning around and stomping out of the room, cursing all the while.

'Are you alright, Manis? I'm sorry; I'm so, so sorry.' The boy picked me up from where I'd fallen, his tears dripping on my fur. He held me against his neck and I licked his cheeks. They were salty-wet. This poor child. This cruel World.

He carried me back to the cupboard and crawled inside it with me. The doors pulled shut; we sat in the dark. I pressed up against his chest even though it was hot and the pounding of his heart filled my head.

'Where are you from, kucing?' he whispered eventually. 'Where is your family? Do you love those bule next door? Do you want to go back to them?'

I let out a meow so soft that I wasn't sure he even heard it.

'I want to go back to my family sometimes. But they can't take care of me. Your bule friends, they have swimming pools and lawns, don't they? My family barely has one room, Manis. A drain for a toilet, salted rice for every meal... Sometimes, not even that.'

He sighed long and deep. 'There were too many of us, you see. How could my parents look after six children? They loved me; I know they did. Ibu used to stroke my hair sometimes. But, in the end, they had to send me away to the pesantren because it was better for me. The kiai told them he would feed me, educate me, give me a chance. My parents couldn't do any of that.'

He plucked me off his chest and set me down beside him. 'I understand what they did. I truly do, Manis. But sometimes, I worry that I am forgetting their faces. They are disappearing, like raindrops drying in the sun. All I have left is a feeling, a scent, a nothing. And this cause: to protect our religion, to defend our nation. The kiai has given us everything. Taught us our letters, given us clothes and food. But...'

I couldn't see clearly in the gloom, but I could hear that the boy had begun crying again. 'But *you*, little kucing. I will not let anyone hurt you. That is not what God would want. That much I know.' His shoulders shook convulsively and I felt myself break into many, painful pieces.

Chapter XIII

Soyabean

Soyabean the Sublime

Oh, my poor stomach; such diabolical agony. Blast Tiktok and his 'plan'. He's insisted I cut back to two meals a day, because, according to His Ratness, it will increase my chances of getting across the wall without a hitch. I can't decide what's more insulting: being called 'fat' by a rat, or having to be in cahoots with a rat at all. Tofu will owe me bucketfuls of kibble for this. Oh, I could do with just a tiny teaspoon of it now. But, no, Soyabean must be thin. Soyabean must be fit. I should take that body-shaming rodent in my mouth and shake him until he learns a little politeness. If only he didn't have a point.

The fact is that there have been one or two times when I've struggled to get up on the garden wall and if we're going to save Tofu, I need to jump over cleanly. The idea is to make sure that Pak Nono sees me leap. He'll be sure to alert all the Orang in the house, and then all I need to do is make sure I'm not caught on the other side for as long as it takes them to come and rescue Tofu and me. I will be a hero once again, and hopefully, that villainous Eman and his troops will get their comeuppance.

The moment is nigh. Tiktok is waiting outside to cheer me on. This is how low I've sunk for Tofu's sake: a sewer rat for a cheerleader. Who would have imagined? The only silver lining is that it's a sunny day and the wall won't be slippery. My paws should be able to get a firm grip on it, if need be.

I pad into the garden and up to the boundary that separates our home from the enemy's. Tiktok, who is keeping low among the bushes, flashes me a ghoulish smile. We both turn to make sure that Pak Nono is sitting out in the driveway, in full view. Now that he's stopped listening to dangdut, he's taken up reading the newspaper instead, on what used to be Pa'harto's favourite chair. The security guard is turning the pages listlessly. It's now or never. If I delay my jump, he'll fold up the paper and be off looking for a cup of tea.

I stand back, focus on the top of the wall and in a flash I am off – up, up and awaaaay, meowing in sonorous triumph. It's glorious. I feel the rush of wind in my fur as

I rise, light and fluffy, like a bright orange soufflé. Oh, a bite to eat wouldn't go amiss now. And, by my whiskers, I've done it! I'm sailing over and across and... Ouch! Hard landing. Ouch! Thorns. Ouch! Ouch! Drat that rat! Couldn't he have warned me about these rose bushes?

I feel like a cactus, I have so many thorns coming out of me, but I must remain soundless. It's too soon to attract attention to myself. I keep my belly close to the floor, my tail stiff and horizontal, as I take a long, slow step out of the bushes. Almost immediately I retreat. Ouch, again! More thorns.

I can hear voices near the front gate. There is the vinegary stink of days-old garbage wafting in the air. I can see plastic wrappings scattered across the lawn – if you can call this expanse of un-watered dirt a lawn. I pivot my ears towards the voices and there is one I recognize: Pak Jubaid, the garbage man.

'I am only a garbage man, but this is too much, Mas. How much sampah can one house generate? And you just stuff it all into torn bags and leave it out for me. It's always spilling about and Jubaid must gather it up with his hands,' the Orang shouts. 'Just because we collect garbage doesn't entitle you to treat us like garbage. Do you understand, Mas?

'Your Mister lives in this big, big house and can't even use a dustbin like everyone else?' The garbage man is a lot more garrulous than I'd given him credit for. I don't think I've ever heard him say more than two words in all the time I've lived in this country. But he's unstoppable today. "Every house on this lane gave me a salary rise for lebaran last year. Every house, but this one. And your house makes more sampah than all the others put together. I will speak to the municipal office if things don't change. We'll boycott this address, and then let's see how your Mister manages.'

'Hold your tongue, you scum. You don't know anything about my master.' Who could this be? I risk a peek and spot the back of a thin Orang wearing a dirty vest and sarong. I think he's the pembantu that Ibu Mari met when Mrs A sent her here to complain about the garbage.

He's about the same size as Pak Jubaid, and the two are almost standing chest-to-chest. The pembantu is wagging his finger in the garbage man's face. 'He's a great man, a righteous man. If you are a true believer, you will bite your tongue, and do your work and make no more fuss, or my Mister will teach you a lesson like you've never had before.'

An alarming thought pops up. If Nono has already raised the alarm, Mr and Mrs A might be on their way. If they arrive now, while the pembantu is at the front gate, he could hold them back for a while. Certainly long enough for those inside the house to get wind of the plan. I need to find Tofu first or there's a risk she'll get hurt. Pak Eman is a vindictive Orang by all accounts. For the plan to work, the element of surprise is necessary.

It's time for the hutong hero to step up. He might be hungry and he might not be young, but he is still a force to reckon with. Taking a deep breath, I step out onto the lawn and meow as loudly as my somewhat dehydrated vocal cords permit. The pembantu jumps violently and stumbles, as though kicked in the gut. He turns, catches sight of me and immediately leaps into action, faster than I'd imagined.

He swings the front door shut in Pak Jubaid's face, ignoring the garbage man's protests and rounds in on me, muttering all the while. 'Where the devil did *you* come from? Dirty creature, polluting our house with fleas and disease! Pak Halim will skin me alive if he thinks I've let filth like you in.'

I am so indignant that I almost stand my ground and give him the 'look'. How dare this weedy Orang in his tattered vest impugn my good character and flea-less body. But I pull myself together at the last moment and make a dash for it. I need to locate Tofu, and fast.

I bound onto the driveway, weaving through the parked cars, my stomach wobbling like jelly. (If it had some food in it, it would probably have held firmer.) Tiktok had described the lay of the land to me; although being a beast of a lower order, his instructions had lacked precision. I knew I needed to get into the house and make my way up the stairs into a large room filled with computers. The problem, according to the rat, was that the house was filled with Orang and my dazzling colour makes it difficult

to be inconspicuous. Having a crazed pembantu running behind me, all the while shouting, 'Catch that devil cat', doesn't help matters either.

I am going so fast that everything is a blur, but I can make out the tall doors that lead into the building. Turning a sharp right at an impressive high speed, I sprint through them to emerge into a huge hall. I take it in: white walls, white floor tiles, no furniture except for a long bench and row upon row of shoes. But I have no time to ponder its strangeness.

The pembantu comes hurtling in behind me and within seconds three young Orang appear, seemingly out of thin air, to assist him. I back into a corner as they approach me, their knees bent and arms spread out to keep me from escaping. When they are almost upon me I let out my most blood-curdling yowl and blindly scratch everything I come into contact with: eyes, ears, necks. Instead of grabbing me, they are suddenly all trying to throw me off, clutching at their torn skin and clothes. I am truly magnificent: Soyabean the Sublime.

'Tofu, I'm coming,' I meow mightily as I bound up the stairs, two at a time. There is no stopping me now. I am like the wind, fast and furious. Ow! Ouch! I missed a step and am thudding back down the staircase. Ow! Ow! I am at the bottom of the stairs again, and unfortunately, the Orang seem to have recovered from my attack.

I pick myself off the floor and, disregarding the terrible pain I am in, start running up again. My empty stomach growls pitifully, but now is not the time to think of food. Tiktok had said the room Tofu was being kept in was to the right of the staircase, off a narrow corridor. The Orang are gaining on me, shouting vile, if unimaginative, threats like 'I'm going to get you!'

No, you're not. Not if Soyabean the Sublime has anything to do with it.

I gain the top of the staircase and spy the room to the right. There are still more Orang emerging from it. 'What's going...?' one of them begins to ask, but I swipe him aside with my powerful paw and, a second later, I am inside the room. It is as the rat had described: all tables, chairs and tangled cables. I look around wildly, trying to spot Tofu. Predictably, she is nowhere to be seen. 'Now is not the time to lurk about!' I want to yell at her. But I have more pressing concerns.

The room is agog. A dozen young Orang blink at each other, before training their gaze on me. I never imagined there to be such a thing as too much attention, but there definitely is. The pembantu and his dastardly accomplices arrive to add to the melee. 'Get that cat, now,' the pembantu shouts. 'Trap him!'

I am slipping through the legs of all the Orang, like a fish with claws. I dive under tables and leap over chairs. Around me, Orang trip on cables and catch their shirts on the edge of furniture. 'Aaaaargh! I'm going to get you,' the pembantu shouts yet again. It's getting old. But where in the World is Tofu? Tiktok had said she hangs out in some kind of cupboard in this room.

I turn round and round in tight circles, trying to find a corner the cat might be hiding in, but no luck. *Wham!* I am flung across the room and hit the wall hard. My breath leaves my body. There is so much pain, it roars in my ears. I can hardly see; the World is swimming.

'Got you now, haven't I?' Through the fug, I see a hazy figure advancing on me. It's the indefatigable pembantu, and he's carrying something in his arms. Even Soyabean the Sublime's brave heart plunges to his paws when he realizes it's a chair. The pembantu swings it high and is about to bring it crashing down onto me. I shrink into a ball because there is not much else I can do. I wish I could cuddle with the children one last time. Or eat a final bowl of tuna.

I squeeze my eyes and prepare for the final blow, but there is none; only a high-pitched screech. I look up to see the pembantu holding onto his bottom hopping around like he's just sat on a collection of Ishaan's toy spears from Papua. And there, standing in front of me, is Tofu as if she had never been gone. She just about has time to quickly touch her nose to mine when another one of the Orang grabs her by the tail and begins swinging her in circles.

I'm readying to attack, but a clear voice rings out. 'Put down that kucing. This instant. Put it down, or you will answer to me.' Who is this new fellow, now? He looks no different from the others: dressed in white, scraggly beard, smooth, young skin. But he walks over to Tofu and picks her up so gently, I sense at once that he is somehow different. Tofu melts into his arms. She *knows* him.

This cat never ceases to surprise the whiskers off me. First, she befriends a rat and now one of these ... these, whatever these Orang are. I stare hard at her and she meets my gaze steadily, telling me that she trusts him. He's a good egg, Tofu's relaxed ears seem to suggest. Hmm. Well, I'll be the judge of that. Even cats have heard of Stockholm syndrome.

'Mas Sigit, what are you doing? We must get rid of these cats before the master sees them,' the pembantu pants. I note with satisfaction that he's still clutching his bottom. But the boy addressed as Sigit only holds Tofu tighter. 'Stay away from us,' he warns.

'What in the name of the blessed Lord is going on here?' A voice rolls across the room like dull thunder. A toad of an Orang swaggers up to us. The effect on the youngsters in the room is instant. They pull themselves up to attention, and avoid eye contact. If there's one thing a cat understands, it's body language. These boys are afraid. They don't want to be blamed.

'What is the meaning of this, Sigit? Another cat in this house! Aduh! The Lord is testing us indeed.'

He sighs heavily, his face blackening like a rain cloud. 'I have had it with these vermin. The black one you are cradling in your arms like a baby is the devil itself. You all saw it bite me.' The Orang holds up his arm. It is bandaged at the wrist. I glance at Tofu and she nods slightly, confirming that the wound is her doing. I feel a flush of pride. She does spend too much time staring at the sky, but when push comes to shove she is fierce.

The fat Orang's ranting continues. 'Why Eman had to bring it here is beyond my wisdom. I can only hope the Lord understands his actions better. But that rice has become porridge and it can't be uncooked.' He falls silent for a moment looking from Tofu to me, and then back at her. I think I prefer his shouting to this quiet. I can hear my blood pounding in my head.

Sigit opens his mouth, but before he can say one word, the fatty holds up his hand, bandage flashing bright, to silence the boy. 'The thing is, Sigit my child, Pak Halim does not enjoy porridge. And if it can't be uncooked, well then, it must be thrown away. It's time to dispose of these cats. They have caused enough trouble already. Our cause is urgent. We must not, cannot, be distracted from it by these trifles.'

Sigit is trembling. I can see beads of sweat dotting his forehead. 'Pak Halim, forgive me,' he stutters. 'But clickbait. You said we needed clickbait. This kucing is already very popular. And if we keep the orange one too, we can double, triple our likes. Please...'

The fat man holds Sigit by the shoulder and grabs Tofu out of his arms. 'We don't need actual animals, boy. Use your brain. Why expose yourself to fleas and scratches?

Just download some cute pictures from the internet. No one will know the difference.'

Holding Tofu roughly by the scruff of her neck, Pak Halim bends down and drags me towards him with his other hand. He turns to face the room. 'Who will volunteer to take this filth outside and get rid of them once and for all?'

I struggle and strain, but the toady one is strong. He holds me away from his body, and try as I might, I can't get tooth or claw near him. I am beginning to panic. Where is Pak Nono? Why is Mrs A not here yet? Something must have gone wrong. And why did that beastly Tiktok not come up with a Plan B?

'Who will do this work?' Pak Halim asks once again. Miraculously, there is silence. No one steps forward. The Orang only look at their toes and shuffle their feet. Pak Halim's voice rises in indignation. 'What? Will not one of my boys help me with this?'

There is no answer except for more shuffling.

'It would appear I have raised a bunch of women!' The sneer is unmistakable, as the kiai, Eman, saunters through the door. His pale, glassy eyes are shining, as though in anticipation of something wonderful. He smiles. 'I started this cat business, so I will end it and show you little girls how it's done.'

Eman stops in front of Pak Halim and bows slightly. 'Pak, with your permission, I will begin with the black one. I really don't like its face.' With that, he grabs Tofu by her neck and begins squeezing.

'No, please, stop!' Sigit launches himself at Eman, tears streaming down his face, but the kiai shrugs him off as if he's nothing more than a mosquito.

I can see Tofu's eyes beginning to bulge, her tongue protruding from her mouth, and I realize I am not Soyabean the Sublime but merely Soyabean the Sorry. I'm sorry, Tofu. I did try my best.

'Di buka, open up!'

I snap my head back towards where the command is coming from. It's Pak Nono!

'If you don't open this gate right now, we will kick it down.'

It's Mrs A! Her voice is shrill with worry. The sound of metal rattling crashes through the windows, even though the blinds are down. They have come! They are breaking down the front gate. It's working! I could leap for joy, were Pak Halim not gripping me so hard.

The Orang in the room begin to move – slowly at first and then faster. In seconds, they are running, shouting instructions to hide this and tear up that. Abruptly, Pak Halim drops me to the floor and starts gathering papers and USB sticks off the tables, stuffing them into his pockets.

Someone stumbles and falls, but the others only trample over him in their hurry. He screams in pain. I swing about looking for Tofu. I can't see her or Eman. The screams multiply.

'Tikus!' an Orang suddenly yells, sounding terrified.

'Tikus!' another one chimes in, leaping onto a chair, only to lose balance and topple it over.

Soon the entire room erupts in shrieks of 'Tikus!' Orang scramble onto tables, clawing at each other to get out of the way.

Even I am taken aback as I behold the scene. The entire room is flooded with rats, dozens of them. I assume it's Tiktok's family. They are not a very attractive sight, but my heart fills with a something – I find it difficult to identify what at first, because it's an entirely new feeling. Then I have it. It's a grudging respect towards the rodent. He is obviously exceptional amongst his species. This must have been his Plan B. The tikus are here.

Chapter XIV

Mrs A

The Rescue

Mrs A was out of breath when she heard the security guard calling out for her. She'd been doing sets of jumping jacks and low lunges, trying to persuade the nasi goreng she loved eating to leave less of an impact on her belly.

'Ibu! Ibu!' Pak Nono's voice was unusually shrill.

Mrs A took a quick swig from the water bottle lying next to her exercise mat and went outside to find out what the guard wanted. She hoped it wasn't a rat sighting again. They'd need Ibu Warsi and her broom to deal with that. Pak Nono was as terrified of the rodents as Mrs A herself.

The security guard looked agitated as he gestured to Mrs A to come closer. 'What is it, Pak?' she asked, jogging lightly down the stairs. 'Is the rat back? Should I call for Ibu Warsi?'

'No, Bu. No rat. Cat!' answered Pak Nono urgently.

Mrs A felt more mystified than ever. 'Cat? What cat?'

'Fat cat,' the security guard replied. 'Orange cat. Soyabean.'

A shard of fear pricked Mrs A. 'What about Soyabean, Pak Nono? Where is he?' She looked about the driveway and garage. When had she seen him last? She couldn't remember.

'Kucing jump, Bu. He jump there. In dirty sampah house.' The security guard pointed to the garden wall that the house shared with their garbage-strewing neighbour.

Mrs A was incredulous. 'Soyabean jumped the wall? Are you sure?' Soyabean had difficulty lumbering onto their bed these days. She found it hard to imagine him being able to scale a wall that high.

'Yes, Bu, Pak Nono see him. He make big meow and jump.'

What on earth had got into Soyabean? He was much more inclined to be napping on silk cushions than to go cavorting about the neighbourhood in the heat. Although, come to think of it, he had been off colour ever since Tofu had gone missing. But then, they'd all been the same. Had she neglected to notice something, Mrs A wondered guiltily for a moment, before springing into action.

'Come with me, Pak. We should go and bring him back at once. The poor cat must be scared witless. And maybe,

I'll finally get to meet this elusive Mister who is never at home. It's time he gets a proper garbage can, whether he wants to or not.' Mrs A strode out of the front gate, Pak Nono following close behind.

A few bedraggled packets of instant noodles lay discarded along the way. Mrs A and Pak Nono exchanged tut-tutting looks. Once they were in front of the neighbour's gate, Mrs A raised a fist and rapped as loudly as she could. There was no response. Pak Nono stepped up beside her and tried his luck with knocking, only to meet with the same result. Nothing.

'I don't like this,' Mrs A muttered. 'Not one bit.'

She took a step back to survey the scene more fully, but it was impossible to see over the high gates. 'Hello!' she called out. 'Anyone home? Our cat has jumped into your garden. We've come to take him back. Can you open up, please?'

There was silence. Pak Nono instinctively put out an arm to nudge Mrs A back. She resisted, remaining shoulder to shoulder with him. 'Di buka, open up,' Nono hollered, giving the gate a light kick. It didn't budge. 'If you don't open this gate right now, we will kick it down,' Mrs A added shrilly.

A soft breeze wafted by, lifting the hair Mrs A had tucked behind her ears onto her cheeks. But there was something else it carried with it. 'Did you hear that, Pak?' Mrs A cocked an ear. 'There's *something* going on inside. Can you hear the shouting?' She stood stock-still for a second, frowning in concentration before straightening up, alarm written across her face. 'Was that meowing? Pak?' She looked at Pak Nono with wide eyes.

The security guard nodded grimly. 'Bu, stand on side, please. Nono will to kick door.'

He took a few steps back, readying to charge. Mrs A found herself wishing the security guard were a bit heftier. He grimaced, flashing his black teeth, and began to run in. But the second before his shoulder would have made contact, the gates were flung open, knocking him over.

Mrs A stared slack-jawed as a stream of young men emerged, some running frantically, others looking about cautiously. Most were clutching laptops, cables trailing on the floor.

'Excuse me, have any of you seen a big orange cat? My cat jumped over the wall into this house,' Mrs A tried asking, but the youngsters hurried on without so much as a glance at her.

'Who lives here?' she shouted at their disappearing backs. 'Where are all of you going? Who can I speak to about my cat? Hello! Can any of you hear me?' Her questions trailed the throng of fleeing men. They were boys really, Mrs A thought. What had so many of them been doing in the neighbour's house? It was quite confounding, but there were no replies and her words were eventually absorbed by the breeze.

Pak Nono was dusting himself off, having recovered from his tumble. He glanced up at Mrs A and shook his head. 'Not good, Bu. Not good place, this house.'

'Yes, it is very strange. Who were all those young people? Have you seen them before, Pak?'

'Never, Bu. Pak Nono always inside Misses' house. Not looking outside. But where cat is?'

'A very good question,' said Mrs A. 'I think it's time we find out. Come on.'

The journalist and security guard walked into the compound slowly, jumpily. Mrs A forced herself to take deep breaths, recalling the instructions of her mediation app. 'Breathe in, breathe out. Follow your breath. Repeat.'

There were several large cars and a motorbike parked along the driveway. 'This way, Bu,' Pak Nono, who was just ahead of her, indicated a door to the right, past all the vehicles. They stepped through gingerly, looking about for any sign of Soyabean. The room they had entered was cave-like with its high ceilings and almost no furniture. 'Not good place,' Pak Nono muttered repetitively.

'Soyabean!' Mrs A called out until she realized she was whispering. But even whispers sounded unnaturally loud in the empty room with its unnervingly bright white walls. She cleared her throat and tried again, louder this time. 'Soyabean! Are you here?'

Why was there no furniture, no paintings on the walls, no sign of family life? What kind of weird person lived in this hulking house? Who were all those boys rushing out of the house? Mrs A was starting to feel very uneasy. She felt for her phone in the pockets of her track pants. Perhaps she had better give Mr A a call to join them. There seemed to be more going on here than merely a case of a neighbour with bad hygiene.

'Ibu, look,' Pak Nono pointed towards a staircase. 'Go up?'

Mrs A nodded, even though her feet felt leaden. 'Yes, Pak. Let's go up.'

But before they could begin to climb, a surging susurration, at first distant, and then ever closer, descended the stairs towards them, like a scrabbling, scaly tsunami.

Mrs A's mouth opened in a silent scream as she felt a hit of revulsion so strong she thought she would vomit. Her body seemed to realize even before her mind could understand that she was looking at a river of sewer rats scampering straight towards her, and so she was as surprised as Pak Nono when she found herself leaping into his arms like a baby.

For a moment, she clung on to the security guard's neck as his arms tried to cradle her body. But Pak Nono shared Mrs A's horror of rats. He dropped her unceremoniously, right into the sea of rodents, hopping about first on one foot and then the other, yelping 'Astaga!'

Mrs A lay on the floor, dazed. Her mind shut down as a flurry of claws and tails slithered over her body. She covered her eyes with her hands and curled into herself, trying not to hold her breath. 'Breathe in, breathe out. Follow your breath,' she repeated to herself. 'In and out. In and out.'

After a few more seconds, she cracked an eye open expecting to shut it again in a hurry, but the room was empty once more, as swiftly and unexpectedly as it had been flooded by rats.

Pak Nono was hovering over her sheepishly. 'Sorry, Bu. Nono little bit scare with tikus,' he said, eyes cast down.

Mrs A scrambled up. 'Don't worry about it, Pak, but I think we need to go upstairs and get to the bottom of this.'

All caution discarded, she took the stairs two at a time, only pausing at the top. To her right was a closed door and from inside she heard a meow. It had been unmistakable, and yet, she thought that she must have been mistaken, for it was not Soyabean's loud hungry call, but Tofu's high-pitched squeak. Mrs A shook her head hoping to clear it. It was Soyabean who had leapt across the wall into this house. Tofu had been missing for days. The last anyone had seen of her had been the surreal picture circulating of her on WhatsApp, with a jilbab draped over her head. But Mrs A had been unable to trace the source of the photo.

A slow and dreadful clarity began to break through her confusion. Was this neighbour somehow involved in Tofu's disappearance and reappearance on social media? Was that why Soyabean had come here? It made a peculiar kind of sense.

She grabbed the door handle and turned it, striding into the room, ready to take on whatever fresh terrors lurked on the other side. 'Give me back my cat!' she demanded. But her words ricocheted across the room only to boomerang back at her. The room was deserted. She took in the upturned chairs and tables, the tangle of cables and the collections of instant noodle packets. People had left here in a hurry. Of course, she thought, the young men they'd seen rushing out. But what did the rats have to do with it? Had they been fleeing because of the rats?

There was that meow again. Tofu! She turned a full circle trying to locate the direction of the sound before zeroing in on a closet on the far side. Pak Nono had come to the same conclusion.

'There, Bu,' he said, pointing to the cupboard.

Mrs A was suddenly hesitant. Someone was holding Tofu hostage in there. Would it help or hurt for her to confront them? Should she call Mr A for back up first? What if it was too late?

Impulsively, she strode up to the closet and yanked the doors open, her eyes struggling to see in the shadows. A figure lay huddled in the corner, shielding something with its body. As the light filtered in, she could make out that it was a young man and then, like a rabbit emerging from a magician's hat, Tofu squeezed out from behind his prone form.

She trotted up to Mrs A's feet and rubbed her face against them. 'Baby cat!' gasped Mrs A, and bent down to pick her up. She breathed in Tofu's fur. 'Where have you been? Are you okay, Tofu? Are you hurt?'

Tofu stared without blinking at Mrs A, her whiskers quivering.

'Topu? Is name of kucing?' The crouching silhouette straightened up to reveal a puffy-eyed youngster, barely out of adolescence. He reached out to stroke Tofu. 'Sigit have secret name for kucing: Manis. Means sweet. But Sigit know that not real name.' He looked at Mrs A, the veins in his scrawny neck bulging. 'You are next-door bule? Your kucing?'

Mrs A nodded. She felt an inexplicable tenderness towards this boy who seemed to care so much for Tofu. But she didn't want to startle him. He had the look of a hurt animal about him, liable to bolt if panicked.

'Is your name Sigit, Mas? Can you tell me what's going on here? I don't understand why you have my cat.' Mrs A spoke gently, but the boy broke down into great heaving sobs. He shook his head from side to side, unable to reply.

Tofu strained in Mrs A's arms until they loosened. She bounded out and went up to where the young man sat, his head buried in his knees. 'Meow.' Sigit looked up and took the cat into his lap. Slowly, his sobs quietened, although he kept his eyes downcast.

'Come on, Mas. Let's go outside and talk,' Mrs A urged, and this time the boy obeyed. Pak Nono handed him a bottle of water that he'd found. Sigit gulped it down thirstily.

'Sorry, Ibu. I am truly sorry,' he eventually said after they'd all pulled up chairs.

'Why? About what?' asked Mrs A. 'What have you done? Have you seen my other cat, Soyabean? An orange cat.'

But Sigit continued talking as though he couldn't hear the questions. 'Sigit know inside heart this work not good, but Sigit family very poor. They give Sigit to kiai; think he good man, love God. But, Bu...' The boy looked Mrs A in the eye for the first time. There were such wells of sadness in them that she felt like crying herself.

'But what, Sigit? It's okay. You can tell me.'

'But we do many bad thing, Bu. Sigit know telling lie not good, but...' The boy broke into a fresh round of sobs.

Pak Nono spoke up in Bahasa Indonesia 'Sigit, who does this house belong to? You need to help us to help you. Pull yourself together, brother. No one will hurt you.'

'Pak Halim,' replied the boy, his voice muffled. 'The kiai brought us here to Pak Halim's house.'

'Who is *us*?' asked Pak Nono.

'Nine or ten boys from the pesantren. We worked here almost all the time. Fighting infidels.' Sigit gestured to the empty tables. 'We posted negative stories on social media about people.'

'Which people?'

'People that Pak Halim and kiai Eman selected. Bad men, the wicked, the dirty. Atheists and communists, like that journalist Hendra.'

Pak Nono shot Mrs A a look, warning her not to interrupt. The boy was finally talking. It wouldn't do to scare him again. 'Do you know where Halim and Eman are now? Any idea?'

Sigit shrugged. 'They ran away when the tikus came.'

'The tikus! Yes, we saw many of them. What can you tell us about them? Are there always so many in the house?'

'A few, Pak. Never so many. I've never seen anything like so many.' Suddenly, Sigit bolted off his chair, eyes wide with an epiphany. 'I think...' he hesitated before continuing, 'I think, maybe the tikus were here to rescue the cats. It sounds crazy, Sigit knows. But no matter how crazy, that is what must have happened.'

Mrs A, who could only follow the broad outlines of the conversation, wondered if the boy was feverish. Or maybe her Indonesian was even worse than she'd thought. He couldn't seriously have been suggesting that an army of rats had tried to free her cats. But, *cats*, he'd said cats in the plural. So he had seen Soyabean!

'Where is the other cat, Mas?' Mrs A asked urgently. 'Did you see him?'

'Fat one, Bu?' Sigit switched to English.

'Yes, yes, fat one,' replied Mrs A eagerly.

The boy looked down at his toes, his voice dropped an octave. 'Sorry, Bu. Sigit get Manis, your Topu, for keeping safe. But he took fat one.'

'Who, Sigit? Who is *he*? Please, please tell me.'

Vroom! The noise exploded into their conversation, scattering them all like shrapnel towards the window at the side of the room. At first, Mrs A only noticed that the sky was darkening, threatening to spill. It was after she'd pressed her hands against the windowpane that she saw Eman zooming out of the driveway on a motorbike. The kiai had on a bulging backpack and, clearly visible, out of the narrow opening at the top was the head of a cat – orange fur flying in the humid wind, a silent meow on his pulled-back lips.

It was Soyabean.

Chapter XV

Tofu

Keeping Vigil

The boys are all hands. I try to bear it when they cup my head, stroke me, hold me. I try not to squirm; they are anxious. Soyabean's absence fills the house.

Yesterday morning, I heard Nico asking Ishaan, 'Everyone keeps disappearing. Will you go away too?'

'No, little fellow,' I wanted to tell Nico, 'your brother will always be by your side. You will always be loved.' But I knew that the world was neither fair nor safe, and that my words would have only been so much hot air, as words were. I didn't trust words at all. But then, I am a cat. A cat sitting under a frangipani tree chatting with a rat.

Tikus was trying to comfort me. He twitched as he asked about my appetite. 'Are you eating? You need to keep up your strength.'

I didn't have the heart to tell him that being comforting was not a rat's forte. What rats were good at was sniffing out information, and I nudged him along those lines. 'I'm fine, Tikus, really. Everyone is treating me like a queen. They don't need to of course, because *I* am fine. Soyabean should be our focus now. Is there any news at all?'

The rat's eyes glinted in the sun. It was hot underfoot. 'I've circulated a description of Soyabean for those who haven't seen him, and all tikus are on the lookout. He paused briefly before squeaking on: 'There was one false alarm.'

I cocked my head.

'Oh, it was nothing. Just young, Nephew Number Nine–Tikus thought that he'd spotted a cat fitting the description in a kampung in Depok. But Niece Number Thirteen–Tikus was with him and, to be honest, she's a bit cleverer. She said the cat that Nephew Number Nine–Tikus had seen was much too skinny to be Soyabean. Niece Number Thirteen–Tikus was one of the tikus who helped rescue you, so she's actually seen Soyabean for herself. And my poor nephew is a kampung tikus, he doesn't have much experience with the shape of house cats like you.'

I looked at him, perhaps a bit blankly, which is why he must have felt compelled to add an explanation. 'I don't mean you personally. Just, you know, cats that have enough to eat.'

I thought of my Mama and my brothers. We were not the same shape either – them and me. They were misshapen. I was shapely. But before I could follow my thoughts any further, Tikus hissed and shrank into himself. I turned to find Mrs A staring at us most strangely. She looked from Tikus to me, and back. My Ren mother was terrified of rats. Tikus needed to get out of here this instant before she summoned Ibu Warsi and her broom. Unfortunately, there was little cover between where we were standing and the hole in the garden wall from where Tikus could escape.

But Mrs A did not call out or scream or run away. She only looked at us. And then she turned on her heels and began walking back into the house, clicking her fingers for me to follow. 'Come on back in, Tofu,' she said, walking away swiftly. 'We don't want you disappearing again. It's been like a relay with you cats as it is.' It was almost as though she hadn't seen Tikus at all, which made more sense to me than the idea of her having seen the rat and just ignoring him.

I twitched my nose at the rat, indicating that he should leave, but he needed no encouragement and was already scampering off. Then I headed into the house where I found the usual crowd sitting in the living room. Pak Hendra was sinking comfortably into the blue sofa, with

Debbie and Mr A next to him. Ibu Mari and Ibu Warsi sat on chairs opposite them, while Mrs A paced up and down the length of the room.

These Ren were my World. The only ones missing were Ishaan and Nico, who were in school, Pak Nono, who was in the driveway, and Pa'harto, who no longer came to work.

But the one *really missing* was Soyabean. What was Eman doing to him? Just the question felt like a punch to the gut. All I knew for sure was that Soyabean was not safe. And the longer he was gone, the greater the danger.

When they'd found him, Pak Halim had blamed everything on Eman. Given the circumstances, I suppose this was not very surprising. Yet, somehow I thought there might be some truth to the claim. Halim was bad, but the kiai was truly loathsome.

The police had caught our neighbour hiding at his parents' home all the way on Lombok island a few days after Mrs A and Pak Nono had rescued me. It turned out that the house next door had been the centre of something called a fake news network. It was a peculiar thing, this fake news: a very Ren thing. Like calling a black cat white and everyone somehow believing it, instead of trusting their own eyes and brains. How could anyone believe that someone as good as Pak Hendra was a bad man because the Ren claiming so had also posted a picture of a cat wearing a jilbab? I thought it unintelligent. Or maybe cats were just not clever enough to understand the intricacies of lies.

Pak Halim had confessed that he paid young men from poor families to spread falsehoods about people like Pak Hendra on social media. Eman supplied the boys from the pesantren, and Pak Halim insisted that the whole enterprise had been the kiai's idea. The neighbour was now with the police, but Eman had vanished. Ibu Mari said he had not come home and he hadn't been seen at the pesantren either.

Everyone was on the lookout for the kiai and a large, orange cat: the police, the tikus, even Ibu Debbie's Indonesian Atheist group. But so far, there had been no trace of either. Mrs A had hardly eaten in days, even though Ibu Warsi was forever putting out plates of her favourite snacks. Pak Hendra had more or less moved into the house. I suppose we were keeping a vigil of sorts.

I jumped up onto Mr A's lap, who put his arms around me. His cheeks were sunken with exhaustion. He'd been driving around looking for Soyabean for hours every day, even though Mrs A told him it was pointless.

'Does anyone here actually believe Halim? That he has no idea where Eman is?' Mrs A asked without slowing her pacing.

'Sit down, Bu. You're making us dizzy,' said Pak Hendra gesturing to an empty chair.

Mrs A ignored the suggestion and repeated, 'Does anyone believe it? I mean the gall of the man! He's bleating on about being some kind of hero. "I fed those boys from my own money. I gave them Indomie. I gave them milk."' Mrs A raised the pitch of her voice to mimic the wheedling tone of the neighbour.

'Does it really matter, Bu?' Pak Hendra dragged a hand through his hair, tiredly. 'Truth or not, I doubt we're going to get any more information out of him. And for what it's worth, I'm not sure he knows much more. I think it's quite likely that Halim was just the shell. My money is on Eman being the peanut.'

Ibu Mari groaned and buried her head in her hands, but Ibu Warsi spoke to her gently, in Indonesian. 'Warsi is here, Mba. There is no need to worry. If that Eman tries anything funny, his bottom will meet my broom.'

Ibu Debbie shot them a dark look. 'I'd like nothing better than to give your husband a hiding myself,' she said. 'But if you do hear from him, anything at all, you must tell the police immediately. Let them handle it. Pak Eman is a lot more dangerous than we might even be able to imagine.'

Mrs A raised an eyebrow. Ibu Debbie's voice cracked ever so slightly as she explained, 'I just mean that he's already had innocent people beaten up. Jailed even.

Deliberately. He is a thoroughly empty man. I think he's empty of feelings, of morals, of happiness. Men like that are bad news.'

'If only they were fake news,' laughed Pak Hendra.

Debbie glared at him. 'It's not funny...' she began, but her voice was drowned out by the sound of ojeks. 'Who's that?' asked Debbie.

Mrs A shrugged. 'I'm not sure. We aren't expecting anyone.'

'I'll go look.' Mr A picked me up and carried me with him to the main door. He opened it just as Pak Nono came jogging up the stairs with four boys following behind.

I squirmed out of Mr A's grip and ran straight to Sigit. The others hung back as he knelt to stroke my head. I gave his fingers a lick. They were salty and a little grubby. This Ren could do with some grooming. It happens when you lose your mother too soon; my Da Ge was the same. The bravest and kindest cat in Beijing, but not the cleanest.

'Come in, Sigit,' said Mr A waving him inside. 'Bring your friends too.'

'Sigit can carry Manis? Your kucing?' the boy asked, still crouching by my side.

Mr A smiled. 'You don't need to ask me. Ask her. If she's okay with it, that's all the permission you need.'

I clambered into Sigit's lap without further fuss and he scooped me up.

'It's funny how it often feels like cats can understand us talking,' Mr A said, turning to return inside, the boys close on his heels.

Pak Nono went back to the driveway.

'Sigit! Is everything okay? Come sit down. Can we get all of you something to drink?' Mrs A asked as we entered the drawing room.

I noticed Ibu Warsi slipping away towards the kitchen. Sigit did not meet anyone's eyes. He just stood there, holding me close to his chest, staring at the floor.

'What is it?' Mrs A asked, walking up to him. 'Are you unwell?' Sigit set me down on the carpet and then turned towards Pak Hendra who, like everyone else in the room was looking quizzically at the boy.

'Pak, Sigit very sorry,' he mumbled, before switching to Indonesian, '*Mohon ma'af.* I've done you a great wrong.'

Pak Hendra held his arms open. 'No, Sigit. I should be the one who is sorry. Every Indonesian should be sorry that your parents were forced to entrust you to the likes of Eman. You don't need to apologize, young man. Pak Hendra is strong. It takes a lot more than fake news to shut me down!'

Ibu Warsi was back in the room, carrying a tray with glasses of water that she held out to the boys. Sigit's friends drank thirstily, but he himself refused the drink. 'Ibu,' he said nervously, addressing Mrs A. 'Sigit have news.'

The room hushed and time seemed to slow down. The buzz of far away traffic filtered through the stillness. It was Pak Hendra who finally broke the spell. 'News? What kind of news?'

'Kiai come to Sigit room in pesantren today. These, my friend: Adi, Agung and Bagus,' Sigit waved a hand at the other boys, who clasped hands to their hearts and bent their heads, almost in unison. 'They with me when kiai come.'

'What did he want? Was Soyabean with him?' Mrs A's voice was shrill.

'No, Bu, no kucing with Pak Eman. But,' Sigit hurried on as Mrs A's face crumpled, 'but, kiai have kucing. He told Sigit give bule message.' The boy spoke so quickly his words tumbled over each other.

'Here, have a sip,' Mr A interrupted, handing the boy a glass of water. 'Take your time. You have nothing to be scared about. Tell us what Eman wanted you to say to us. Try and remember every detail. Okay?'

'He say if bule pay him money, he give back kucing. He want you meet him in Lippo Mall, in Kemang. No police. No friends. Only you. He say he good man and all fault is Pak Halim.' Sigit was almost panting with urgency. 'He say you give money and he go away. You get back kucing. No more problem. But if you get police, you not see cat again.'

'What time does he want to meet?' asked Mrs A, grabbing her purse off the floor. 'And how much money does he want?'

'At three o'clock, Ibu, in Lippo Mall. He want,' Sigit lowered his voice, '100 million rupiah.'

'Wait a minute,' protested Mr A. 'Does anyone trust this man to keep his word? Shouldn't we call the police?'

'I'd expect rats to fly before trusting the kiai to keep his word,' Pak Hendra said. 'He's a snake hiding behind the stones alright. And yes, we should call the police. Immediately.'

'No. Not now.' Mrs A's tone was rough. 'We need to get Soyabean back first.'

'And how are we going to do that? You want to pay off that villain?' asked Mr A. 'If we try and do this ourselves, it could end badly for everyone, including Soyabean.'

'For heaven's sake. We don't have much time. It's two-thirty already.' Mrs A had begun striding towards the front door, but she stopped and looked back. 'Let's just go; only the two of us. Like the kiai wants. Pak Hendra and Debbie can follow with the police – if they can manage to get their attention in time. But we can't lose this opportunity. We can't!'

Mr A exhaled loudly. 'Fine, let's do it. But I think it might be too late. I was out this morning, and the road to Kemang was totally jammed. I think they want to get the MRT open before the elections. The traffic is insane.'

'Can take on ojek.'

'What?' Mr A swivelled to face the voice. It was one of Sigit's friends, Bagus.

'What did you say?' Mr A asked again. Bagus' face had turned a flaming red and he suddenly seemed tongue-tied, but Sigit had come alive.

'Yes!' Sigit exclaimed. 'Yes. Very good idea.' He walked towards Mr and Mrs A, shoulders thrown back, until he was standing between them. 'You will come on ojek?' he asked. 'With us?' The As exchanged quick nods and it was decided.

I sat still as a storm broke all around me. Ojeks shot out of the driveway. Pak Nono clanged the gate shut. Pak Hendra and Debbie shouted into their phones. My stomach flip-flopped. I felt like something was going to give.

Chapter XVI

Soyabean

Kampung

I am befouled by the kiai. The rascal has grabbed me, manhandled me most outrageously, stuffed me in a backpack and is now hurrying away somewhere. I think we are going downstairs; I can feel the descent, although I can't see much. I try to meow, but I'm squeezed in so tight that I begin to choke.

Tantalizing sounds filter into the backpack: tikus squealing, Orang screaming, and, if I'm not mistaken, Tofu mewling. But these fade as Eman's huffing and puffing becomes the dominant note. It is obvious he is running away, but where to? And why with me? I would give up a dinner of tuna steak to sink my teeth into this Orang's smug face. Well, maybe not a fresh tuna steak, but a can of tuna most definitely.

Eman goes still. His breathing is as heavy as the darkness. We are somewhere windowless and forlorn. All of a sudden, I hear running. If it could, my heart would soar straight out of my body and through the opening of the backpack.

Mrs A's voice is ringing out, clear as a bell, 'Soyabean! Are you here?'

I begin to struggle. I must break out of this infernal backpack. I try bucking and twisting, but Eman swings the backpack off and smacks me on the side of my head. I have a bad feeling that this is his signature move. The pain is sharp and hot, and I go limp.

After a wait, which feels interminable, although it might only be a few minutes – being beaten mercilessly can have adverse effects on the most infallible of internal clocks – we are on the move again. It is light once more, and I venture a peek. But before I can get my bearings, there is a thud, a heave and a loud vroom. *Astaga naga*! A whiplash of air has me gasping. First, it was too little, and now too much. I would marvel at the irony were I not too busy choking.

The kiai rides the ojek out of the driveway like a maddened brute. Once we're on the road, we zigzag through the traffic alarmingly. Luckily, the backpack I've been imprisoned in is securely fastened onto Eman's back. But my eyes are aflame with the pollution and the wind. I've never been out in the World like this before. It's a different, and rather less appetizing, bowl of sardines to our outings to the cat groomers in the As' air-conditioned car.

Within minutes, we are out of the neighbourhood and onto a broad main road. But the macet is impenetrable. Cars, vans and ojek are stacked up, one behind the other, nothing moving. I crane my neck every which way to try and glean a clue about where we are, or, more importantly, where we might be going. Unfortunately, being a pet cat means I am rather limited in my geographic knowledge.

The road seems to have a big construction site dividing it into two. A mechanical monster is trundling up and down it. Huge blocks of concrete pipes and metal sheets line the area. Eman swears – for a religious leader, the kiai's language is overly colourful – and glues his thumb to the ojek's horn. Its peeee-peeee noise is swallowed up by the general cacophony on the road. No one pays him much attention.

Eman swears again. Such ignoble turns of phrase! They have my ears burning, as though smarting eyes weren't enough for a cat to handle. And then he heaves the ojek off the road and onto the paved surface adjacent to the construction site. In a second, we are zipping along once again, macet-free. For once, I know where we are. It's the busway, a path meant only for special buses. Mr A had driven our car on the busway once, and ended up getting a big fine from the police and a long lecture from Mrs A. But today, there is no police officer in sight; more irony, and still no respite from choking to be able to appreciate it.

I lose track of how long we've been going, but eventually the kiai takes us off the busway and we squeeze past the jam of cars into a narrow side road. Open ditches line the street, and there is a rather unpleasant odour in the air. It smells of dirt and also, strangely, of hunger. Speaking of, I cannot remember when I last ate. Being kidnapped on an empty stomach is even worse than just being kidnapped.

We turn into another lane and then another. This is nothing like our neighbourhood. Instead of big houses and high walls, there are shacks, and you can look right into crowded rooms buzzing with flies and babies. The kiai is driving very slowly now, honking at the shabby children who play on the road. A mother chicken and her troop of chicks scatter in front of our ojek. A wrinkled old lady is hanging laundry on a line fastened right over the sewer. This place feels familiar. A bakso seller is blaring music from his cart. I can't quite place it at first, but then I have it. This is a bit like an Indonesian hutong. It must be one of those kampung places that Tofu is always bleating about.

'Yunqi,' she'd muse ever so often. 'Why am I in this comfortable house, when there are kampung tikus who die of hunger every day?' As far as I was concerned then, the fewer tikus the better. Even now, I wouldn't exactly describe myself as a champion of kampung rodents.

But it's true that on the 'dying of hunger' front I am fast developing some sympathy.

I wonder what happened to Tofu. I only hope she is back home safe, or all my heroism will have been for naught. Last I could remember the boy, Sigit, had snatched her out of Eman's hands once the tikus made their entrance. Unfortunately, that had freed up the kiai to grab me instead. She's not as brave as me, silly Tofu. She's a delicate cat. Her tummy is so easily upset, it's ridiculous. A quick purr ripples through my body at the thought of her lying curled up safely on a dark shelf amongst Mrs A's sarees, her favourite spot in the house.

But soon, the purr turns into the rumble of an empty stomach mixed with the plummeting sound of a cat's heart dropping to his feet thinking about his bleak prospects. How on earth is anyone going to find me in this stinky kampung? And I'm still not sure why Eman has brought me along for the ride, although I am quite sure it's not for any reason that would give me cause for cheer. I'm in a bit of a sambal all right.

Many twisting turns later, the kiai is finally pulling up next to what is obviously the standard architecture in these parts: an open sewer framed by a clothes line leading into a room crammed with pots and pans, a large bed, a worn-out rug, three children and a baby.

'So, you're back? Have you got any money? Or is your God going to provide?' A female Orang emerges from a door set to the back of the room. Perhaps it is the kitchen?

She is dressed in a sarong and dirty grey top, a dishcloth slung over her shoulder.

I am swung around indecorously as Eman takes off the backpack and enters the shack. It's hard to make out exactly what is going on until the kiai discards the pack, with me still in it, in a corner of the room. Even though I am dizzy, I'm finally able to crawl out. The bag's drawstrings have loosened with all the motion.

'Keep your mouth shut, woman,' Eman growls. 'A glass of teh tarik. I need to think.'

One of the children, a little girl, begins crying soundlessly, her face screwed-up, tears coursing down her cheeks and yet no sound escaping her lips. I sidle up to where she is sitting cross-legged on the floor and rub the back of my head against her knee. Luckily, no one notices either of us, but the girl instantly stops her sobbing and smiles. Beholding me has that effect on little Orang.

The female Orang shows no signs of getting any tea for Eman. She drags the dishcloth off her shoulder as though unsheathing a weapon and starts to shout shrilly. 'Why has the Lord cursed me in this life? Does money grow on trees, Pak Kiai? And where have you been in any case? I don't see you for Lord only knows how long, and then you come dancing in demanding teh tarik! It's not like I'd ever expect you to come with something nice to eat for the children, but how about a "How are you, Ipah?" Is even that too much for you?'

'Ipah, don't push my patience,' Eman says with a look that could curdle milk to yogurt. 'It's been a difficult day. I need to think.'

'You need to think. *You*!'

It is clear to me that Ibu Ipah is not possessed with a calm temperament. Why this is so becomes abundantly clear as she continues her tirade.

'While you are having your difficult day, no doubt at your rich friend's fancy house, Ipah has been standing with the baby by the main road for hours. I have to give the baby medicine to keep it sleeping, so it does not cry. A mother has to drug her baby. It makes me feel like the devil to do it. But what choice do I have, Eman? It's not like you support us.'

The kiai raises his voice to match Ipah's. 'How many times have I told you not to do this dirty work? What would people think if they knew that a kiai's woman was working as a sampah jockey? Getting in and out of cars with strangers. Where are your morals, woman?' Eman spits – *splat!* – on the floor.

I think it's a bit much that he calls the other Orang 'sampah' and then so unceremoniously expectorates himself.

Ibu Ipah is ready with her answer. 'That is how I make money, Eman. Your Ipah does nothing wrong. What is sampah about being a jockey? My customers just need an extra passenger in the car so they can drive on the highway during rush hour. You know the rule. If there are less than three people in the car, it must take the side roads. These people are busy, important. They have jobs to get to and cannot waste time stuck in macet. So we help them out. What's wrong with it? It is how I get food on the plate. You want teh, but if I was not a jockey where would the money for the teh and the milk come from? Not from you, I am certain.'

The girl has been stroking me throughout this conversation, and now she takes me into her lap and holds me close. Admittedly, I am not at my most groomed, but even at the worst of times, I remain lovably fluffy.

I notice that the baby is lying still on what is a very stained rug. It's not like any baby I've seen before. There is a fly sitting right at the corner of its eye, but it does not move to shoo it off. I think of Nico and Ishaan, and how wriggly they are all the time. My heart starts beating faster as I feel something unfamiliar. Yikes! I do believe its empathy. Soon I'll be mooning away about yunqi like Tofu.

There are two other children in the room, both boys. They are very thin; I can see their ribs as they sit on prayer mats like the one Ibu Warsi has. They are facing a wall, but I notice that every once in a while, they steal a glance at their parents. Parents? Is it just me or is everything confusing? Is the kiai their father? Then what about Ibu Mari? Who is this Ipah? The base affairs of Orang are honestly beyond feline comprehension, and it's a jolly good thing that.

I tune back into the conversation in which Eman has returned to scowling mode and his favourite topic. 'You should stay at home like a pure woman and pray. God is great. He rewards the pious and provides, if you have faith.'

Ibu Ipah sinks down to the floor. 'It looks like you'll have your prayers answered soon enough, Pak. They're saying the MRT will be ready very soon. You know what that means? No more restrictions on passenger numbers in cars on the highway. No more jockeys. No more money. Who will feed my children? The Lord should just take my life now. Why delay?'

'You women are so hysterical. Why be so dramatic?' sneers Eman.

'Dramatic! Who is being dramatic?' screeches Ipah, brandishing the dishcloth. 'If you don't like it here, go home to your precious Ibu Mari. I might be a jockey, but at least I don't demean myself as a servant to bules. Go to her for your teh, Eman. And speaking of your wife, have you finally found the courage to tell her about us?'

My ears prick up. I would like to know the answer to this as well.

It's clear from Eman's expression that it's a no.

Ipah appears to surmise as much. 'How much longer are you going to keep us stashed away like sampah in a dustbin? How much?' she screams.

I can feel the little girl's hot breath rise and fall as she clutches at me. I would let her squeeze me like this for hours if I thought it would allow her to forget about this hellish place. Now that I've caught this empathy bug, it seems to be intent on staying put.

Eman squats down next to Ipah and raises his hand as if about to strike her. I am already groaning from the clobbering he'll give me once I've unleashed my claws on him. But before I can make my move, the kiai appears to deflate. Instead of hitting Ipah, he slaps his own forehead.

'Can you be quiet for once, woman! Now is not the time for your prattle. There is trouble. I must think of something, otherwise that Halim will leave me hung out to dry. I'm not sure he can be trusted under pressure. These rich men are all the same: too soft.'

Ipah takes Eman by his shoulders and looks into his eyes. They are a strange colour. Too light, almost milky, for his face. 'What's wrong, Eman? What has that dog, Halim, done?'

The kiai shakes his head. 'I don't know for sure. Halim is an idiot. A rich idiot, but I can't trust him. Even my own boys from the pesantren have turned on me. All because of that ugly cat.' His pale eyes flash and he looks towards me. It is clear from his expression that he does not wish me well.

Ipah looks at me too. It's the first time she's noticed that I'm even in the room. 'Do you mean *that* cat?' she asks. 'Why have you brought it here?'

'No, not that cat. Another one.' Eman looks worried. It's a fetching change from his standard glower-scowl.

'Never mind,' he shakes his head. 'It's too complicated for a woman to understand.'

Even I can tell that Ipah is not the type of Orang to be brushed off easily. 'What is too complicated for me? I'm smarter than you and Halim put together and multiplied by all your pesantren lackeys. What trouble are you fools in?'

'We've been found out,' says Eman, who looks sullen again. 'The boys dared to defy me just to protect the bule's kucing. Not this orange one; another wretched black creature. And then the tikus appeared and everyone began squealing like children. The young men these days have no discipline.'

Ipah is staring at Eman as though he were raving like a mad man, but she says nothing, and the kiai continues what I realize must sound like an improbable flow of events. 'Even then I could have got everything back in hand, but the she-devil bule started hammering at the gates just then and the cendol-livered boys panicked. They made a run for it, and let in the bule and her servant. Halim disappeared and I had no choice but to make a getaway.'

The baby on the rug is finally beginning to stir. It rubs its face, unsettling the flies. The girl pushes me off her lap and crawls towards the baby. I have a bad feeling. About everything. Ipah turns towards me. There is no place for me to back into. 'So,' she clears her throat and speaks slowly. 'Why is *this* cat here?'

'Look at him,' replies Eman. 'Fat and well-fed, isn't he? These bule treat their animals like little Gods. They deserve to be punished just for that. He got into Halim's house somehow; must have jumped over the wall. And I took him. I don't really know why, but I do know it will upset his atheist-loving owners. That's enough cause.'

The kiai scrambles up and starts towards me. 'Maybe I should kill it now. At least I can be of some service to the Lord by ridding His beautiful world of filth like this.'

'Do not touch that kucing!' Ipah's voice is clear and loud, and suddenly quite melodious to my ears. 'This cat is valuable. The bule will pay you for returning it. Do it! Get some money from them, and then we can all leave. I'll take you back to my village.' Ipah grabs Eman's leg and pleads: 'We'll do some farming; stay with my parents. I'll cook for you. We can be happy, I promise. Please, listen to me this once.'

The kiai hesitates. Anything that gives him pause from attacking me is good news as far as I am concerned. 'But what about our fight?' he says. 'We can't just give it up. It is God's will that we take down His enemies. And the election is very close.'

Ipah gets off the floor and stands up, hands on her hips, dishcloth back on her shoulder. 'Listen, Pak. Leave Mari. She is no good for you. Take the money from the bules and let us go away. Your fight is righteous, yes, but it is not a matter of today or tomorrow. The pure-hearted have been fighting it from before time, and the fight will go on after this election and beyond. Let's take some time to rest and recover before the next battle. It's what the Lord would want. I'm sure of it.'

A great wailing fills the room and all of us, even I, who am known for my nerves of steel, start in shock. The baby is crying like there will be no tomorrow.

Chapter XVII

Mrs A

Mall Melee

The mall's entrance was obscured by a sea of stalls, their white awnings aflutter in the breeze. Mrs A remembered distractedly that weekends at Lippo Mall featured an Artisanal Food Fair. She threaded her way past tables laden with herb-crusted kale chips and homemade almond butter. It was a melee; ladies toting designer handbags stepped out of expensive cars while nannies soothed testy infants into prams.

Mr A, Sigit and his friends followed close behind, their faces strained tight. They had made it to the mall with only minutes to spare. The macet had been dreadful, as predicted. The ojeks were now parked illegally on the side of the road leading up to the Food Fair; there had been no time to find proper parking.

Once in the air-conditioned lobby, the sudden hush felt uncanny. The pesantren boys were overcome with shyness. The mall was a foreign country to them; the models advertising the clothes and shoes being sold in the shops were white-skinned and blonde. An entertainer was playing the theme song from *Beauty and the Beast* on a grand piano. The young men had never heard the song before. Nor had they seen a piano in person. They gaped like fish.

'Hurry,' urged Mrs A, pulling on Sigit's hand as she jogged towards the escalators. The kiai was supposed to be waiting for them in the basement, next to ACE, a sprawling hardware store. She'd been wondering about Eman's choice of meeting point. Was there any logic to it? Perhaps it was because he'd likely be carrying Soyabean in a bag. A kiai with a bulging bag would probably draw less attention outside a hardware store, rather than the French fashion boutiques that dotted the rest of the mall.

They sprinted down the escalators, Mrs A in the lead once more. She knew this mall well, ACE in particular, having spent an inordinate amount of time there in her early days in Indonesia. The shop was the source of many things in the As' home, from the nails on the walls to the anti-mosquito citronella candles on the verandah.

They passed a bookstore on their right and a beauty salon on the left. Only the length of a supermarket separated them from ACE, when Mrs A spotted the kiai. She stopped in her tracks, almost causing the others to bump into her. But before anyone could exclaim, she'd turned around, finger on her lips and a fierce expression that commanded silence.

She held out her arm, finger pointing to the far end of the corridor, where, amidst a grove of plastic Christmas trees, right outside the main entry into the hardware store, Pak Eman lurked, complete with a telltale bulky bag on his shoulder. Mr A moved stealthily to the front of their motley gaggle. He gestured for them to move to one side of the passageway, out of Pak Eman's direct line of sight.

They squished up against the wall of a pharmacy for a few moments, hearts cantering, and then began to creep forward. They'd already discussed that the best-case scenario was one where they could sneak up on the kiai and wrest Soyabean away from him before he'd even had the time to realize what was going on. No one had expected it to be so easy, but suddenly, there seemed to be a genuine chance that they could pull it off. Pak Eman appeared unexpectedly interested in the Christmas trees and was gazing at the fairy lights as though entranced.

The kiai was thirty metres in front of them, his back to the group. They moved forward and gained ten metres, and then another. Mr and Mrs A exchanged a brief, incredulous glance. Was their outrageous luck going to hold? Eman was fingering the plastic needles of a large tree, oblivious to the goings-on just behind him.

Mrs A indicated that the others should stay put. She had decided to sprint the few remaining steps between the group and Eman, and to grab the bag off his shoulder before anyone could say '*Astaga!*' But as she hurled herself forward, her right thigh slapped against the handbag she was carrying. 'Welcome back. Today we'll explore ways to allow the breath to flow at its own natural pace. Start by taking a comfortable position.'

Mrs A froze, stunned. Her phone's meditation app had never sounded louder or been more unwelcome. The kiai jumped, as if stung and pivoted to face her, his stance wide and combative.

He spoke in Bahasa Indonesia. 'You've come?'

'Iya,' replied Mrs A as steadily as she could. 'Yes.'

'Where is my money?' Pak Eman asked, ominously soft-spoken.

Mrs A turned to Sigit, who had come up to stand next to her and began to interpret. 'Kiai want money,' he explained.

'Well, he isn't getting a rupiah from us. And we want our cat back immediately, no conditions.' Mr A had walked up to Pak Eman and stood chest-to-chest with him. The kiai stared at him unflinchingly and began to speak.

'Pak, Ibu, Eman your friend. Not bad man. Look, orange cat here, in bag. Just give money and Eman go away. Far away. No problem for anyone,' Sigit translated.

'What do you mean, *no problem* for anyone?' Mrs A asked. 'Do you think Pa'harto would agree with you not being a problem? Or Pak Hendra? Or Ibu Mari? Do you know how much danger they have been in because of your lies? Do you know how much your wife has suffered? Do you think the parents of the children in your pesantren will agree that you are *not a problem* for having used these young boys and infected them with hate?'

Mrs A had begun to shake. 'Pak Eman, hand over our cat to us and surrender to the police. They are already on their way. If you do this, there will truly be no problem for anyone.'

The bag on the kiai's shoulder was jumping compulsively, muffled meows emanating from its insides. He held on to it tightly and took a step back, but a wall of Christmas trees prevented his retreat. He tried pleading again. 'You already have Halim. He bad man. Always telling kiai to do bad thing. Eman happy Pak Halim in jail. Now Eman just want little money, and bule have nice cat back.'

'Pak Eman,' Mr A interjected. 'The only place you are going is to join Halim in jail. The likes of you are a plague. We are foreigners, yes, but we have come to love and respect your country; the country you are destroying with your poison. You say you are pious, but you have no goodness in you. And if there is a God, She knows this too.'

Eman's face, which had been a mask of contrition, flared into a snarl. He spat on Mr A's shoes and heaved the bag around onto his other shoulder. 'You bule get out Indonesia now, or we throw you out. Kiai no want your dirty money. Eman make mistake coming here, listening to no-good woman. But, Mister, you also make mistake to coming here and talking at kiai like this. You know what good Indonesian do to atheist? I show you on cat.'

Mrs A screamed as Pak Eman tore open the bag and pulled a bedraggled-looking Soyabean out by the scruff of his neck. The cat was rigid, eyes bulging with terror. The kiai was also screaming.

Only Sigit who continued to translate back and forth, stood his ground. 'Bule come near Eman; Eman will kill fat cat here only. You can see what we do to godless sampah.'

'Excuse me, but what are you doing to this cat?'

Everyone turned towards the owner of the haughtily enunciated words. An aristocratic Ibu, with a helmet of hair-sprayed hair and false eyelashes that fanned out like the wings of an eagle, tottered forward on six-inch stilettos, arms outstretched towards Soyabean.

Eman shoved the lady hard as she approached him, sending her sprawling to the ground, where miraculously her hair remained intact, even as she began to bawl, holding on to her injured ankle. Within moments, a dense crowd had gathered, a murmur rippling and rising as people took in the Ibu lying on the floor, the poor pesantren boys, the anxious foreigners and the man at the centre of it all, who was dressed like a kiai and manhandling a cat. Some wondered if it was a weird kind of store promotion for ACE's Christmas trees.

Pak Eman stared about him wildly, but looked reassured by the number of jilbabs he saw. He began to address the crowd, 'Bapak-bapak and Ibu-Ibu, in the most Kind and Merciful God's name, let me tell you about me. I am a respected kiai, who has devoted his life to defending the Faith in Indonesia. I have sworn to protect the righteous. The biggest threat to the purity of our country are people like these bule, you see here.'

A forest of suspicious eyes turned to look at the As; a few lips curled in threatening grimaces. Eman continued, gaining confidence as he spoke. 'I am a man of God. And it is my duty, just like it is the duty of every one of you who loves our country, to drive out these debauched communists from our motherland's sacred soil. Tell me, do you want a communist Indonesia? A Chinese Indonesia? A Christian Indonesia?'

With every question, the kiai's voice rose, until his voice was a roar, reverberating in the air. A roar that transformed into an inglorious yowl as Soyabean, who had been trying all along to turn his head around enough to get a bite of Pak Eman's arm, finally succeeded. Every tooth in the cat's mouth sank deeply into the kiai's flesh and there it stayed, even as the kiai cursed and spat.

Mrs A, who had been frozen, suddenly found her legs and leapt forward, but the kiai kicked her and simultaneously managed to yank Soyabean off with his other hand. He bayed like a wounded werewolf and thrashed the cat with all his might, until Soyabean went flaccid and lifeless.

Mr A was about to throw himself on Pak Eman, when Sigit managed to grab Soyabean from the kiai. Now that the cat was dead, Pak Eman had fast lost interest in it. He began to survey the space for the best escape route.

Sigit cradled the cat in his arms and began to speak. 'My name is Sigit, and I am a simple village boy from East Java. I have studied in a pesantren for many years. And while I do not claim to be very clever or even very good, I love God and I know God loves us. Do you really think He would want us to murder innocent animals? Do you really think He would want this?'

The crowd stood silent before the young man, their mood unreadable. Mr and Mrs A held each other tightly, their hearts broken. And then, a sob – not much louder than a sigh – broke the spell. A middle-aged man, dressed in the ACE shop attendant uniform, had begun to cry, his shoulders trembling.

'What a beautiful kucing this was,' he gasped. 'I can't even imagine what I'd do if someone attacked my sweet Nasi so brutally.'

Other voices joined in. 'My Bobo is the best dog in the world and I've had it with these gatekeepers of everyone's morality telling me he is dirty,' said a plain-faced lady carrying a bag of vegetables. 'Bobo is my child, and I don't want anyone saying otherwise.'

'Nothing wrong with pets,' muttered a recently manicured woman, who'd been holding her fingers out to dry through the whole drama. 'Give you more love and less trouble than children, let me tell you.' She guffawed, amused at her own daring.

A few people had begun to go up to Sigit and ask to stroke Soyabean.

'What soft fur.'

'Poor kucing.'

'He looks well-fed. Must have been loved by the owners.'

The ACE shop attendant had finally pulled himself together and now held out his arms to Sigit, asking to hold the cat. Sigit carefully transferred Soyabean to him. The cat looked angelic, a ball of ginger fluff. 'What a gorgeous kucing,' the shop attendant crooned over and over again.

There was not an eye in the crowd that remained dry. The hairsprayed Ibu had gathered herself off the floor and was comforting Mr and Mrs A, who were blinking as though uncertain that anything was real. The shop attendant buried his head in Soyabean's round tummy, readying for a fresh bout of sobbing, when he started. He'd felt a movement. The dead cat had moved. 'The Lord is merciful!' he cried out, as Soyabean opened his deep green eyes and meowed. It was a weak sound, but Mrs A could swear it sounded approving. Almost like he was saying, 'Yes, it's true; I am a gorgeous kucing.'

But everything had taken on a surreal quality for Mrs A by now, and she couldn't be sure of anything. She blinked hard to try and shrug off the strange lethargy that had descended on her. She needed to hold Soyabean. Had he

actually died and then come back to life in the hands of an ACE attendant? Was last night's spicy rendang causing strange dreams? Was she in fact a cat who had gone to sleep and dreamt that she was Mrs A?

'Out of my way. Move.' To make things even stranger, Mrs A now found herself staring at a breathless Debbie. She held Mrs A by the shoulders and looked at her with concern. 'Are you okay, Bu? What's going on here? The police are on their way. Where is Pak Eman?'

Mrs A felt like she'd been slapped. Where *was* Pak Eman? She swivelled around looking for the kiai, but there was no trace of him. Only the bag in which he'd been carrying Soyabean lay on the floor, as deflated as a balloon stamped on by a careless toddler.

Chapter XVIII

Tofu

A Pause

Mrs A had not been able to stop grinning today. She didn't even lose her temper at breakfast, when Nico took over an hour to finish, pushing his cereal around in a bowl while asking her rapid-fire questions.

'Mama, why is a dinosaur not a hippopotamus?'

'Mama, where was I before I was born?'

'Mama, what is the opposite of red?'

'Mama! Mama?'

Mrs A only beamed at the barrage of questions and clutched the magazine that was delivered with the morning post. It had her article from Lombok published in it and it seemed to mean a lot to her. 'Bhineka Tunggal

Ika,' she'd said showing it to Mr A. He read out the title: 'Faithful Aim: A food fight brings out complex communal relations on an Indonesian island.'

'Yup,' she'd laughed. 'It does. And complicated does not mean impossible, after all!' I didn't always understand what went on in the mind of Ren, but I was glad for her. When Mrs A was happy, I felt the clouds lift.

We'd all been keeping close to each other since Soyabean had been rescued. It was so easy to lose what you loved. All it took was one bad egg and the blink of an eye. Yunqi was the most fragile of threads tying us to this life. Even a pair of rusty, blunt scissors could cut it loose.

This time, the thread had held. Things had ended well; although in some ways they hadn't ended at all. The kiai had still not been found and perhaps he never will be. So there was no end to this story – only a pause.

But I think that a pause was good enough. Some of the best things happened in pauses. Like the first night Soyabean was back, and the whole family snuggled together in Ishaan's room. It wasn't a large bed and I was not a cuddly cat, but the need to scrunch up against legs and tummies and tails had been strong in all of us.

This morning was the first day the new driver, Pak Suminder, came to work. He looked nice enough: a brief moustache, kind eyes. He'd told Mrs A in his job interview that although he'd worked for more than fifteen years as a driver, his true passion was singing at weddings.

I imagined he would get on with Pak Nono, who was back to blaring dangdut on the radio for hours on end. The security guard had a spring in his step these days, as though he couldn't stop his toes from tapping. I was just a cat, and I might well have been wrong, but I suspected his bounciness had something to do with Ibu Mari.

The children's nanny had begun to spend all her free time with him. Since Pak Eman's disappearance, she was like a bird let out of a cage. The two sipped their tea and giggled at each other. Sometimes she brushed a speck of dirt off Pak Nono's uniform. Ibu Warsi gave them the occasional dirty look if she passed by, but it was only half-hearted. The cook seemed to be finding it harder and harder to be sincerely disapproving.

The other day, I caught her looking at Soyabean with what could only be described as a fond expression as he'd wolfed down the chicken livers she'd ladled into his bowl. Soyabean's appetite wasn't any worse for his kidnapping. If anything, he was eating with doubled vigour, abetted unexpectedly by Ibu Warsi. She'd dispensed with all the store-bought bags of kibble. 'This food, no good,' she'd announced to Mrs A one day, and ever since, she'd taken it upon herself to serve us home-cooked treats.

I did feel the occasional twinge when I was eating freshly steamed salmon belly, knowing as the flavours burst in my mouth that Da Ge and my other siblings would never enjoy such luxury. Soyabean says I am a gloomy cat. Perhaps.

Once Nico finally finished his breakfast, Pak Suminder drove the boys to school. Mr and Mrs A came out onto the verandah to wave them goodbye. It was almost cool and Mrs A shivered slightly in the breeze. For once, I was glad of my fur. I licked at the knot of tangled hair under my chin; I was due a good brushing.

'Doesn't it feel odd to have a new driver?' Mrs A said, looking at the empty space in the driveway where the car had been moments before. 'Pak Suminder seems really nice,' replied Mr A. 'True,' she shrugged. 'But he's not quite Pa'harto.'

'No, of course not. But Pa'harto's happy. He was getting on in any case, and now he can spend time with his grandchildren and eat pisang goreng to his heart's content. I forgot to mention it to you, but he called meyesterday.'

Mrs A perked up. 'And?'

'And he wants to come and visit next weekend. To see the kids. And his beloved kucing!' Mr A chuckled.

I smiled, although if a Ren were looking at me they wouldn't be able to tell. Cat smiles are not in the lips, they're in the whiskers. It would be a treat to see Pa'harto again.

'I need to get going soon,' Mr A had his brisk-office voice on. 'What are you up to today?'

'I'm finishing off a piece on what can be done at a policy level to tackle fake news. And Pak Hendra is coming over later for lunch.'

'Yes, well, I have a bad feeling there's going to be a lot more fake news rather than less,' Mr A said. 'Pak Halim and friends are just the tip of the iceberg. And Pak Eman will, no doubt, be stirring up trouble again whenever he resurfaces.'

'Certainly, it's the not the last anyone's heard from Pak Eman, but I think Indonesia is resilient enough to deal with the likes of him. Look at the election results! Pak Halim and Pak Eman were hardly the only bigots spreading fake news. But the President won. He won because, in the end, people know what is right and what is not.' Mrs A leant her chin on Mr A's shoulder. 'I can't help feeling optimistic,' she said. 'I know it can make me sound naive, but did you see all those people at Lippo Mall? They came through. There's a decency in people that Pak Eman will never be able to corrupt,' Mrs A said.

Mr A tucked a strand of her hair behind her ear. 'Perhaps you're right. I hope you are.'

She took his hand in hers. 'Pak Hendra and I will be discussing the latest in Debbie's friend, Agus', case. We've been able to hire a really good lawyer, who says it might just be possible to get him out of jail early. But it won't be easy.'

Mr A squeezed her hand. 'What did you say to me earlier? "Complicated doesn't mean impossible."' All of us in the verandah smiled, lips and whiskers. If I kept this up, Soyabean would no longer be able to accuse me of being gloomy.

'It's Ibu Ipah's first day at work today. I shouldn't be late,' Mr A said. A few days after Soyabean had returned home, we'd discovered that the rotten-fish kiai had had two wives. It was Ibu Mari who'd told the As. The other wife, Ipah, had landed up at her doorstep one evening with a baby and several children in tow. Eman had abandoned them without a word and they hadn't had a proper meal in days.

'Ipah children hungry,' Ibu Mari had said briskly, as she'd stood before the As. 'Can help?' The nanny should have been a cat. She had the directness of one. Mr and Mrs A had met Ibu Ipah that evening and, after much discussion, Mr A offered to try and find her a job at his office. She was now going to start work as a cleaner there.

Mr A left to catch a taxi and Mrs A disappeared back into the house, but I stayed out in the garden. It was rare for it to be so cool. There was only a single wispy cloud drifting in the sky, changing shape as it moved.

I walked up to the frangipani tree. The fallen flowers were still heavy with water from the rain last night. I thought of how the pomegranate tree in our home in Beijing had changed into this frangipani tree and how this huge bungalow had replaced our small courtyard home. We'd changed shape too, growing older and, in Soyabean's case, fatter. But I suppose it was all like the cloud. We – the cats and Ren and tree – were still the same cloud, just shifting outlines as we moved in time.

'So, the cat is out of the bag!'

I knew that it was Tikus even without turning around. 'What do you mean?' I asked, whiskers smiling.

The rat came up beside me. 'Nothing, just thinking of Soyabean stuffed in Pak Eman's bag. And now he's out.'

'Tikus! Has it taken you all this time to think up of that terrible joke?'

'Well, Tofu, some of us have to forage for food and dodge brooms. We don't all have the luxury of time, not to mention Ibu Warsi's cooking.'

'But I sneak food out for you all the time!'

'I just like making you feel guilty, silly cat!'

Tikus nudged me with his scaly tail and for a second I prepared myself for a wave of revulsion. But it never came. The only wave I felt was one of affection, and also the certainty that Tikus was part of our cloud too.

Glossary

Indonesian (Bahasa Indonesia)

Iya:	Yes
Mukena:	Religious veil
Sampah:	Garbage
Orang:	Person
Macet:	Traffic
Pak:	Mr/father
Ibu/Bu:	Mrs/mother
Tikus:	Rat
Ojek:	Motorcycle taxi
Pisang goreng:	Fried banana
Jilbab:	Hijab
Sarong:	Wrap-around skirt/dhoti
Kiai:	Imam/religious leader
Pembantu:	Domestic helper

Pemangku:	Supervisor
Kampung:	Village/slum
Mujur:	Luck
Reformasi:	Literally: Reformation. Used to indicate the Post-Suharto era in Indonesia that was marked by a more open and liberal political environment.
Hujan:	Rain
Kucing:	Cat
Kebaya:	Female outfit in Indonesia
Bhinneka Tunggal Ika:	Unity in diversity
Gamelan:	Percussion musical orchestra
Satay:	Skewer
Bakso:	Meatball
Rendang:	Meat (usually beef) in spicy coconut gravy
Ke sini:	Come here (imperative)
Dangdut:	Genre of popular music in Indonesia
Sambal:	Spicy sauce
Selamat siang:	Mid-morning greeting
Jalan Antasari:	Main road in Jakarta
Bule:	Foreigner
Rumah sakit:	Hospital
Pesantren:	Religious school (usually boarding school)

Bagus:	Good
Dungu:	Idiot
Bajai:	Autorickshaw
Mas:	Brother (Javanese)
Manis:	Sweet
Astaga:	An exclamation
Di buka:	Open up! (imperative)
Teh tarik:	Condensed milk tea
Jockey:	Passenger for hire to allow motorists to circumvent highway restrictions
Cendol:	Green, gelatinous jelly
Orang Rimba:	Indigenous tribes in the forests of Sumatra
Sabar:	Patience

Chinese (Mandarin)

Ren:	Person
Yunqi:	Luck
Nai Nai:	Grandmother
Chengyu:	Idiom
Da Ge:	Older brother
Hutong:	Alleyway in Beijing
Yangui:	Nightmarish ghosts

Acknowledgements

Terimah Kasi: Andreas Harsono, Ibu Narni, Ibu Heni, Pak Suharto, Pak Nono, Pak Sunadi, Pak Sumindar, Ibu Tinah, Ibu Ipah.

Thank you: Ruchika Gokarn, Beverley Naidoo, Tuva Kahrs, Udayan Mitra, Ananth Padmanabhan, Sohini Basak.

Always grateful to my family: Julio, Gitanjali, Swaminathan, Shekhar, Kiran (to whom this book owes its title), Ishaan, Nico, Tania and Jaan.

Biggest thanks of all to Tofu and Caramel.

About the Author

Pallavi Aiyar is an award-winning foreign correspondent who has reported from across China, Europe, Indonesia and Japan. She is the author of several books of fiction and non-fiction, including the bestselling China memoir, *Smoke and Mirrors*. She currently lives in Spain with her family – human and feline.

ALSO BY
PALLAVI AIYAR

'Fables are universal, and the issues *Chinese Whiskers* deals with are too. This is Aiyar's first novel, and with any luck the adventures of Tofu and Soyabean have only just begun.'

– India Today

'The cats have a way of purring their way into your heart, and you'll find it hard not to finish this novel in a single sitting.'

– Mail Today

Soyabean, a middle-class cat looked after by a cynical but kind grandmother, and Tofu, a dustbin cat, are brought together when they are adopted by foreigners who have arrived in Beijing. Their life as pampered pets is interrupted when Soyabean is offered a job as a model for a new brand of cat food. At the same time a mysterious virus is sickening people across the city and it is cats that are being blamed. *Chinese Whiskers* is a heartwarming story of cats and humans will make you laugh and tear up, and think again about the battles that we all fight between the corruption of modern living and the ideals of traditional life.

ALSO BY
PALLAVI AIYAR

'[A] smart, insightful book about modern China.'
– *The New York Times*

'Spurning the usual West-centric perspective on China, Pallavi Aiyar brings a sharp assessing eye to her intractably complex subject. In brisk, often entertaining, prose, she exposes the rich paradoxes and ironies of both authoritarian China and democratic India.' – Pankaj Mishra

Winner of the Vodafone–Crossword Readers' Choice Award 2008, Pallavi Aiyar's best-selling debut recounts her five-year long experience of China. China is at an historical point where tradition and modernity, communism and capitalism, chaos and control, rub up against each other on a daily basis. In order to remain in power through this period of far-reaching transformations, the Chinese Communist Party must walk a tightrope, balancing and mediating the conflicting needs and aspirations of its various constituencies. Smoke and Mirrors spotlights these contradictions and describes the different strategies the Party and the people deploy to manage them.